ALL
FACTS
CONSIDERED

ALL FACTS CONSIDERED

The Essential Library of Inessential Knowledge

KEE MALESKY

John Wiley & Sons, Inc.

Published by John Wiley & Sons, Inc., Hoboken, New Jersey
Published simultaneously in Canada

Design by Forty-five Degree Design LLC

Library of Congress Cataloging-in-Publication Data:
Malesky, Kee, date.
All facts considered : the essential library of inessential knowledge / Kee Malesky.
p. cm.
"Published simultaneously in Canada"—T.p. verso.
Includes bibliographical references and index.
ISBN 978-0-470-55965-9 (cloth); ISBN 978-0-470-88199-6 (ebk);
ISBN 978-0-470-88200-9 (ebk); ISBN 978-0-470-88201-6 (ebk)
1. History—Miscellanea. 2. Science—Miscellanea. 3. Arts—Miscellanea. I. Title.
D10.M35 2010
001—dc22
2010016888

Printed in the United States of America

10 9 8 7 6 5 4 3 2

For my dear parents,
Joe and Marilyn Shields,
who taught me to love reading,
and that education is never wasted

Feed your head

Contents

Introduction

FACTS ARE CARVED IN STONE, or they're dissipated by time; they're stubborn, or they're counterrevolutionary; they're sacred, or they obscure the truth. They're immutable, or they squirm. They evolve, they're influenced by opinion and points of view, and they're modified by disputation and community consensus. Facts speak for themselves, or they're ventriloquists' dummies. They are food and air for the mind, or, like cows, they're easily frightened away. They should be worshiped, or judged in the open market.

Facts mean different things to history, to science, and to art. A fact is a datum of experience, but it is subject to interpretation and therefore distortion. Research can bolster or destroy a fact. Individual perspective provides context and shades of meaning.

Facts can migrate from rumor to certainty and then to apocryphal story or folklore or even to myth and legend. Did the young George Washington chop down a cherry tree?

The tale originally appeared in the early 1800s in the first biography of the "father of his country." Mason Locke Weems, a traveling pastor and bookseller, claimed to have heard the story from a slave in the Washington household at Ferry Farm, Virginia. Accepted as true by the American reading public, it was perpetuated in the dozens of editions of the book over many decades and was even retold in *McGuffey's Readers.*

By the 1930s the story had been dismissed as "wholly imaginary" and as "one of the more interesting, if absurd, contributions ever made to the rich body of American legend." When Grant Wood painted *Parson Weems' Fable* in 1939, he was criticized for debunking the Washington myth and making the future president look smug. There was even a version of the incident in which the Washingtons lived on the bank of the Rio Grande and George chopped down a huisache tree with his machete!

Despite its total lack of historical provenance, the original story is still widely known, and a 2008 article about archaeological excavations at Ferry Farm would say only that the cherry tree tale "has never been proven." The old adage applies: Never let the facts get in the way of a good story.

Facts and information are the nourishment, the lifeblood, the raison d'être, and also the bane and despair of librarians and researchers. Librarians tend to be generalists, people who know a little bit about a lot of things. Maybe that sounds superficial, but it makes a great reference librarian. We store up facts and information (and occasionally even knowledge or wisdom), connect them, organize and describe them, and make them accessible to the world. It's that simple and that infinitely complex. Frontline reference work, at the desk of any library—public, corporate, academic, or news media—is living on the edge; it means that you might be hit with any question about any topic at any time, from the gross domestic product of Bhutan to the latest Elvis sighting, from the casualty figures of the Hundred Years' War to metallurgical microstructure analysis. Life is never dull, and we learn something new every day.

I am—we all are—Sherlock Holmes: deducing, eschewing factoids, chasing down the fact, wherever it leads. Sometimes it leads nowhere; the fact cannot be verified as accurate, and therefore it isn't usable. Former National Public Radio host and reporter Alex Chadwick often provided us with fact-checking challenges. He sent this note to the news managers about the librarian's tenacity and good judgment:

> [The librarian] was especially helpful today in chasing down the particulars of a fact that I wanted to include in a script. It was about 5:00 this morning west coast time. . . . She persisted over the course of about 45 minutes in trying to establish the fact—its supporting data grew increasingly frail, but I liked this fact quite a lot and kept asking her to go down one more route. She finally concluded that we could not establish this fact, despite my affection for it, so I left it out of the script.

The facts in this collection have been chosen by me—and, as the surrealist Marcel Duchamp pointed out in the 1930s, the act of selection can elevate an ordinary object to "the dignity of a work of art." These are facts that I like or that I find useful, interesting, amazing, or worth sharing, but this book does not contain *all facts*. I did *consider* all facts, or as many as I could recall, imagine, or pluck from the brains of my friends and colleagues. I did not attempt to be comprehensive or all-inclusive in my selection. In one volume, I cannot cover every topic, every culture, every country, every phenomenon in human history. The absence of a fact from this volume should not be interpreted to mean that the fact does not exist.

The majority of these facts do not come directly from questions that I have answered for NPR reporters and editors. But many of them are based on, or inspired by, journalists' queries. If one of these facts reminds you of a story you heard on the radio, it still doesn't mean that I researched it. I am not *the* NPR librarian; I'm one of a team of searchers who support NPR's editorial process.

Most facts, I have discovered, are not so easily stated in a clear and succinct manner. No individual fact can contain the whole story. The big picture requires many facts, plus nuance, opinion, and perspective. Any attempt to boil down or abstract a piece of information inherently implies that some (or many) details will be omitted. I apologize if, in trying to tell a fairly complete but necessarily truncated story, I have left out your favorite detail.

I can state that all these facts have been verified to at least a reasonable extent, but I know that events may change them and that their meanings will be modified; I can therefore make no guarantee for the permanence of any fact. Every fact has at least one good citation to back it up, but I consulted as many reputable sources as necessary to ensure that I had a decent grasp of the fact before I attempted to wrestle it into a couple of paragraphs. I always stayed true to the original sources, and as a result some quotations of historical materials contain unusual spellings.

Nailing down the proper frame in which to organize the facts was naturally of equal importance. Knowledge is inherently ambiguous and any system of classification is arbitrary; one could argue that it's absurd even to attempt to sort things into categories. But sort we must because it's in our nature, and because it's necessary to make information manageable. (Managing information is something that all librarians do every day.)

To organize the facts in this collection, I considered the ways in which philosophers—Aristotle, Aquinas, and Bacon, among others—have classified human knowledge in the past and settled on the "Figurative System of Human Knowledge" from the eighteenth-century *Encyclopédie* compiled by Denis Diderot and Jean Le Rond d'Alembert, which was itself based on Ephraim Chambers's *Cyclopaedia* and Francis Bacon's *Advancement of Knowledge*. D'Alembert explained their system as a "general distribution of human knowledge into history, which is related to memory; into philosophy, which emanates from reason; and into poetry, which arises from imagination." Diderot and d'Alembert created their Tree of Knowledge, "which communicated the idea that knowledge grew into an organic whole, despite the diversity of its branches."

In the spirit of arbitrariness and uncertainty, I felt free to shape this tree as it suits my facts, which goes against the nowadays more common and unfortunate inclination others have to shape their facts to suit the trees upon which they will hang.

Remember that annoying kid in your elementary school who raised her hand for every question, even if she didn't know the answer? That was me. I like to know things, and I like to share information. But I didn't realize I was born to be a librarian until I was in my mid-thirties. While studying for my master's degree, I worked in NPR's Broadcast Library, cataloging finished programs and retrieving audio for the staff. Soon I was in the Reference Library—fact-checking, doing background research, finding experts, and providing guidance in grammar and pronunciation; I started out with print collections and evolved to embrace new technologies, right up to blogging and tweeting.

I've always believed that being a librarian is a vocation, a calling, and not just a job. What we do matters in the world. Every moment of the day, I must be open to learning something that will help me to be a better librarian. If you live in the world and you pay attention to what is happening around you, you acquire information. My brain is stuffed with zillions of facts after twentysomething years of answering questions for NPR reporters, hosts, and editors. Facts float around among my little gray cells and have a tendency to percolate to the surface at the oddest moments. I wake up at 4 a.m., wondering whether the Romans really sowed the fields with salt after the Battle of Carthage in the Third Punic War (I doubt it) or how many states have had two Senate elections in the same year. It's time to spill out some of those facts onto the page and maybe make room for more.

PART ONE

ON MEMORY AND HISTORY

Memory, from which comes History: History concerns facts, and facts concern either God, or man, or nature. The facts which concern God belong to sacred history. The facts which concern man belong to civil history, and the facts which concern nature belong with natural history.

—JEAN LE ROND D'ALEMBERT

Battles and Bigwigs

Ancient and Modern, Sacred and Civil History

The Start of History

History begins with writing, with the ability to document events, traditions, laws, and myths and to record and preserve them for posterity. *Homo sapiens* developed spoken language tens of thousands of years ago, but writing—the inscribing of characters or signs with an instrument on a surface to represent language and to communicate or record information—is a much more recent achievement. The earliest examples of writing are from Sumer and Egypt, with China and Central America developing their systems a bit later.

First, people needed counting devices (such as sticks, pebbles, or clay tokens) to keep track of commercial transactions and personal possessions. These led to systems of simple visual symbols to express ideas or objects; these are called pictograms. Next, logograms evolved;

these represented specific words, but they could not easily express abstract concepts.

Around 3300 BCE, the Sumerians developed the first phonetic system by using a word symbol to stand for other words that had a similar sound but were difficult to represent with a picture symbol. The final step was the development of individual alphabetic characters, each of which represents a single sound. In *The Book before Printing*, David Diringer writes, "Alphabetic writing is the last, the most highly developed, the most convenient and the most easily adaptable system of writing."

Ancient Crossroads

Persia (which changed its name to Iran in 1935) was one of the world's first civilizations; it has evidence of Neolithic Aryan (peoples who spoke Indo-European languages) settlements from nearly ten thousand years ago. Persians are a non-Arab people who migrated from central Asia. According to *National Geographic*, "If you draw lines from the Mediterranean to Beijing or Beijing to Cairo or Paris to Delhi, they all pass through Iran, which straddles a region where East meets West. Over 26 centuries, a blending of the hemispheres has been going on here—trade, cultural interchange, friction—with Iran smack in the middle." The Elamites established the first known Persian dynasty in the third millennium BCE. Another Aryan people, the Medes (the ancestors of the Kurds of today), created a unified empire in the northwestern part of that region around 625 BCE. Cyrus the Great, who issued what some consider the world's first declaration of human rights, overthrew the Medes and established the Achaemenid Empire, expanding Persian control and influence from Egypt to India—making it one of the largest empires in history. His descendants, Darius and his son Xerxes, invaded Greece but were defeated and expelled from Europe in 479 BCE.

In the next century, Alexander the Great conquered Persia and ended the Achaemenid dynasty. After about a hundred years of Alexander's Seleucid Empire, the Parthian and Sassanid dynasties reestablished Persian rule until the Arab invasion in the seventh century CE. The Persians, the Kurds, the Turks, and others then converted to Islam.

The Rome of China

The story of Xi'an, one of the oldest cities in China, began long before cities were invented: archaeologists have discovered fossils of early *Homo erectus* nearby that may be a million years old, and there was a Neolithic village in the area at least eight thousand years ago. Qin Shi Huang, the first emperor of a unified China, selected Xi'an for his capital in the third century BCE, and it rivaled such Western cities as Rome and Athens.

In 1974, parts of Qin's burial complex (the largest mausoleum ever discovered) were identified and excavated. Eight thousand life-sized clay figures, known as the Terra Cotta Warriors and Horses, were found along with actual chariots, weapons, armor, and other funerary art. Their role was to guard Qin in the afterlife and allow him to rule the universe from his tomb. The site also included figures of acrobats and musicians whose role was to provide eternal entertainment for the emperor.

Throughout the centuries, thirteen Chinese dynasties established their primary centers at Xi'an, and it became the eastern terminus of the Silk Road, the network of trade routes that linked the East with the West.

Just the facts, ma'am.

—Jack Webb (Sgt. Joe Friday on *Dragnet*)

The Face of Amateur Archaeology

Heinrich Schliemann (1822–1890) was a German businessman and an amateur archaeologist who made his fortune speculating in the U.S. stock market and serving as a military contractor during the Crimean War. An autodidact with a romantic attachment to the ancient world, he wanted to prove the historicity of Homer's *Iliad* by finding the location of Troy—this was when most people thought the Trojan War was merely a legend.

In 1871, he began excavating around Hissarlik in Turkey. Because scientific technique had not been developed yet for archaeological fieldwork, Schliemann destroyed several incarnations of Troy in his attempts to find Priam's city. His wife was photographed wearing the "jewels of Helen," although the treasures he found there probably date back to well before Homeric Troy.

Schliemann did find the location of Troy, however, and subsequent excavations have uncovered evidence of nine iterations of that city, including one level that revealed a collapsed and burned fortification.

Working next in Mycenae, Schliemann excavated shaft graves near the Lion Gate and located the remains of several chieftains wearing golden masks. Schliemann is said to have sent this telegram to the king of Greece: "Today I gazed upon the face of Agamemnon." The text of the message is probably apocryphal, and the face was not Agamemnon's. The tombs were hundreds of years older than the era of the Trojan War, which probably occurred between 1300 and 1200 BCE.

Not the face of Agamemnon

Did Schliemann do more harm than good? Was he just a self-promoting embellisher, a looter and a smuggler, or did he go so far as to fabricate some artifacts? The debate on his motives and accomplishments continues, as does the archaeological work at Troy and Mycenae.

Pristine Civilization

The Olmecs of southern Mexico are often called the Sumerians of the New World because they are probably the oldest culture in Mesoamerica—a pristine civilization (one of a handful of ancient societies in the world that developed independently of any known preexisting cultures). The name *Olmec* means "rubber people" in the Aztec language, but it is not known what name these people called themselves. They flourished in the Veracruz and Tabasco region near the Gulf of Mexico from about 1200 to 400 BCE and seem to have developed a sophisticated and diverse economy.

Archaeologists have discovered more than a dozen Olmec giant stone heads—the first monumental sculpture in this hemisphere. The Olmec may also have been the originators of the Mesoamerican ball game, the precursor of the volleyball-like Aztec game called *ulama* or *ullamaliztli*, which is still played today; rubber balls, figurines of ball players, and remains of playing courts have been unearthed in Olmec areas.

Debate continues on whether the Olmec were a "mother culture," one that strongly influenced subsequent societies, or a "sister culture," one whose "interactions through the region produced shared attributes of religion, art, political structure and hierarchical society."

Go Goth

In contemporary pop culture, a Goth is a young person who listens to Alien Sex Fiend and dresses exclusively in black. However, the Goths were a collection of Germanic tribes who probably originated in Scandinavia and migrated south and east in the early years of the Common Era. As they moved, they were influenced by the culture and technology of the Roman Empire, as well as by Turkish and Persian societies. In the fifth century, they overran Rome, replacing the declining imperial society with their own civilization, modifying Roman culture and institutions, and profoundly changing the future of Europe.

Barbarians at the Gate

When was "the sack of Rome"? The Eternal City has been attacked a number of times, with varying degrees of damage. The first raiders were the Gauls in 387 BCE, but according to legend the Romans were awakened by sacred geese honking in the night and were able to defend themselves from the attack. Later attempts were made by Alaric and the Goths in 410 CE, by the Vandals in 455, and by the Suebians in 472. Once the Gothic kings ruled Rome, they saw the city assaulted by the Ostrogoths in 535 and 553. The Saracens arrived in 846, followed by the Normans in 1084. Finally (thus far) in 1527, mutinous troops of the Holy Roman Emperor Charles V (mostly supporters of Martin Luther) surpassed the horrors of the early barbarians, looting churches and palaces, assaulting nuns, and torturing and killing citizens and prelates. Pope Clement VII had to escape from the Vatican through the Passetto (the secret passageway) into the fortress of Castel Sant'Angelo, and the event essentially ended the Italian Renaissance.

Lost Knowledge

There is no doubt that there was a magnificent library in ancient Alexandria, Egypt, perhaps the greatest and largest collection ever assembled up to that time. It is also certain that the library had vanished by the Middle Ages, but who destroyed it and how are unanswered questions (and possibly unanswerable, because earthquakes and floods have put that part of Alexandria under water today). There are several legends; you can pick your villain: two pagans, a Christian, or a Muslim may have destroyed the library.

In 48 BCE, Julius Caesar, aligned with Cleopatra against her brother, set fire to ships in the harbor. The flames spread to nearby buildings, destroying at least a book warehouse, if not the main library building. Three hundred years later, the Emperor Aurelian invaded Egypt, and much of the city was burned. The patriarch of Alexandria, Theophilus, is alleged to have sent a mob to raze the library and the surrounding pagan temples in the late fourth century. The story with the least historical evidence has Caliph Omar ordering the burning of the books because they either contradict the Koran and are heretical or agree with it and are therefore superfluous. Maybe it was just the centuries of humidity that claimed the scrolls of Alexandria.

Dating Epochs

In order to break from the regnal dating system used by the Roman emperors, early Church scholars chose the birth of Jesus as the starting point of their calendar, and the term *anno Domini* ("year of our

Lord," or AD) gradually became popular. The abbreviation BC, for the years "before Christ" (the English translation of *ante Christi*), appeared much more recently.

For the last couple of centuries, some non-Christians have substituted the terms CE ("common era") and BCE ("before the common era"). Now many scholars and academics have adopted these terms as more inclusive. This change is far from universally accepted, although Kofi Annan, former secretary-general of the United Nations, endorsed the idea in 1999: "The Christian calendar no longer belongs exclusively to Christians. . . . There is so much interaction between people of different faiths and cultures . . . that some shared way of reckoning time is a necessity. And so the Christian Era has become the Common Era."

Lovers Asunder

As star-crossed as any Shakespearean lovers (and perhaps an inspiration to the Bard), Abelard and Héloïse were brilliant thinkers who gave themselves up utterly to love and paid the price for scandalizing twelfth-century France. He was the most popular philosopher and teacher in Europe; she, already incredibly well educated for a woman, became his student. Abelard described her in a letter to a friend:

> Dear Héloïse . . . Her wit and her beauty would have stirred the dullest and most insensible heart, and her education was equally admirable. . . . I saw her, I loved her, I resolved to make her love me. The thirst of glory cooled immediately in my heart, and all my passions were lost in this new one.

They fell in love, had a child, and were married (secretly, and over her objections) to protect the advance of his career. Her family sought revenge and arranged to have him castrated. Héloïse and Abelard fled Paris, each taking monastic vows, and rarely saw each other again. But they did correspond by letters, some of which have been preserved. Héloïse wrote in one of them:

> I will still love you with all the tenderness of my soul till the last moment of my life. . . . If there is anything that may properly be called happiness here below, I am persuaded it is the union of two persons who love each other with perfect liberty, who are united by a secret inclination, and satisfied with each other's merits. . . . I have renounced life, and stript myself of everything, but I find I neither have nor can renounce my Abelard. Though I have lost my lover I still preserve my love . . . do not forget me—remember my love and fidelity and constancy: love me as your mistress, cherish me as your child, your sister, your wife!

When Héloïse died, twenty years after Abelard, legend claims that they were buried together at the Paraclete, the abbey he had founded. But during the French Revolution their remains were moved or destroyed; today they have a tomb in Père Lachaise Cemetery in Paris, but it is unknown if either of them is actually buried there.

Abelard and Héloïse

Cradle Books

Anything printed from about 1455 to the end of 1500—in the first decades of printing with movable metal type in the West—has a special name: *incunabula* ("incunables," in English), or "cradle books," because "they belong to the childhood of the art of printing." Still strongly influenced by medieval manuscripts, the first printers made books that resembled the work of scribes and were decorated by hand. The Bibles printed by Johannes Gutenberg and his associates are usually considered the first Western printed books. Gutenberg's workshop in Mainz, Germany, printed about 150 oversized copies of the Bible—the process required six men to set the type and took several months. Only twenty-one complete copies still exist.

In the 1490s, Aldus Manutius established a press in Venice to print editions of ancient Greek classics, and he invented italic type (said to be based on the handwriting of the humanist scholar and poet Petrarch). Aldus wanted to publish beautiful books in small, affordable copies; he developed the octavo format (eight to ten inches tall), which made the works easy to transport—these were the forerunner of modern pocket editions. Aldus may also have invented the semicolon; one of his books contains the oldest known example in print. It's impossible to overestimate the revolutionary impact on literacy and the accessibility of information that began with the invention of the printing press in fifteenth-century Europe.

Out of Africa

The first African to come to the New World may have been Pedro Alonzo Niño (1468–1505?), who was not a slave but a pilot and a navigator for Christopher Columbus on his first voyage. It's possible that there were earlier trading contacts between Africa and the Americas, but historians are still debating the evidence. Africans were certainly involved in other European explorations: thirty black men were with Vasco Núñez de Balboa when he reached the Pacific Ocean in 1513; Africans accompanied Hernando Cortés to Mexico and Francisco Pizarro to Peru; and they ventured into Canada and the Mississippi Valley with the French. And, around 1780 or 1790, it was a black man from Haiti, Jean Baptiste Point du Sable, who constructed the first non-Native dwelling at a trading post that would later be named Chicago.

No Prenups?

Henry VIII of England (1491–1547) had six wives: Catherine of Aragon, Anne Boleyn, Jane Seymour, Anne of Cleves, Katherine Howard, and Katherine Parr. They are easily remembered as, respectively, divorced, beheaded, died, divorced, beheaded, survived. Technically, though, both divorces were actually annulments.

Henry VIII

Naming the Big Apple

Nieuw Amsterdam, founded as a commercial center by the Dutch East India Company, became New York (for the first time) in 1664, when the English captured the colony and sparked the Second Anglo-Dutch War in Europe. At the end of that conflict, the English traded Nieuw Amsterdam for Suriname in South America, and the name *New York* first appeared on an official document on September 16, 1664.

A decade later, during the Third Anglo-Dutch War, the future greatest city in the world again became Dutch: it was called New Orange in 1673–1674, until the Treaty of Westminster returned it permanently to English control. The English named it for James, the Duke of York and brother of King Charles II. On January 1, 1898, the modern metropolis we know was created when surrounding towns in Brooklyn, Queens, Staten Island, and the Bronx were consolidated into the Greater City of New York.

The Cost of Wars

The cost (in 2008 dollars) and the numbers of casualties in American wars are as follows:

American Revolution (1775–1783): $1.825 billion; between 4,400 and 6,800 battle deaths
War of 1812 (1812–1815): $1.177 billion; 2,260 battle deaths
Mexican War (1846–1849): $1.801 billion; 1,733 battle deaths
Civil War—Union (1861–1865): $45.199 billion; 140,414 battle deaths
Civil War—Confederacy (1861–1865): $15.244 billion; 94,000 battle deaths
Spanish-American War (1898–1899): $6.848 billion; 385 battle deaths
World War I (1917–1918): $253 billion; 53,513 battle deaths
World War II (1941–1945): $4.114 trillion; 292,131 battle deaths

Korean War (1950–1953): $320 billion; 33,629 battle deaths
Vietnam War (1965–1975): $686 billion; 47,393 battle deaths
Persian Gulf War (1990–1991): $96 billion; 146 battle deaths
Afghanistan War (2001–): $321.3 billion; 906 battle deaths
Iraq War (2003–): $739.8 billion; 3,489 battle deaths

The costs do not include veterans' benefits, war debts, or assistance to our allies; casualties do not include civilians, noncombat deaths, those wounded or missing in action. (Information for the Iraq and Afghanistan wars is correct as of August 5, 2010.)

The Gateway Gap

The Cumberland Gap is a natural passageway through the Appalachian Mountains near the point where Virginia, Tennessee, and Kentucky meet. Since prehistoric times, people and animals have used the narrow gap to travel through instead of over this section of the mountains, which were a significant barrier to the westward expansion of the colonies.

In 1750, the first Europeans found the pass after hearing descriptions of it from Native Americans. Daniel Boone and a small party explored the gap in 1769, but raids by the Shawnee discouraged their efforts for the next few years (Boone was captured for a brief time, and one of his sons was killed). Then, in 1775, "Boone with about thirty axmen hacked out a road" through the pass and constructed a small village that would be called Boonesboro. The Cumberland Gap became the primary route across the Appalachians, and allowed settlers to reach the Mississippi River.

By 1810, more than a quarter of a million people had passed through the gap, including the parents and grandparents of Abraham Lincoln. Describing the view of the White Rocks that tower thirty-five hundred feet above the valley, Boone said, "These mountains are in the wilderness, as we pass from

There's a world of difference between truth and facts. Facts can obscure the truth.

—Maya Angelou

the old settlements in Virginia to Kentucke, are ranged in a S. west and N. east direction, are of a great length and breadth, and not far distant from each other. Over these nature hath formed passes, that are less difficult than might be expected from a view of such huge piles. The aspect of these cliffs is so wild and horrid, that it is impossible to behold them without terror."

Eighteenth-Century Networking

Paul Revere wasn't the only man out for a midnight ride on April 18, 1775. With the news that British soldiers were on the march, Revere initiated an eighteenth-century form of networking. Part of a broad social circle, Revere knew everyone of import, and everyone knew him. As he rode from town to town, he alerted local leaders, who called out their militias and additional messenger relays.

At Lexington, Revere warned Samuel Adams and John Hancock that they might be in danger of arrest; more riders were dispatched, and the news quickly spread. Within a few hours, word of the redcoats' military incursion had traveled more than thirty miles. Hundreds of colonial militia headed for Lexington and Concord.

The previous September, the Massachusetts colonials had been taken unaware when British troops mounted a secret raid on the powder stores at Somerville. Rumors spread that people had been killed and war had started, and soon men were pouring onto the roads toward Boston in what became known as the Powder Alarm. Not wanting to be surprised again, the provincials refined and expanded the alarm system. It proved very effective at Lexington and Concord seven months later, as the American Revolution began.

Built by Bondage

Washington D.C., the "capital of the free world," was built primarily by slaves. It was a sparsely populated region in the 1790s, so massive efforts were required to turn the bucolic area between Rock Creek and the Anacostia River (then called the Eastern Branch of the Potomac) into a capital city by 1800. Since there weren't sufficient white laborers to handle the huge construction project, local slaveholders hired out their slaves for the task.

The District of Columbia became a major hub for the American slave trade until Abraham Lincoln abolished slavery there in 1862. Twelve U.S. presidents were slave owners. In July 2009, Congress passed a resolution that instructed the architect of the Capitol to place a marker in the visitor center to acknowledge that "No narrative on the construction of the Capitol that does not include the contribution of enslaved African Americans can fully and accurately reflect its history." The marker is made from stone that was quarried by slaves.

The U.S. Capitol

Battling for Booze

The ancient Celts knew how to ferment and distill grains in the first millennium BCE, and their *uisge beatha*, or "water of life," is now called whisky (in Scotland and Canada) or whiskey (in Ireland and the United States). The spelling difference is considered significant by distillers and drinkers because the process and the ingredients vary. In 1794, one of the first antigovernment protests in the United States was the Whiskey Rebellion, a demonstration against a tax that had been levied on distilled spirits to help pay off the national debt from the Revolutionary War. Whiskey, to the early Americans, was "an informal currency, a means of livelihood, and an enlivener of a harsh existence," so they strongly resisted the tax.

After some violent incidents in western Pennsylvania, President Washington mustered a citizens' army of thirteen thousand men and accompanied them to Carlisle as they mobilized. He didn't see any action, however, because he returned to Philadelphia and put Governor Henry "Lighthorse Harry" Lee of Virginia and Secretary of the Treasury Alexander Hamilton (the tax had been his idea) at the head of the army as it rounded up and arrested the suspected leaders. The insurrection quickly ended, and the tax was repealed in 1803.

Presidential Secrets Revealed

James Madison and Zachary Taylor were second cousins. Madison's grandfather, Ambrose, married Frances Taylor in 1721; she was the sister of Zachary Taylor, the future president's grandfather.

Madison was the shortest president so far—only five feet four inches.

John Quincy Adams was the first chief executive to be photographed, but it was after he left office.

Martin Van Buren was the first president to be born in the United States; all the earlier presidents were born in the colonies.

The only president who never married was James Buchanan, although he came close in 1819. His fiancée, Anne Caroline Coleman, called off the nuptials and died a week later, possibly by suicide. Buchanan never commented on his relationship with her.

William McKinley was the first president to ride in an automobile.

Warren G. Harding was the first president to speak over the radio.

To the Pacific

In January 1803, President Thomas Jefferson sent a secret message to Congress, requesting funds for an expedition to explore the western areas of the continent. Meriwether Lewis and William Clark began preparing their Corps of Discovery in the summer, after the announcement of the Louisiana Purchase. Jefferson's instructions to Clark included this directive: "The object of your mission is to explore the Missouri river, & such principal stream of it as by its course and communication with the waters of the Pacific ocean whether the Columbia, Oregon, Colorado or any other river may offer the most direct & practicable water communication across this continent for the purposes of commerce." The Corps supplied itself with three boats; two horses; hatchets; mosquito curtains; twelve pounds of soap; fifty dozen "Rush's Thunderclapper" pills and other medicines; rifles and gunpowder; navigational instruments; mirrors, combs, handkerchiefs, tobacco, and face paint as gifts for Native Americans; several books, maps, and tables for finding longitude and latitude; and other gear that cost about $2,300 in total.

Facts are many, but the truth is one.

—Rabindranath Tagore (*Sadhana*, 1913)

After traveling through what today are about a dozen states, from Illinois to Oregon, on November 7, 1805, Clark wrote in his journal, "We are in view of the opening of the Ocian, which Creates great joy. This great Pacific Octean which we been So long anxious to See. and the roreing or noise made by the waves brakeing on the rockey Shores (as I Suppose) may be heard distictly." They were actually looking at the wide estuary of the Columbia River; they reached the Pacific a few weeks later. The complete trip covered about eight thousand miles, and the explorers recorded and described hundreds of species of plants and animals that had previously been unknown to science.

Melancholy Meriwether

Meriwether Lewis did not enjoy the glory of his accomplishment; in his mind, the great expedition had been a failure. The hoped-for goal—finding an easy all-water passage through the Rocky Mountains to the Pacific Ocean—was not met; he thought that the Great Plains were too arid for farming; and some of the Native Americans they encountered were unfriendly and resistant to settlers or trading. Lewis was depressed, malarial, drinking heavily, taking opium and snuff, and facing financial ruin. He had attempted suicide at least twice.

On the night of October 11, 1809, at Grinder's Inn on the Natchez Trace in Tennessee, Lewis shot himself in the head, but he was only slightly wounded. With a second pistol, he then fired a shot into his chest, but that didn't kill him, either. At dawn, servants found him cutting himself with a razor. He died just after sunrise and was buried on the site of the inn.

When William Clark heard the news, he wrote, "I fear, O I fear the weight of his mind has overcome him." A few years later, Thomas Jefferson described Meriwether Lewis this way: "Of courage undaunted, possessing a firmness and perseverance of purpose which nothing but impossibilities could divert from its direction . . . of sound understanding and a fidelity to truth so scrupulous that whatever he should report would be as certain as if seen by ourselves."

Books a Million

The first U.S. federal cultural institution was the Library of Congress, founded in 1800. Burned by the British in 1814, it was renewed by the purchase of 6,487 volumes from Thomas Jefferson's personal collection, at a cost of $23,950. Today, it is the largest library in the world, "with nearly 145 million items on approximately 745 miles of bookshelves. The collections include more than 33 million books and other print materials, 3 million recordings, 12.5 million photographs, 5.3 million maps, 6 million pieces of sheet music, and 63 million manuscripts." Every day, ten thousand items are added to the library. Half of the book and serial collections are in languages other than English—470 languages. The Library of Congress holds the largest collection of incunables (fifteenth-century printed books) in the Western Hemisphere. Among its more precious holdings are a cuneiform tablet from 2040 BCE; the first extant book printed in North America, *The Bay Psalm Book* (1640); the 1507 Waldseemüller map, the first document on which the name *America* appears; and one of the world's few perfect copies of the Gutenberg Bible on vellum. In addition, there are more than a hundred thousand comic books.

The Library of Congress

Numismatically Speaking

Paper money was first issued in the United States by an act of Congress in 1861, to help finance the Civil War. Called demand notes, they were non-interest-bearing treasury notes. The Massachusetts Bay Colony issued the first paper money in the colonies in 1690, and during the Revolutionary War, the Continental Congress issued notes that were easily counterfeited and quickly devalued.

At the end of 2009, the value of U.S. currency in circulation was $888.3 billion. The Bureau of Printing and Engraving produced 2,636,800,000 one-dollar bills in fiscal year 2009. Although many people think that the two-dollar bill is fake, as of April 30, 2007, there was $1,549,052,714 worth of them in circulation worldwide. Different denominations of U.S. currency have different life spans, as shown below:

DENOMINATION	LIFE SPAN
$1	21 months
$5	16 months
$10	18 months
$20	24 months
$50	55 months
$100	89 months

Presidents in the Line of Fire

Abraham Lincoln is often cited as the only sitting U.S. president ever to be under actual fire in wartime. Bullets whizzed near him during his visit to Fort Stevens on the outskirts of Washington on July 12, 1864, as Lieutenant General Jubal Early's Confederate forces attacked the city.

However, a strong case can be made that Lincoln was not the first president to be in danger on a battlefield while in office. On August 24, 1814, James Madison rode from the White House toward

Bladensburg, Maryland, where British troops were gathering as they planned to attack the capital. Madison arrived just as the British did, and shooting soon commenced. As the British fired artillery and rockets, it was suggested to Madison that he move to the rear. This he did, but it was soon apparent that the battle was lost, and he headed back into town. The victorious British then burned Washington.

Artist, Inventor, Bigot

Samuel Finley Breese Morse (1791–1872) is known primarily as the inventor of the telegraph, but he started out hoping for a career as a great artist. He studied in London with Benjamin West and at the Royal Academy of Arts, and later he studied in Paris and Rome. One of his more famous works is *Gallery of the Louvre*, in which he copied the paintings he considered the best in the museum's collections as if they were gathered together in one salon.

When Morse returned to the United States, he became known primarily as a portrait painter. His artistic work didn't compensate him sufficiently, so Morse then turned to the subjects he had studied in college: chemistry and electricity. Working with collaborators in the 1830s, Morse developed the idea for long-distance communication using electrical signals transmitted via wire, with a code to represent the letters in the message.

What's usually left out of writings about Morse are his views on immigration and slavery. He ran unsuccessfully for mayor of New York in 1836 on the anti-immigrant Nativist Party ticket, and he was an enthusiastic supporter of the Know-Nothing movement. He held rabid anti-Catholic views.

The Jesuits, he asserted, were "proverbial through the world for cunning, duplicity, and total want of moral principle." They had too much influence on their adherents, he believed. The "great body of emigrants to this country are the hard-working mentally neglected poor of Catholic countries in Europe. . . . They are not fitted to act with judgment in the political affairs of their new country." Morse continued, "We have in the country a powerful religious-politico sect, whose final success depends on the subversion of these democratic institutions, and who have therefore a vital interest in promoting mob-violence." Morse was also a defender of slavery: "Are there not in this relation [of master to slave], when faithfully carried out according to Divine directions, some of the most beautiful examples of domestic happiness and contentment that this fallen world knows? Protection and judicious guidance and careful provision on the one part; cheerful obedience, affection and confidence on the other." Some writers claim that Morse modified his positions and became more tolerant in his later years.

Samuel F. B. Morse

The First and the Last Man Killed

Fort Sumter, South Carolina, April 14, 1861: Federal troops, under the command of Major Robert Anderson, surrender after thirty-four hours of bombardment to Confederate General P. G. T. Beauregard. The Civil War had begun.

As the Federal troops lowered their flag and honored it with a one-hundred-gun salute, there was a premature discharge of the cannon and a huge explosion. Private Daniel Hough (1st U.S. Artillery) became the first man killed in the War Between the States.

The last man to die in action was also a Union soldier, Private John Jefferson Williams of the 34th Indiana Infantry. On May 13, 1865, nearly a month after the surrender at Appomattox, an inconsequential battle—no more than a skirmish—occurred along the Rio Grande at Palmito Ranch in Texas. Despite an informal truce between the Confederate and Federal forces, Union commander Colonel Theodore Barrett ordered his men to push inland on a raid. The Confederates were better armed, with artillery and cavalry, and soon the Union forces retreated. Private Williams was the only casualty, and his regiment gave his family a medallion honoring him as the last man killed in the Civil War.

The Kidnapped President

Eleven years after Abraham Lincoln was assassinated, there was an attempt to kidnap his corpse and hold it for ransom. On Election Day in 1876, thieves tried to "steal the bones of the martyr president," as one newspaper headline put it, but they were interrupted by the Secret Service, which had been tipped off by an informant. Widely described as inept, the would-be grave robbers were quickly arrested, tried, convicted, and given brief prison sentences.

President Lincoln did not rest very peacefully during the nineteenth century: historians count as many as seventeen times that his body was buried, exhumed, inspected, or reburied. But since 1901, he has remained in his Oak Park Cemetery tomb in Springfield, Illinois, protected by two tons of concrete.

The Great Hunger

The Irish Famine (in Gaelic, *An Gorta Mór*, "the Great Hunger") had a terrible impact on the country: a million people died of starvation or disease, and at least another million emigrated. In the mid-1800s, Ireland was "wretched, rebellious and utterly dependent on the potato." When blight hit the potato crop beginning in 1845, the people were devastated. Little was done by the British government to alleviate their suffering; indeed, merchants and landlords actually exported food from Ireland during the worst years of the famine. Some Protestant groups offered to feed the hungry—if they would convert from Catholicism; those who did were called *soupers*, because they traded their souls for a bowl of soup. British economist and Oxford professor Nassau William Senior wrote at the time that the famine "would not kill more than one million people, and that would scarcely be enough to do any good."

The Prince of Cranks

An especially colorful character in U.S. history who is now mostly forgotten was Ignatius Loyola Donnelly. Born in Philadelphia in 1831, he moved to Minnesota in his mid-twenties, worked as a farmer, and then began a career in politics. Elected as a Republican to the U.S. House of Representatives, he later joined the Greenback Democrats (a farm-labor coalition that supported currency reform) but was defeated for reelection. He served as lieutenant governor of Minnesota, was a state legislator for the Farmer's Alliance Party, and ran for vice president in 1900 on the "Middle of the Road" Populist ticket.

Donnelly also worked as a lobbyist, edited newspapers, and was one of the early supporters of the Populist Party. A brilliant and popular orator, he was known as the Prince of Cranks and a quack historian because in "literature as in politics, he made it his concern to espouse unusual and unproved theories." He wrote books—now considered pseudoscience or science fiction—on the lost continent of Atlantis as well as on his theory that a prehistoric comet that struck the earth accounts for all the sand and gravel on the planet.

Another book aimed to prove that Francis Bacon wrote the works of William Shakespeare. Donnelly's novel, *Caesar's Column: A Story of the Twentieth Century*, imagined the United States in the year 1988, when plutocracy had created a cruel, morally corrupt society. He wrote elsewhere that America comprised only two classes: tramps and millionaires.

Donnelly died on January 1, 1901 (which was considered the first day of the twentieth century).

The King of Censors

Anthony Comstock, a man "possessed of a curious, vague sense of sin," was born in 1844, served uneventfully for the Union in the Civil War, and then began working with the Young Men's Christian Association in New York City. In 1873 he formed the New York Society for the Suppression of Vice and immediately began crafting anti-obscenity legislation. He brought the bill to Congress and it was passed, making it illegal to use the mail to disseminate "obscene, lewd, or lascivious" material; however, his idea of pornography included contraception and any sort of information about sex. The bill became known as the Comstock Law, and its birth control provisions remained on the books until Margaret Sanger began her campaign against such laws in 1916. Some Comstock-inspired state regulations were still in effect until the 1960s. The obscenity portions of his bill were used to suppress not only information about sex and birth control but also works of art and literature, including poems and plays by Walt Whitman and George Bernard Shaw and the painting *Matinée de Septembre* ("September Morn") by French artist Paul Chabas, which depicted a young girl standing at the edge of a lake, nude but demurely so.

Shaw said, "Comstockery is the world's standing joke at the expense of the United States. Europe likes to hear of such things. It confirms the deep-seated conviction of the Old World that America is a provincial place, a second-rate country-town civilization after all." Comstock was also appointed as an official, though mostly unpaid, agent of the U.S. Post Office, and he used his powers to prosecute many offenders. Comstock had no regrets about his approach to censorship, and he even bragged that he was responsible for four thousand arrests and fifteen suicides. His work inspired J. Edgar Hoover, the future head of the FBI, to study and use similar methods.

The New York Society for the Suppression of Vice

A Visit from the Merry Monarch

The first visit to the United States by a foreign head of state was in 1874, when King Kalākaua of Hawaii (then also known as the Sandwich Islands) spent about two months touring the country. He met with President Ulysses Grant and his cabinet, and Congress held a reception for him. Before he arrived in Washington, he was questioned by reporters who asked about the upcoming meeting with Grant.

"It would not be courtesy to President Grant," said the king, who was nicknamed the Merry Monarch, "to speak of state affairs in the public newspapers. Do not suppose me offended at your question. I am sufficiently familiar with your American institution of 'interviewing,' which was fully explained to me in San Francisco, to recognize your right to question anybody on any subject whatever, but reasons of state are higher than considerations of journalism."

The Golden Door

More than twenty-five million immigrants, passengers, and ship crew members were processed through Ellis Island from 1892 to 1924; only 2 percent were rejected, usually for medical reasons. The first new American to arrive was Annie Moore, a young girl from Ireland ("rosy-cheeked," according to the *New York Times*) who had traveled with her two brothers to join their parents in New York. The high point of immigration through Ellis Island was 1907, when more than a million people were received, including 11,747 on a single day in April. After 1924, the island's function reversed, and it was used primarily to detain and deport people who had entered the United States illegally or violated the conditions of their admission. During World War II it housed "enemy aliens." Closed from 1954 to 1976, Ellis Island is now open as a museum and genealogy center. In 2009, there were 1,840,160 visitors, and about twelve million people have used the American Family Immigration Center database on the Internet since 2001.

The Bonus Expeditionary Force

The Bonus Army—fifteen to twenty thousand World War I veterans who demanded a bonus that had been promised to them by Congress—descended on Washington in 1932 in one of the first major marches on the city. The veterans lived in abandoned buildings and built a large shantytown (referred to as a "Hooverville") in Anacostia Park, across the river from downtown Washington.

The payment of the bonus had been deferred until 1945, but because of the Depression, a bill was introduced to make the payments

> *The truth is more important than the facts.*
>
> —Frank Lloyd Wright (quoted in *Context*, vol. 11, no. 14, May 6, 1994)

immediately. When that bill was voted down in Congress, the Hoover administration thought it was time for the Bonus Army marchers to leave. They didn't, and soon the U.S. Army, led by Douglas MacArthur, George Patton, and Dwight Eisenhower, was brought in to clear the protesters from the city. Tanks swept through downtown, and soldiers armed with machine guns, bayonets, and tear gas burned the camps. The marchers and their families dispersed, but they came back again in 1933 and 1934 to lobby the Roosevelt administration. The bonus was finally granted in early 1936, and the incident influenced Congress to enact the GI Bill for veterans of World War II.

Temp Jobs

When a sitting U.S. senator leaves office for any reason, he or she is replaced by an appointee in most states (a few require special elections instead). After interviewing a historian of the Senate, NPR's Ken Rudin reported, "The largest number of Senate appointees was during the 79th Congress (1945–1946), when there were 13 appointed senators (out of 96 at the time)."

APPOINTEE	REPLACED (REASON FOR VACANCY)	SUBSEQUENT SERVICE
Frank Briggs (D-MO)	Harry Truman (became VP)	Lost seat
Thomas Hart (R-CT)	Francis Maloney (died)	Did not run for reelection
Milton Young (R-ND)	John Moses (died)	Elected to six terms
Edward P. Carville (D-NV)	James G. Scrugham (died)	Lost primary
William Knowland (R-CA)	Hiram W. Johnson (died)	Elected to two terms
James Huffman (D-OH)	Harold H. Burton (became Supreme Court justice)	Lost seat
Charles Gossett (D-ID)	John Thomas (died)	Lost primary

APPOINTEE	REPLACED (REASON FOR VACANCY)	SUBSEQUENT SERVICE
William Stanfill (R-KY)	Albert B. Chandler (became baseball commissioner)	Did not run for reelection
Thomas Burch (D-VA)	Carter Glass (died)	Did not run for reelection
George Swift (D-AL)	John H. Bankhead II (died)	Did not run for reelection
Spessard Holland (D-FL)	Charles O. Andrews (died)	Elected to four terms
Ralph Flanders (R-VT)	Warren R. Austin (became U.S. Ambassador to UN)	Elected to two terms
William Umstead (D-NC)	Josiah W. Bailey (died)	Lost primary

Throwing Off the Shackles

In the twentieth century, especially after World War II, many African nations began the excruciatingly difficult process of breaking from colonial rule and forging their own national identities as they ended the political partitions of the nineteenth century. The United Nations passed a resolution in 1960: "The General Assembly . . . Recognizing the passionate yearning for freedom in all dependent peoples and the decisive role of such peoples in the attainment of their independence . . . Solemnly proclaims the necessity of bringing to a speedy and unconditional end colonialism in all its forms and manifestations." Some countries changed their names.

NAME	COLONIAL NAME	YEAR OF INDEPENDENCE
Ghana	Gold Coast	1957
Guinea	French West Africa	1958
Mali	French West Africa	1960
Senegal	French West Africa	1960
Benin	French West Africa	1960

(Continued)

(Continued)

NAME	COLONIAL NAME	YEAR OF INDEPENDENCE
Niger	French West Africa	1960
Burkina Faso	FWA, Upper Volta	1960
Mauritania	French West Africa	1960
Chad	French Equatorial Africa	1960
Central African Republic	French Equatorial Africa	1960
Congo	French Equatorial Africa	1960
Gabon	French Equatorial Africa	1960
Democratic Republic of Congo	Belgian Congo	1960
Tanzania	Tanganyika and Zanzibar	1961, 1963
Uganda	British East Africa	1962
Kenya	British East Africa	1963
Malawi	Nyasaland	1964
Zambia	Northern Rhodesia	1964
Botswana	Bechuanaland	1966
Equatorial Guinea	Spanish Guinea	1968
Guinea-Bissau	Portuguese Guinea	1974
Mozambique	Portuguese East Africa	1975
Djibouti	French Somaliland	1977
Zimbabwe	Southern Rhodesia	1980
Namibia	South West Africa	1990

Presidential Nanas

The only U.S. president to have a grandparent still living when he took office was John F. Kennedy. His maternal grandmother, Mary Josephine Hannon Fitzgerald, watched on television as JFK was inaugurated in 1961, and he used her Bible to take his oath of office. President Barack Obama's grandmother, Madelyn Dunham, died just days before he was elected in 2008, but she had already mailed in her absentee ballot.

A Rare Honor

In its entire history, the United States has conferred honorary citizenship on only seven individuals: Winston Churchill; Raoul Wallenberg; William and Hannah Penn; Mother Teresa; Marie-Joseph-Paul-Yves-Roche-Gilbert du Motier (better known as the Marquis de Lafayette); and the Polish nobleman and hero of the American Revolution, Casimir Pulaski (added in November 2009). The Senate is considering honorary citizen status for Holocaust victim Anne Frank.

Marquis de Lafayette

He Should Have Said It

As famous as the phrase "Follow the money" is, it was never actually uttered by Mark Felt, also known as Deep Throat, the long-anonymous source for Bob Woodward and Carl Bernstein in their investigation of the Watergate burglary that led to the downfall of Richard Nixon in 1974. Nor does the line appear in the book *All the President's Men*; it was written for the movie version, and screenwriter William Goldman told NPR's Daniel Schorr in 1997 that he came up with the phrase while discussing the script with Woodward.

Plenty of Presidents

Three times in the history of the United States, there have been five former presidents still living:

1861, at Abraham Lincoln's inauguration: Martin Van Buren, John Tyler, Millard Fillmore, Franklin Pierce, and James Buchanan (Tyler died on January 18, 1862).

1993, at Bill Clinton's inauguration: Richard Nixon, Gerald Ford, Jimmy Carter, Ronald Reagan, and George H. W. Bush (Nixon died on April 22, 1994).

2001, at George W. Bush's inauguration: Ford, Carter, Reagan, Bush, and Clinton (Reagan died on June 5, 2004).

Killed in the Line

The Committee to Protect Journalists (CPJ) keeps track of violence against reporters, editors, producers, and other media people: murders, threats, abductions, attacks, imprisonments, and harassments. At the end of May 2010, the group had confirmed 811 cases since 1992 in which a journalist was killed in the line of duty, in "direct reprisal for his or her work; in crossfire; or while carrying out a dangerous assignment," according to the CPJ Web site.

The majority of those killed were print or broadcast reporters (54 percent) who were murdered (72 percent) by political groups (30 percent). Most journalists were covering war or politics (94 percent); the majority of the deaths (141) were in Iraq.

The committee also advocates for journalists who are imprisoned; in December 2009, it counted 136, with China, Iran, and Cuba at the top of the list of incarcerators.

Party Changers

In April 2009, Pennsylvania's Republican senator Arlen Specter changed parties, but the switch backfired when he lost the 2010 Democratic primary. In the years since the direct election of senators began, a dozen other U.S. senators have pulled the big switcheroo—six Democrats and six Republicans:

Joseph Lieberman, Connecticut: Democrat to Independent, 2006
James Jeffords, Vermont: Republican to Independent, 2001
Bob Smith, New Hampshire: Republican to Independent, then back to Republican, 1999
Ben Nighthorse Campbell, Colorado: Democrat to Republican, 1995
Richard Shelby, Alabama: Democrat to Republican, 1994

Harry Byrd Jr., Virginia: Democrat to Independent, 1970
Strom Thurmond, South Carolina: Democrat to Republican, 1964
Wayne Morse, Oregon: Republican to Independent, 1952, then to Democrat, 1955
Robert LaFollette Jr., Wisconsin: Republican to Progressive, 1934, then to Republican, 1946
Henrik Shipstead, Minnesota: Farmer-Labor to Republican, 1940
George Norris, Nebraska: Republican to Independent, 1936
Miles Poindexter, Washington: Republican to Progressive, 1912, then to Republican, 1915

SCOTUS: Confirmed or Rejected

According to the U.S. Constitution, the president must submit Supreme Court justice nominations to the Senate for confirmation. The Web site of the Senate notes, "Since the Supreme Court was established in 1789, presidents have submitted 159 nominations for the Court, including those for chief justice. Of this total, 123 were confirmed (seven declined to serve)." The following twelve nominees to the Supreme Court of the United States (SCOTUS) had the most "no" votes from the Senate, in the years since World War II:

Robert Bork: 58 (rejected 42–58, October 23, 1987)
Clement Haynsworth: 55 (rejected 45–55, November 21, 1969)
G. Harrold Carswell: 51 (rejected 45–51, April 8, 1970)
Clarence Thomas: 48 (confirmed 52–48, October 15, 1991)
Samuel Alito: 42 (confirmed 58–42, January 31, 2006)
Elena Kagan: 37 (confirmed 63–37, August 5, 2010)
William Rehnquist (for chief justice): 33 (confirmed 65–33, September 17, 1986)
Sonia Sotomayor: 31 (confirmed 68–31, August 6, 2009)
William Rehnquist: 26 (confirmed 68–26, December 10, 1971)
John Roberts (for chief justice): 22 (confirmed 78–22, September 29, 2005)

Potter Stewart: 17 (confirmed 70–17, May 5, 1959)
Sherman Minton: 16 (confirmed 48–16, October 4, 1949)

Some nominations were handled by a voice vote, so no count is available.

Six SCOTUS nominees have been unanimously confirmed by the Senate:

Morrison Waite: 63–0 (January 21, 1874)
Harry Blackmun: 94–0 (May 12, 1970)
John Paul Stevens: 98–0 (December 17, 1975)
Sandra Day O'Connor: 99–0 (September 21, 1981)
Antonin Scalia: 98–0 (September 17, 1986)
Anthony Kennedy: 97–0 (February 3, 1988)

One man, Edwin Stanton (who had been President Lincoln's secretary of war), was nominated to the Court in 1869 and was approved by the Senate, but he died before he could be sworn in.

Deviations and Wonders

The Natural History of Land, Sea, Animals, and Vegetables

Planet Earth 101

Age: 4.6 billion years
Weight (mass): 5,973,700,000,000,000,000,000,000 kilograms
Surface area: 196,937,500 square miles (71% water, 29% land)
Circumference at equator: 24,901 miles
Circumference at the poles: 24,859 miles
Speed of orbit (average): 18.62 miles/second

Forest Primeval

The immense primordial forest that once covered all of eastern Europe exists today in just one tiny, undeveloped remnant: the Białowieża Forest (known as the *Belovezhskaya Pushcha* in Russian). It's now a 360-square-mile park that straddles the border between Poland and

Belarus, with stands of ancient oaks—some up to six hundred years old—as well as herds of wisent (European bison), wild horses, European elk, and wild boar. For much of its history, the forest was a royal hunting preserve and was therefore protected, which accounts for its survival. The Białowieża Forest is now a UNESCO World Heritage site.

Lunar Labels

Native American peoples and other cultures mark the seasons by naming the full moons. A *blue moon* is a second full moon in a single month.

January	Wolf Moon or Old Moon
February	Snow Moon or Hunger Moon
March	Worm Moon or Sap Moon
April	Pink Moon or Egg Moon
May	Flower Moon or Planting Moon
June	Strawberry Moon or Rose Moon
July	Buck Moon or Thunder Moon
August	Sturgeon Moon or Green Corn Moon
September	Harvest Moon or Fruit Moon
October	Harvest Moon or Hunter's Moon
November	Beaver Moon or Frosty Moon
December	Cold Moon or Long Nights Moon

(The Harvest Moon is the full moon closest to the autumn equinox, so it can occur in either September or October.)

A full moon

The Greatest Lakes

There are 5,472 cubic miles of water—or about 6.025 quadrillion gallons—in the five lakes that make up the Great Lakes system (Superior, Huron, Ontario, Michigan, and Erie). They form the

Facts are stubborn things; and whatever may be our wishes, our inclinations, or the dictates of our passions, they cannot alter the state of the facts and evidence.

—John Adams ("Argument in Defense of the British Soldiers in the Boston Massacre Trials," December 1770)

largest group of freshwater lakes in the world, with 18 percent of the planet's fresh surface water; only the polar ice caps hold more. The Web site of the Great Lakes Historical Society is called "inland seas.org."

A Deep Blue Lake

The intensely blue Crater Lake, in the Cascade Mountains in southern Oregon, is a caldera (collapsed volcano) lake that was created about seventy-seven hundred years ago after the cataclysmic explosion of Mount Mazama. It is 1,943 feet deep, making it the deepest lake in the United States and the seventh deepest in the world. There are no rivers or streams that feed or drain the lake, but it does get about sixty-six inches of rain and forty-five feet of snow per year. Its brilliant blue appearance is due to its depth and clarity, and it stays clear because the lack of incoming streams means that less sediment or pollution can enter the lake. Crater Lake was made a national park in 1902.

Deep in the Ocean

Creatures that live in the Mariana Trench—the deepest place on the planet (more than a mile deeper than Mount Everest is high)—are among the oceans' more unusual species. The Mariana Trench is an area of extreme cold and darkness and crushing pressure, with no plant life. Microorganisms predominate, but tube worms, siphonophores, crabs, and anglerfish can live around hydrothermal vents, where hot, mineral-rich water breaks through the earth's crust, providing nourishment for the bacteria at the bottom of the food chain. The trench, which is located below the Northern Mariana

Islands southwest of Guam, is more than fifteen hundred miles long. It's the boundary where two shifting tectonic plates are colliding, part of the Pacific Ring of Fire where most earthquakes and volcanic eruptions happen. The deepest point of the trench, called Challenger Deep (after the British vessel that surveyed the trench in 1951) is about thirty-six thousand feet below the surface.

Anglerfish

Jaws

Between 1990 and 2008, there were 1,076 shark attacks in the world, almost half of them (429) in Florida waters. Also high on the list of unprovoked incidents of "shark-human interaction" are Australia (122), South Africa (78), and Hawaii (66), according to the *International Shark Attack File*, which is maintained by the Florida Museum of Natural History.

Few of these attacks were fatal, and there's been a "gradual reduction in the yearly number of attacks since reaching an all-time high of 79 in 2000." In July 2009, nine shark attack survivors went to Washington to support passage of the Shark Conservation Act, "which would strengthen the ban on shark finning in U.S. waters and encourage shark conservation programs around the world." Finning is the practice of removing a shark's fin for use in gourmet food preparations and throwing the shark back into the sea, where, rendered helpless without its fin, it will drown or be eaten.

Jaws and Julia

Julia Child (1912–2004), the incredibly famous chef, master of French cuisine, and star of public television, worked as a research assistant for the Office of Strategic Services (the forerunner of the CIA) during World War II. One of her assignments was with the Emergency Sea Rescue Equipment Section, for whom she helped develop a shark repellent. (However, she refused to allow it to be called her "first recipe.")

The scientists in her section discovered that dead sharks release a sulfur compound that live sharks find intolerable, so they extracted the substance and put it in pellet form, which could then be used by shipwrecked sailors or downed pilots to keep the sharks from attacking. Child later said that the navy was hesitant to use the pellets at first, because it didn't want to acknowledge that sailors might be eaten by sharks. The repellent was also used to coat explosive devices in order to prevent sharks from accidentally bumping into them and causing them to detonate.

Arid Areas

A desert (from the Latin *desertus*, for "abandoned place") is an arid area, with little or no precipitation or vegetation, but not necessarily a place that is hot and sandy. Antarctica is the largest desert on earth (5.3 million square miles)—a polar desert—and it is shrinking as climate change and other factors melt the ice shelves.

The Sahara is the largest hot desert, more than three million square miles—as large as the continental United States. Some sources claim that the Sahara is advancing southward, but there is actually a complicated fluctuation of drought and greening; the desert expands and retreats, due to both environmental and human factors.

Flatland

The Republic of Maldives is the world's flattest country: its highest point is less than eight feet above sea level. It is also one of the more disparate nations, with 1,190 atolls (coral islands) that comprise 115 square miles of land spread over approximately 35,000 square miles of the Indian Ocean. Only about 200 of these islands are inhabited; their big industries are tourism and processing fish and coconuts.

The 2004 Indian Ocean tsunami had a devastating impact on some parts of the atolls, and they had to redraw all their maps. President Mohammed Nasheed held an underwater cabinet meeting in October 2009 to draw attention to the country's serious environmental concerns.

"What do we hope to achieve?" he asked, adding, "We hope not to die. I hope I can live in the Maldives and raise my grandchildren here." Nasheed promised to make Maldives the world's first carbon-neutral country within ten years, but he has a backup plan to move the entire population to a new (unspecified) home if they lose their battle with the rising sea.

Chew on This

Chewing gum has been around for eons. To be more precise: humans have been chewing plant exudates—gums, tars, resins—since Neolithic times, because they sweeten the breath, hold off hunger and thirst, taste good, and have medicinal properties. In ancient Greece, people chewed resin from the evergreen mastic tree (*Pistacia lentiscus*), which probably gave us the word *mastication*.

In the New World, the sapodilla tree of Mexico and Central America produces chicle, a natural latex similar to rubber that was used for centuries by the Maya and the Aztec people. The first commercial chewing gum product in North America, called State of Maine Pure Spruce Gum, was introduced in 1848. By the 1890s, the Wrigley Company of Chicago dominated the industry with its Spearmint and Juicy Fruit brands.

Today, synthetic gum base is used for most chewing and bubble gum products. In many cultures, gum chewing has been considered vulgar, impolite, or an indicator of immoral character, and we've all been told by a teacher or a parent at some time to "just spit it out."

Put That in Your Pipe

Cannabis has a very long history of use by humans—for rope, textiles, and paper, in magic and in medicine, and for its psychotropic properties—all the way back to ancient China, where archaeological evidence indicates the use of hemp and marijuana as early as 10,000 BCE. Also widely used in ancient India and Nepal, it's even mentioned in the Vedas: "Siva brought the marijuana plant down from the

Himalayas for their use and enjoyment." Cannabis has been identified as the largest cash crop in the United States, greater than corn and wheat combined. But marijuana use became illegal throughout the world in the twentieth century, perhaps in part due to the influence of the plastics, timber, and pharmaceutical industries, which saw cannabis products as competition. Medical use—for pain relief, appetite stimulation, and so on—is now legal is some states and countries. Some scientists think that the need to alter one's consciousness is nearly as fundamental as the need for food and shelter.

A cannabis plant

Lunar Lagomorph

Patterns in the dark and light areas of the moon (the seas and the highlands) cause many of us in the West to see a "man in the moon." In some other parts of the world, people see a rabbit or a hare. Buddhists have a sweet tale of self-sacrifice to explain how a hare came to be on the face of the moon; it has been handed down in many versions in Eastern cultures. The Sanskrit word for moon is *sasin*, "marked with the hare." As told in Sri Lanka:

> The Buddha was wandering through a wood when he met a hare who asked him how he fared. "I am poor and hungry," the Buddha replied. "Art thou hungry?" asked the hare. "Make a fire, friend, and then kill, cook, and eat me." The Buddha thanked him and lit the fire. But as the hare leapt into the flames the Buddha plucked him out unharmed and placed him in the Moon.

Volcanic Explosivity

The volcanic eruption of Mount St. Helens on May 18, 1980, produced 1.4 billion cubic yards of uncompacted ash, which traveled around the earth in fifteen days and left detectable amounts for twenty-two thousand square miles. Fifty-seven people and countless wildlife were killed.

On August 24, 79 CE, Mount Vesuvius erupted, spewing 3.4 billion cubic yards of rock and ash and burying Pompeii under about ten feet of debris. As Pliny the Younger described it, "A cloud . . . was ascending, the appearance of which I cannot give you a more exact description of than by likening it to that of a pine-tree, for it shot up to a great height in the form of a very tall trunk, which spread itself out at the top into a sort of branches." As many as twenty-five thousand people were killed in Pompeii, Herculaneum, and the surrounding area.

Mount Vesuvius erupting

The eruptions of St. Helens and Vesuvius are both rated five (very large) on the Volcanic Explosivity Index.

Freak Waves

Scientists have been surprised to learn that rogue waves really are natural ocean phenomena; they're not just sailors' tales that belong in the category of sea monsters and mermaids. Also called freak waves or extreme waves, they're usually defined as spontaneous ocean waves that are "more than 2 times the significant wave height" (which is "the average height [from trough to crest] of the highest one-third of waves" observed). They are a danger even to large cruise and tanker ships. Researchers are still debating the causes, but rogue waves seem to occur where strong currents run against the primary direction of the waves or where shoals or coastal variations allow smaller waves to combine and amplify. The wind may also play a role. There are reports of 80- to 110-foot waves hitting oil-drilling rigs, barges, and freighters, and some scientists think that rogue waves might account for some disappearances in the Bermuda Triangle.

In 1995, the *Queen Elizabeth 2* was hit by a ninety-five-foot wall of water in the North Atlantic. The ship's captain said that it "looked as if we were heading straight into the White Cliffs of Dover." There is at least one example in which freak waves may have occurred in fresh water. The SS *Edmund Fitzgerald*, which sank in a gale on Lake Superior in 1975, may have been struck by two unusually large waves.

If you can't picture what a rogue wave can do, watch the first half hour of the 2006 movie *Poseidon*.

Underwater Caves

The Blue Holes of the Bahamas have absolutely no relation to black holes, the regions in space where not even light can escape the intense gravitational pull of a supernova. Kelsey Ramos of the *Los Angeles Times* explains: "Named for their vibrant color as seen from above, [blue holes] are subsurface voids that contain fresh, marine or mixed waters that extend below sea level. They are open to the surface and may provide access to submerged caves." Their apparent blueness is just the reflection of the sky. Sea-level changes in past ice ages left the islands with numerous caves and sinkholes, which are home to crustaceans, sponges, annelids, and fish and are very popular with scuba divers. Local myths about a sea monster called a lusca that lives in the caves are probably sightings of giant octopuses or just decomposing mounds of whale blubber.

Sometimes Speed Is of the Essence

The world's fastest bird is *Falco peregrinus*, the peregrine falcon, which in a stoop (a steep dive) can fly more than 200 miles per hour. On land, the cheetah (*Acinonyx jubatus*) is the fastest animal in short bursts of running—up to 70 miles per hour—and can accelerate from 0 to 60 miles per hour in under 4 seconds. (By contrast, according to *Motor*

Facts do not "speak for themselves", they are read in the light of theory.

—Stephen Jay Gould (*The Richness of Life: The Essential Stephen Jay Gould*, 2006)

Trend magazine, the 2009 Corvette "blitzes from 0 to 60 . . . in a scalding 3.3 seconds"). The sailfish (*Istiophorus platypterus*) can swim almost as fast as a cheetah can sprint. Among our insect friends, the dragonfly (Odonata) travels up to 38 miles per hour, and the Australian tiger beetle (*Cicindela hudsoni*), on its six skinny legs, can run 5.6 miles per hour.

A cheetah

The Roots of Red Hair

The hair color inaccurately referred to as *red* is the rarest human hair color; only 1 to 2 percent of the population enjoys the privilege of "red" hair, which has existed for only the last forty thousand years. It's caused by a variant in the melanocortin 1 receptor gene (MC1R, sometimes called the *Celtic gene*), which was discovered in the 1990s in Scotland, the country with the highest proportion of auburn-haired people in the world. Famous redheads in history include Alexander the Great, King David, Mary Magdalene, Queen Boudicca (or Boadicea), Richard the Lionhearted, Erik the Red, Leonardo da Vinci, Galileo Galilei, Christopher Columbus, Thomas Jefferson, Antonio Vivaldi, Vincent van Gogh, Emily Dickinson, James Joyce, and Katharine Hepburn.

Fish or Weapon?

The Natural History of Crafts and Manufactures

The Highest Honor

Beginning in the earliest days of the republic, the U.S. Congress has presented gold medals to convey the "highest expression of national appreciation for distinguished achievements and contributions." The first medal was awarded to George Washington by the Continental Congress in 1776, and until the 1860s, all the recipients were military men. Then Congress expanded the eligibility to include artists, writers, musicians, scientists, explorers, athletes, and others.

Some awards have been made years or decades after the events, some posthumously. Recipients of the Congressional Gold Medal—not to be confused with the Medal of Honor, which is a military award—include Joe Louis, Louis L'Amour, and Fred Waring (all three on the same day in 1982); Frank Sinatra and Mother Teresa of Calcutta (1997); the Little Rock Nine (1998); the Navajo Code Talkers (2000); the Tuskegee Airmen (2006); the Dalai Lama (2006); Arnold Palmer (2009); and all 650 members of the 1980 Summer Olympics team.

A Special Span

The Brooklyn Bridge, dubbed the Eighth Wonder of the World on the day it opened, was then the longest suspension bridge, at 1,595 feet and 6 inches. Each of its four suspender cables, from which the roadway hangs, is 15¾ inches in diameter. Each cable contains 5,434 steel wires wrapped by almost 244 miles of wire, for a total of 3,515 miles of wire in each cable. The weight of the new bridge, not including the masonry, was 14,680 tons.

On May 25, 1883, the bridge's first full day of operation, 1,800 vehicles and 150,300 pedestrians crossed between Brooklyn and Manhattan (which were still separate cities). Regarding the traffic, the *New York Times* predicted, "The preparations are thus completed for about the most helpless and extensive dead-lock that is to be seen anywhere." These days, the Brooklyn Bridge carries more than 131,000 vehicles each weekday.

Fish or Weapon?

A *torpedo* is an elongated explosive projectile that travels underwater. In the animal kingdom, it's also the name of a member of the family *Torpedinidae*—the electric rays. The fish torpedoes are flat and shaped like a disk and don't look like the weapon at all. The origin of the name is the Latin verb *torpere*, which means "stun, make numb, or paralyze"—what the sting of an electric ray will do.

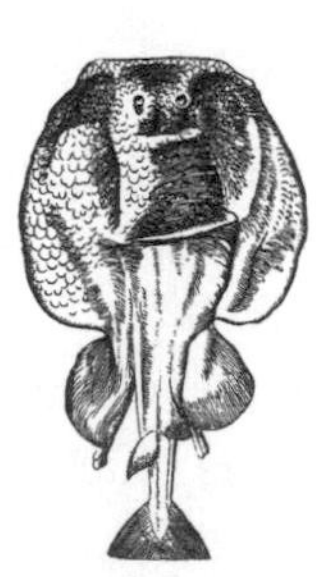
An electric ray

In early experiments in torpedo weaponry, before 1800, the devices were more like mines: round explosive charges without propulsion, which could be towed to a vessel or floated below the surface in an attempt to blow it up. So, in 1864, at the battle of Mobile Bay, when Admiral David Farragut said, "Damn the torpedoes, full speed ahead!" he meant "Ignore those floating bags of gunpowder!"

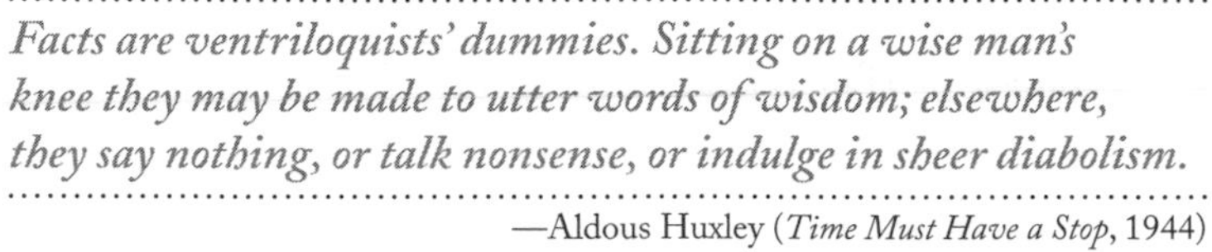

Facts are ventriloquists' dummies. Sitting on a wise man's knee they may be made to utter words of wisdom; elsewhere, they say nothing, or talk nonsense, or indulge in sheer diabolism.

—Aldous Huxley (*Time Must Have a Stop*, 1944)

Rockets' Red Glare

The "rockets' red glare" that Francis Scott Key described in "The Star-Spangled Banner" (1814) came from Congreve rockets, which had been designed by Sir William Congreve a decade earlier. They were iron tubes of various sizes filled with black powder as a propellant, topped with a cylindro-conoidal warhead.

Launched from a wooden pole, they had a range of half a mile to two miles. Their main advantage was that they were self-contained and portable: they didn't have to be fired from a cannon, yet they had a similar destructive force. Wildly inaccurate, they were effective when they hit the target.

In the Battle of Bladensburg during the War of 1812, veteran British troops fired Congreve rockets at poorly trained U.S. militiamen and routed them. The men broke and ran so quickly that the skirmish became known as the "Bladensburg Races." The British then set fire to the Capitol (including the Library of Congress), the White House, and other public buildings in Washington.

If you have ever set off bottle rockets in your backyard on the Fourth of July, you know what a Congreve rocket is (at least, a small one).

Bombs Bursting in Air

Key's phrase "bombs bursting in air" also has an interesting back story. Henry Shrapnel (1761–1842), an English artillery officer, used his personal fortune to develop what he called spherical case shot, a "shell . . . filled with bullets and contain[ing] a [timed] bursting charge which is only just sufficient to open it and allow the bullets to continue to travel along paths not diverging very much from the trajectory of the shell before bursting." In 1803, the British government conducted extensive tests of Shrapnel's case shot, and it was adopted by the Board of Ordnance.

Shrapnel shot, as it was called, was first used against the Dutch in Suriname the next year. It was also fired at the Battle of Baltimore in 1814 and was a significant factor in the British victory over Napoleon at Waterloo. The Duke of Wellington's chief artillery officer claimed that without this weapon, the British would not have been successful; "hence on this simple circumstance hinged entirely the turn of the battle."

Bombs bursting in air

By World War I, all armies were using shells based on Shrapnel's original design—to devastating effect. In the following decades, however, they became obsolete, replaced by high-explosive projectiles that don't use gunpowder or bullets.

The word *shrapnel* originally referred to the shell, then to the bullets that were dispersed; now it means "any metal fragment of a bomb, projectile, or mine sent flying by its explosion." Military secrecy prevented Shrapnel from receiving the public recognition he thought he deserved for his invention, and he died "a disappointed man" at age eighty.

From Featherie to Polymer

The first balls that were used to play the game of golf were made of wood. The featherie, introduced in the early 1600s, was the real beginning of the modern golf ball. Made of wet leather stuffed with wet feathers, it was a hard, durable ball, because the leather contracted as it dried while the feathers expanded as they dried. Handcrafted featheries were very expensive, but they were in use for more than two hundred years.

The gutta-percha ball, or guttie, was made from the sap of certain tropical trees and was introduced in 1848. Gutties could be mass-produced, so they were considerably cheaper than featheries and thus opened up the game to nonwealthy players. The early gutties were smooth-surfaced, but golfers began to notice that balls with nicks and scratches tended to fly farther, so soon a variety of dimples and other patterns began to appear. For many years, the bramble design, which made the ball look like a raspberry, was dominant.

> *Facts are to the mind what food is to the body.*
>
> —Edmund Burke (*The Forbes Book of Business Quotations*, 1997)

In 1898 a ball was developed that had a solid rubber core wrapped with rubber thread and a gutta-percha cover. Other experimenters tried balls with a core of compressed air (but they had a tendency to explode), mercury, cork, or metal. Modern balls use new materials—polymers, silicone, synthetic rubber—to optimize the aerodynamics and get better distance and spin ratios.

Hard as Rock

Cement and concrete aren't the same thing; the former is an ingredient of the latter. Several types of concrete were known to the ancient world, but the Romans perfected the technology and used it extensively, including in the construction of the walls and the dome of the Pantheon (the dome weighs almost five thousand tons).

Cement is made of calcium, aluminum, silicon, iron, gypsum, and other ingredients. The formula for concrete is 6 percent air, 11 percent Portland cement, 41 percent gravel or crushed stone (coarse aggregate), 26 percent sand (fine aggregate), and 16 percent water. There are 150 billion grains in one pound of cement.

The White City

The buildings of the Chicago World's Fair of 1893 (properly known as the Columbian Exposition) gained fame as the White City and influenced American architecture for decades—which was longer than the buildings themselves lasted. Designed to be temporary, the buildings were constructed with an iron or a wooden frame and covered with a material called *staff*. Invented in Europe, staff was a mixture of plaster, cement, and jute (or hemp) fibers, which made lightweight and moderately sturdy structures.

Only one of the exposition buildings survives today. Because it was meant to house valuable paintings and sculpture, the Palace of Fine Arts was built of brick and given a top layer of staff. In the 1920s, Julius Rosenwald, the head of Sears, Roebuck & Company, donated funds to have the crumbling facade made permanent, so the staff was stripped off and replaced with limestone. The palace reopened on June 19, 1933, as the Museum of Science and Industry and is one of Chicago's most popular tourist destinations today.

The White House

The Executive Mansion, or the White House, as it came to be known, measures 168 feet by 85 feet and 6 inches (or 152 feet wide, with the porticoes) and sits on eighteen acres of fenced land. Made of painted sandstone in the late Georgian architectural style, the White House has 132 rooms (including 35 bathrooms) that total about 55,000 square feet, and it requires more than five hundred gallons of paint to cover the exterior.

The original, palatial design by Pierre L'Enfant was four or five times larger, but it was scaled down in the final plans because "many Americans were opposed to such monarchical pretensions," and L'Enfant was replaced by architect James Hoban. The total construction cost (1792–1800) was $232,372.

The White House

John Adams was the first president to reside there. Until the 1860s, the White House was the largest residence in the country.

Rising from the Ashes

San Francisco's Fairmont Hotel ("the most conspicuous structure on the sky line of the city") was still under construction but almost ready to open on April 18, 1906, when at 5:13 a.m. an earthquake of at least 7.7 magnitude struck the city. It lasted under a minute, but it was one of the nation's worst natural disasters. The interior of the empty hotel was seriously damaged by the quake and by subsequent fire, although the exterior walls of the building remained.

The hotel reopened one year later, rebuilt by Julia Morgan, the first woman to graduate from the École des Beaux-Arts in Paris and from the University of California–Berkeley's civil engineering program. Morgan was also California's first female licensed architect, and she designed a number of buildings and residences for William Randolph Hearst, including Hearst Castle at San Simeon.

Pleasant Transit

The word *highway* is very old; the *Oxford English Dictionary* has tracked its use back to the year 859. In the 1890s, the term *parkway* was introduced; the idea was that a parkway would be surrounded with trees and grass, thus designed for "pleasant transit."

The Merritt Parkway was built in the 1930s as a scenic highway, winding through the lush forests of southern Connecticut; its sixty-eight original bridges each had a different art deco or art moderne design (the work of architect George L. Dunkelberger). Another beautiful parkway is the Natchez Trace, a 450-mile road that commemorates an ancient trail that was used for thousands of years by Native Americans. Nicknamed the Devil's Backbone for its hazards (from both beasts and men), the road connects Natchez, Mississippi, with Nashville, Tennessee.

In California, the most scenic part of the Pacific Coast Highway is the 139-mile stretch from Morro Bay to Monterey: stunning ocean views; redwood, cypress, and pine groves; jagged rocks and granite cliffs. All three roads are on the list of National Scenic Byways.

A City for "Useful Manufactures"

The nation's first planned industrial city was Paterson, New Jersey. In 1778, Alexander Hamilton, then a colonel in the Continental Army, stood on the banks of the Passaic River, marveling as the water plummeted seventy-seven feet down the Great Falls. He envisioned it as the great energy source that could power a city of factories.

In 1792, as secretary of the treasury, Hamilton formed an investment group called the Society for Establishing Useful Manufactures, which founded mills and other industrial projects. Textiles—cotton, hemp, sailcloth—became the first big industry in Paterson, followed by steel, iron, firearms, and railroad locomotives.

Paterson reached its economic height in the early twentieth century, when its abundance of silk mills gave it the name Silk City. But along with industry came labor issues, including a historic six-month silk workers' strike in 1913. Like many northeast industrial towns, Paterson faded after World War II and is today one of the more economically depressed areas in the state of New Jersey. In April 2009, the Great Falls were designated a National Historical Park.

The Salad Dressing of the St. Lawrence

Thousand Island salad dressing is actually named for a thousand islands—more precisely, 1,864 islands in the St. Lawrence River between the United States and Canada. According to the 1000 Islands tourism bureau, "To become an official part of the count, an island must meet two criteria: it must be above water 365 days a year and it must support two living trees." For the past century, two hotels, in the towns of Clayton and Alexandria Bay, New York, have been fighting (good-naturedly, I'm sure) over the right to claim that they originated the mayonnaise-based condiment.

All Things Peanut

George Washington Carver, agricultural scientist, educator, and artist, is well known for his work with peanuts and sweet potatoes. He found more than three hundred uses for the peanut, including many nonfood products: hand lotion, laundry soap, wood stains, paper, axle grease, hen food, and a cure for dandruff.

From the sweet potato, he produced ink, library paste, vinegar, synthetic rubber, silk and cotton dyes, and flour that was used by the U.S. government in World War I. He also developed face powder, wallpaper, and paint pigments from the Alabama clay soil; paper and rope fiber from cotton; and rugs, fuel bricks, synthetic marble, and wall board from recycled materials.

In childhood, Carver had shown some talent for needlework and basket making, and all his life he loved to paint the flowers and plants that he studied. When he died in 1943, Carver left his entire estate to the Tuskegee Institute, where he had worked and taught for fifty years. He is buried there beside his friend and colleague, the first president of Tuskegee, Booker T. Washington.

Spoiled Milk

Cheese is one of the accidental inventions in human history. In almost all parts of the world, in the earliest days of civilization, people drank the milk of sheep, goats, cows, buffalo, or other local ungulates (hooved mammals). People noticed that milk would spoil quickly if it sat in containers made from an animal stomach. The curdling was caused by the action of an enzyme (rennet) in the stomach on the protein (casein) in the milk. The resulting solids (curds) could be pressed and salted, making them easier to preserve and transport than milk.

Polyphemus, the Cyclops in Homer's *Odyssey*, was a cheese maker; Odysseus (Ulysses) and his men stole and ate some of his cheeses. A two-thousand-year-old piece of carbonized cheese was found in the ruins of Herculaneum, an ancient Roman town. In Wisconsin and the Netherlands, where large amounts of cheese are produced and consumed, people are often called "cheeseheads," and they don't seem to mind. A cheese connoisseur is called a *turophile* (*tiri* means "cheese" in Greek).

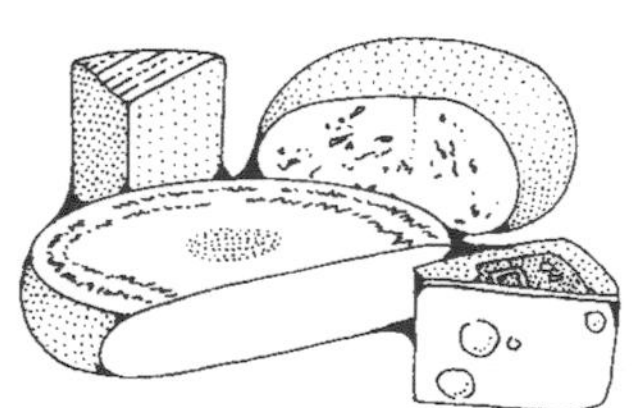

Spoiled milk in cheese form

Italian Food Translated

Saltimbocca: jump into the mouth
Linguini: little tongues
Arrabbiata: angry style
Tiramisu: lift me up
Orecchiette: little ears
Puttanesca: in the style of a prostitute
Vermicelli: little worms
Strozzapreti: strangled (or choking) priest

Tiramisu—the very popular dessert of mascarpone cheese, espresso, ladyfingers, and Marsala wine—was not a Renaissance delicacy (it requires refrigeration). It doesn't have a long tradition in *cucina Italiana*; no recipes or published references have been found from before the 1980s. It was probably invented by a pastry chef in Treviso, Italy, who now lives in Baltimore.

Something to Write On

The word *paper* comes from *papyrus* (*Cyperus papyrus*), a reedlike water plant grown extensively in the Nile Delta. By the third millennium BCE, the Egyptians had developed a process of pressing strips of papyrus into sheets to create a material that could be used for writing as well as for mats, sandals, and even cloth. Sheets of papyrus were glued together to form scrolls, the original form of the book.

A rivalry between the libraries of Alexandria and Pergamon (in modern Turkey) seems to have led to Egypt's withholding supplies of papyrus, and parchment—which had been developed in Pergamon—began to replace papyrus around 200 BCE. Parchment is made from animal skins: goats, sheep, calves, and even donkeys. The skins are washed, treated with lime, stretched, scraped, and rubbed with chalk and pumice to produce a smooth white surface. The best quality of parchment is vellum, and it is still used today for important documents and some drum heads and bagpipes.

Paper as we know it was invented by the Chinese about two thousand years ago. After first using wood or silk as a writing surface, they tried hemp and mulberry fibers, but eventually they discovered that pounding rags or rope into pulp produced a superior product. The Arabs learned the technique from Chinese papermakers, and the industry was established in Baghdad by 800 CE. From there, it spread to Europe and the West.

Steinway Grand

A concert grand piano is one of the more complex devices built by human hands. Steinway pianos, still entirely handmade, have about twelve thousand individual parts. To make one instrument in the company's Long Island City, New York, factory takes nearly a year and about 450 skilled artisans: case makers, plate fitters, grand finishers, belly makers, stringers, and fine-tuners, among many others.

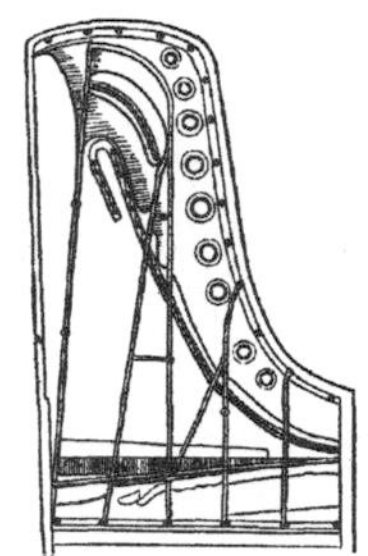

The inside of a Steinway grand piano

PART TWO

ON REASON AND SCIENCE

Reason, from which comes Philosophy: Philosophy, or the portion of human knowledge which should be related to reason, is very extensive. There is almost no object perceived by the senses which has not been transformed into a science by reflection. . . . God, man, and nature will therefore furnish us with a general division of philosophy or of science (for these words are synonyms); and philosophy or science will be science of God, science of man, and science of nature.

—JEAN LE ROND D'ALEMBERT

Links in the Chain of Being

The Science of God: Theology, Religion, and Superstition

The Great Chain of Being

The *scala naturae*, the "ladder of nature" or "chain of being," is an idea attributed to Aristotle (although he did not use that term), who attempted, in his *History of Animals*, to classify all types of creatures. Here is the usual depiction of the ladder:

God
Humans
Other mammals
Birds
Fish
Insects
Plants
Rocks

For Aristotle, the species were immutable and fixed, and this view continued to be profoundly influential for centuries. It was, however, disputed and modified by many philosophers, until finally the great chain of being had been transformed into the "contingent chain of becoming."

One God

According to the *Stanford Encyclopedia of Philosophy*, "Theists believe that reality's ultimate principle is God—an omnipotent, omniscient goodness that is the creative ground of everything other than itself. Monotheism is the view that there is only one such God." It's not quite that simple, however; there are some variations. Within Christianity, for example, the doctrines of the Trinity (God in three persons) and of the nature of Jesus (both human and divine) seem to contradict the single God concept. The terms *henotheist* and *monolatrist* were coined to describe someone who worships one supreme being while allowing that other gods might exist. The idea of monotheism first developed from ancient pantheistic systems.

Two Natures

The religious and philosophical concept of Manichean duality is named for Mani, a Babylonian prophet of Persian descent who lived in the desert of Mesopotamia in the third century CE and was a member of a Christian sect known as the Elchasites. Mani taught that there were pairs of opposing entities that existed from eternity: light versus darkness, life versus death, and good versus evil. In his view, the salvation process was "the ultimate recovery . . . of the Light particles which have become trapped in the material world."

Facts are the air of scientists. Without them you can never fly.

—Ivan Pavlov (letter, "Bequest to the Academic Youth of Soviet Russia," 1936). Also widely attributed to Dr. Linus Pauling.

Three Fates

In Greek mythology, the Three Fates (or Moirae, "apportioners"; the Roman equivalent were called Parcae) are the "divinities of the duration of human life," who assign "to every man his fate or share." Clothoe, the spinner, reels out a thread of life for each newborn; Lachesis, the measurer, determines the length of the thread and assigns our destiny; and Atropos, the unavoidable, cuts the thread and ends each life. (The Roman names are Nona, Decuma, and Morta, respectively.)

As with most myths, there are other versions. In the *Iliad*, Homer combines all three Fates in one deity. In Scandinavia, the Fates (called the Norns, "those women who shape what must be") are three sisters: Urd (the past), Verdandi (the present), and Skuld (the future). Artists often depict the Three Fates as "aged and hideous women"—Clothoe with a spindle or a book, Lachesis pointing to the globe, and Atropos with a blade or a sundial.

The Three Fates

Four Truths

The Four Noble Truths, the central tenets of Buddhism, teach that "suffering is part of life; there are causes of suffering (emotional attachment, ignorance, and selfishness); there is a state of transcendence of suffering; and there is a path that leads to that state." The Middle Way (moderation) and the Noble Eightfold Path can help us to transcend the cycles of rebirth and attain enlightenment and utter peace. The eight elements of the path are right views, right intentions, right speech, right conduct, right livelihood, right effort, right mindfulness, and right concentration.

Five Pillars

Islam (derived from the Arabic word *aslama*, which means "submission") is the faith founded by Muhammed in the seventh century CE. In Islam, God is called Allah and is the same God worshipped by Jews and Christians. All three are thus known as People of the Book. Muslims believe that any activity done in obedience to Allah is an act of worship. The framework of daily life for a Muslim is focused on the Five Pillars of Islam:

Faith (*shahadah*): Believe in one God and that the Prophet Muhammed is His messenger.

Prayer (*salat*): Pray toward Mecca five times each day to remember God and thank Him for His grace.

Alms (*zakat*): Donate a portion of one's wealth to the poor.

Fasting (*siyam*): Go without food and drink from before dawn to sunset during the month of Ramadan to empathize with the poor and learn self-discipline.

Pilgrimage (*hajj*): Visit Mecca and perform the *hajj* once in a lifetime, if one is able and has the means.

A Six-Pointed Star

Though frequently associated with Judaism today, the Star of David (or Shield of David)—*magen David* in Hebrew—does not appear in early rabbinic writing. It's a recent addition to Jewish iconography, and probably was originally intended to represent the shape of King David's shield.

Although the hexagram—two interlocking equilateral triangles—was used in ancient times and is a good luck symbol throughout the Middle East and North Africa, the Star of David began to be used by Jews only in the Middle Ages, appearing on a flag in Prague in the fourteenth century and on synagogues in the seventeenth century.

In 1897, Theodor Herzl selected the star as the symbol of the Zionist movement, and it was chosen for the flag of the new state of Israel in 1948. In Nazi Germany, Jews were required to wear yellow stars on their clothing. The Magen David Adom (the Red Star [or Shield] of

There are no facts, only interpretations.

—Friedrich Nietzsche (*Notebooks*, Summer 1886–Fall 1887)

David) is Israel's emergency disaster service, akin to the Red Cross of Christian countries and the Red Crescent of Muslim countries.

Seven Happiness Beings

In Japanese mythology, there are Seven Lucky Gods, or Gods of Good Fortune (from *shichi fukujin*, or "seven happiness beings"). Strongly influenced by Indian and Chinese religious characters a thousand years ago, the seven gods developed into significant cultural icons in Japanese culture. Especially at the New Year, they "journey harmoniously together on a ship of treasure [the Takarabune] to share all of the positive qualities that are embodied by their cheery symbolism." Although there are variations in their descriptions (and, of course, in the spellings), these are the Seven Lucky Gods:

Hotei, the Laughing Buddha

Hotei	The god of happiness; also called the Laughing Buddha or the Santa of Japan
Jyuroujin	The god of longevity and wisdom
Fukurokujuzin	The god of wealth; the twin of Jyuroujin
Bishimon	The god of warriors; the guardian of the treasure house
Benzai	The goddess of flowing water and of knowledge, art, music, and beauty
Daikoku	The god of the household and prosperity
Ebisu	The god associated with fishing and merchants

Eight Immortals

The Eight Immortals were mythological archetypes of Taoism in early medieval China, and they continue to be popular religious and secular symbols today. Representing "male, female, the old, the young, the rich, the noble, the poor, and the humble Chinese . . . [they] are the gods who punish evildoers and encourage people to do good,

Han Xiangzi, the flute player

help those in distress and aid those in peril." Their powers are represented by talismans, or instruments: "the fish-shaped drum that can tell the future; the precious sword that can subdue monsters and drive away evils; the flute that can make everything grow; the lotus flower that can bring self-cultivation; the bottle gourd that can save all living things from misery; the fan that can make the dead come back to life; the jade clapper that can purify the environment; and the flower basket that has great magic power." The legend is commemorated and celebrated at the Temple of the Eight Immortals, the largest monastery in Xi'an and an important and popular site for Taoist celebrations.

Nine for Hindus

The number nine is of great significance in Hinduism, the oldest living religion on earth. Nine is "closely associated with the process of creation in the cosmic time cycle." Hindus have nine beliefs that summarize their spirituality: one all-pervasive Supreme Being; the divinity of the Vedic scriptures; the endless cycles of creation; karma, the law of cause and effect; the reincarnation of the soul; personal rituals that create connections with unseen worlds; personal discipline and an enlightened guide as essential; the sacredness of all life; and the idea that all paths to God deserve tolerance and understanding. There are also nine modes of devotion and nine *dravyas* ("materials" or "substances"): earth, water, fire, air, ether, time, space, mind, and self. Hindus celebrate Navaratri, or Navratras, the nine auspicious nights, a festival that honors the mother goddess Shakti, who is "the emanating power, the essence and the creative manifestation of the Supreme Being."

Get your facts first, and then you can distort them as much as you please.

—Mark Twain (*The Wit and Wisdom of Mark Twain*, 1999)

Ten Commandments

When people discuss placing the Ten Commandments in public spaces, I always wonder: Whose version do they plan to use? Judaism numbers them one way, and the early Church numbered them another way, based primarily on the Catholic desire to circumvent the prohibition of statues and images. (That commandment was a definite nonstarter, like circumcision and kosher dietary laws, among the pagans whom the Church hoped to convert.) The Protestants, except for Lutherans, follow the Jewish numbering almost exactly, differing only at the beginning.

Thus, your eighth commandment might be my seventh. The commandments are listed—but not numbered—three times in the Bible: twice in Exodus and once in Deuteronomy. The following wording is from the Book of Exodus, according to the King James translation, with modifications provided by the Catholic catechism:

PROTESTANT (OTHER THAN LUTHERAN)	CATHOLIC AND LUTHERAN	JEWISH
1. Thou shalt have no other gods before me.	1. I am the Lord thy God. Thou shalt not have strange gods before me.	1. I am the Lord thy God, who brought thee out of the land of Egypt, out of the house of slavery.
2. Thou shalt not make unto thee any graven image, or any likeness of any thing that is in heaven above, or that is in the earth beneath, or that is in the water under the earth: Thou shalt not bow down thyself to them, nor serve them: for I the Lord thy God am a jealous God, visiting the iniquity of the fathers upon the children unto the third and fourth generation of them that hate me; And showing mercy unto	2. Thou shalt not take the name of the Lord thy God in vain.	2. Thou shalt have no other gods before Me. Thou shalt not make unto thee a graven image, nor any manner of likeness, of any thing that is in heaven above, or that is in the earth beneath, or that is in the water under the earth; Thou shalt not bow down unto them, nor serve them; for I the Lord thy God

(Continued)

PROTESTANT (OTHER THAN LUTHERAN)	CATHOLIC AND LUTHERAN	JEWISH
thousands of them that love me, and keep my commandments.		am a jealous God, visiting the iniquity of the fathers upon the children unto the third and fourth generation of them that hate Me; And showing mercy unto the thousandth generation of them that love Me and keep My commandments.
3. Thou shalt not take the name of the Lord thy God in vain: for the Lord will not hold him guiltless that taketh his name in vain.	3. Remember thou keep the Sabbath Day.	3. Thou shalt not take the name of the Lord thy God in vain; for the Lord will not hold him guiltless that taketh His name in vain.
4. Remember the Sabbath day, to keep it holy. Six days shalt thou labor, and do all thy work: But the seventh day is the sabbath of the Lord thy God: in it thou shalt not do any work, thou, nor thy son, nor thy daughter, thy manservant, nor thy maidservant, nor thy cattle, nor thy stranger that is within thy gates: For in six days the Lord made heaven and earth, the sea, and all that in them is, and rested the seventh day: wherefore the Lord blessed the sabbath day, and hallowed it.	4. Honor thy Father and thy Mother.	4. Remember the Sabbath day to keep it holy. Six days shalt thou labour, and do all thy work. But the seventh day is the Sabbath in honour of the Lord thy God; on it thou shalt not do any work, neither thou, nor thy son, nor thy daughter, thy manservant nor thy maidservant, nor thy cattle, nor thy stranger that is within thy gates; For in six days the Lord made the heavens and the earth, the sea, and all that is in them, and rested on the seventh day; therefore the Lord blessed the Sabbath day, and hallowed it.

PROTESTANT (OTHER THAN LUTHERAN)	CATHOLIC AND LUTHERAN	JEWISH
5. Honor thy father and thy mother: that thy days may be long upon the land which the Lord thy God giveth thee.	5. Thou shalt not kill.	5. Honour thy father and thy mother; in order that thy days may be prolonged upon the land which the Lord thy God giveth thee.
6. Thou shalt not kill.	6. Thou shalt not commit adultery.	6. Thou shalt not kill.
7. Thou shalt not commit adultery.	7. Thou shalt not steal.	7. Thou shalt not commit adultery.
8. Thou shalt not steal.	8. Thou shalt not bear false witness against thy neighbor.	8. Thou shalt not steal.
9. Thou shalt not bear false witness against thy neighbor.	9. Thou shalt not covet thy neighbour's wife.	9. Thou shalt not bear false witness against thy neighbor.
10. Thou shalt not covet thy neighbor's house, thou shalt not covet thy neighbor's wife, nor his manservant, nor his maidservant, nor his ox, nor his ass, nor any thing that is thy neighbor's.	10. Thou shalt not covet thy neighbour's goods.	10. Thou shalt not covet thy neighbour's house; thou shalt not covet thy neighbour's wife, nor his manservant, nor his maidservant, nor his ox, nor his ass, nor any thing that is thy neighbour's.

Soul Guides

Many belief systems include the concept of a psychopomp, from the Greek words *psyche*, "breath" or "soul," and *pompos*, "conductor." A psychopomp is a nonjudgmental guide for the souls of the dead on their journey to the afterlife.

In ancient Egypt, the god Anubis oversaw the mummification process and led the spirit of the deceased to the entrance of the underworld. Dolphins—"emblematic of the passage of the soul from one state of existence to another"—were frequently depicted in Etruscan tombs. In northern Europe, the Valkyries carried bodies from the battlefield to Valhalla (where fighting resumed).

Barnumbir, the aboriginal Australian name for the morning star, grabs the souls (*mokuy*) of the dead with a feathered string and brings them to their spiritual home. For Buddhists, Jizo is the enlightened being who compassionately protects children who die before their parents do and are thus unable to cross over to the afterlife. In other cultures, it might be angels, shamans, birds, bees, foxes, or even the northern lights that perform this guiding function.

A dolphin

Jesus and Mary

The Catholic theological concepts of the virgin birth and the immaculate conception are often confused. The virgin birth refers to the birth of Jesus to a woman who had not had sexual relations. The immaculate conception is about Mary, not Jesus. It's a dogma of the Catholic Church, promulgated in 1854, that Mary herself was conceived without original sin because she was to be the mother of Jesus. According to a papal bull of Pope Pius IX, "The most Blessed Virgin Mary was, from the first moment of her conception, by a singular grace and privilege of almighty God and by virtue of the merits of Jesus Christ, Saviour of the human race, preserved immune from all stain of original sin."

Cow Protection

Why are cows sacred in India? Hindus do not actually worship cattle; it would be more accurate to say that cows are taboo rather than sacred: they are not to be touched; they are *aghnya*, not to be slaughtered. Cows have been venerated in India since the Vedic era (second millennium BCE). They are associated with mother earth and the Brahman class. They symbolize nonviolent generosity, and the products that they give are used in religious rites. Mahatma

Gandhi wrote in 1950, "The cause of cow-protection is very dear to me. If someone were to ask me what the most important outward manifestation of Hinduism was, I would suggest that it was the idea of cow-protection."

The Piasa

There's a giant bird painted on a high bluff over the Mississippi River, on the Illinois side near the town of Alton. It's the Piasa (*PY-ah-sah*), and it was first seen by non-Native people in 1673 when Jacques Marquette and Louis Jolliet traveled down the river. Marquette described the painted petroglyph in his journal: "While skirting some rocks which by their height and length inspired awe, we saw upon one of them two painted monsters which at first made us afraid, and upon which the boldest savages dare not long rest their eyes. They are as large as a calf; they have horns on their heads like those of a deer, a horrible look, red eyes, a beard like a tiger's, a face somewhat like a man's, a body covered with scales, and so long a tail that it winds all around the body, passing above the head and going back between the legs, ending in a fish's tail. Green, red, and black are the three colors composing the picture."

The true story of the Piasa is lost, but legends have endured about Ouatoga, chief of the Illini, who saved his tribe from the devastations of the "bird who devours man." It may also be a local example of the thunderbird myth shared by many Native American peoples: a huge bird that darkens the sky and brings thunder and lightning. Nearly destroyed from ravaging by man and nature, the painting—now depicting only one bird—has been restored and continues to be visible from the Meeting of the Great Rivers National Scenic Byway, near Alton. The Piasa is also the best-selling postcard at the Alton Regional Convention and Visitors Bureau.

The Piasa

The Numbers of the Faithful

It might be an impossible task to count the number of members of any individual religion, because definitions and counting methodology are likely to vary. That said, here are some estimates of the numbers for the top world religions, according to Adherents.com, an Internet initiative not affiliated with any religious, political, or educational organization.

Christianity	2.1 billion
Islam	1.5 billion
Hinduism	900 million
Chinese traditional	394 million
Buddhism	376 million
Primal, indigenous, animist	300 million

The source identifies an additional 1.1 billion people as "secular, nonreligious, agnostic, or atheist" and 1 million as followers of some form of neopaganism. According to the American Jewish Committee, the world's Jewish population is 13.2 million.

Don't Annoy the Gods

Politicians, corporate executives, and sports superstars may want to take note: Hubris (extreme arrogance, presumption) was the sin most hated by the gods of ancient Greece. They were "relentless in striking down a man who, confident in his own achievement or good fortune, tended to forget his human status."

Jinxed

The evil eye—*malocchio* (Italian), *matiasma* (Greek), or the milder version, the "hairy eyeball" (at least in the Brooklyn neighborhood where I grew up)—is the "idea that a malign glance can do grievous harm to person and property." It's older than Greek and Roman civilizations, and its widespread distribution from India to the Middle East and Europe points to its great antiquity. It may even have existed in Sumer in the third or fourth millennium BCE.

The belief in the evil eye traveled with the waves of immigration to the Americas, where we worry about "jinxing" a positive outcome. Praising someone—especially a child—may invite the evil eye, so such praise must be avoided or balanced with insults. There are also apotropaic (designed to avert evil) rituals, gestures, and amulets that are supposed to cure or prevent the feared bad luck or illness. In Turkey, they say, "*Nazar değmesin*" ("May the evil eye not touch you").

The superstition may have a foundation in the Indo-European concept of "limited good"—that there's a fixed supply of happiness and good fortune in the world, so my success could be at your expense. The evil eye is a manifestation of the spirit of envy. In the first chapter of Bram Stoker's *Dracula*, the protagonist is surprised when "all made the sign of the cross and pointed two fingers towards me. With some difficulty, I got a fellow passenger to tell me what they meant . . . he explained that it was a charm or guard against the evil eye."

An apotropaic gesture

Lucky Seven

In many cultures and religions around the world, seven is a significant and lucky number, although the reasons for its reputation are not always clear. Robert Solomon writes, "Seven is an odd and arbitrary number [with] a long numerological and mystical literature celebrating the supposed magic of seven. . . . It is the perfect number, according to Pythagoras (the sum of three [the triangle] plus four [the square], both lucky too)." According to the wedding planner Web site theknot.com, tens of thousands of American couples chose to be married on July 7, 2007, because they considered it to be an especially auspicious day.

At any time or place in human history, a list of significant sevens would be quite extensive: seven seas; seven continents; seven days of creation; seven against Thebes; seven layers of ox hide in the shield of Ajax; seven wonders; seven heavens; seven seals of seven angels with seven trumpets in the Book of Revelation; Shakespeare's seven ages of man; seven chakras of the human body; the seven-year itch; seven colors in the rainbow; and seven as a winning roll of the dice in the game of craps.

Letters in Plain Sight

The Science of Humanity: Thinking, Remembering, Communicating

A Man of Puzzles

Will Shortz, the crossword editor of the *New York Times* and the puzzle master of NPR's *Weekend Edition Sunday* with Liane Hansen, is the only person anywhere to hold an official academic degree in enigmatology, the study of puzzles. He designed the program himself at Indiana University and graduated in 1974.

The Infinity of Lists

I don't know about you, but I can't live without making lists. Whether they're for shopping, household repairs, work or life tasks, lists bring order, and every time you cross off an item, you get a wonderful feeling of accomplishment. Most librarians—and other well-organized types—consider lists to be an essential element of life, without which everything would descend rapidly into chaos.

Italian semiotician, novelist, and book collector Umberto Eco agrees. When invited by the Louvre Museum to curate an exhibition, he selected as his theme "The Infinity of Lists." He told the German magazine *Der Spiegel*, "The list is the origin of culture. It's part of the history of art and literature. What does culture want? To make infinity comprehensible. It also wants to create order—not always, but often. And how, as a human being, does one face infinity? How does one attempt to grasp the incomprehensible? Through lists, through catalogs, through collections in museums and through encyclopedias and dictionaries. . . . That's why we like all the things that we assume have no limits and, therefore, no end. It's a way of escaping thoughts about death. We like lists because we don't want to die."

Hometown Names

"Labels for locals"—demonyms or residential designations that people give themselves—are usually simple constructions: add *-ite*, *-an*, or *-er* to a place name, and you get *Brooklynite*, *Cuban*, and *Aucklander*, for example.

In some places, it's more complicated. You can't easily put a suffix on Massachusetts and still have a pronounceable word, so the people who live there are called Bay Staters. Similarly, people in Connecticut are Nutmeggers (it's the Nutmeg State). There are many, many irregular forms: people of Glasgow, Scotland, are Glaswegians; the Beatles and other residents of Liverpool are Liverpudlians; everyone in Indiana is a Hoosier.

In Halifax, Nova Scotia, they've chosen Haligonians; and in Manchester, England, they're Mancunians, a term that probably derives from Mancunium or Mamucium, the first-century Roman fort at that location. The Michigan legislature decided in 1979 to officially name the residents Michiganians (rather than Michiganders or Michiganites, both of which are still in popular use). And if you live or work at the Panama Canal, you're a Zonian.

They Carried the Mail

In ancient times, there were networks for the delivery of messages and information for government and commerce in China, Egypt, Babylonia, and the Indus Valley. Augustus Caesar ran a sophisticated relay system throughout the Roman Empire. After the Dark Ages in Europe, merchants' courier services developed, growing rapidly with the invention of printing.

In the United States, the first system was established in 1639 in Boston, with taverns and inns as post offices. The first adhesive postage stamps were introduced in the United States in 1847 (Benjamin Franklin was depicted on the five-cent stamp, and George Washington on the ten-cent stamp). The Pony Express was a brief experiment (1860–1861) that ended with the introduction of transcontinental telegraphy.

Engraved on the façade of a New York post office, "Neither snow, nor rain, nor heat, nor gloom of night stays these couriers from the swift completion of their appointed rounds," is an unofficial motto of the U.S. Postal Service. It's an adaptation of a statement by the Greek historian Herodotus, who admired the messengers of the Persian Empire.

There are more than 36,000 post offices and stations in the country (although some might soon be consolidated), and more than 590,000 postal employees. Letter carriers delivered 177 billion pieces of mail in 2009 to more than 150 million residences, businesses, and post office boxes, which brought in $68 billion in revenue. About one-quarter of that revenue was for what the postal service charitably calls "advertising mail" but what most of us would call junk. The U.S. Postal Service is a sponsor of National Dog Bite Prevention Week, which occurs each year in the third full week of May.

"Neither snow, nor rain, nor heat, nor gloom of night"

Main Street, U.S.A.

According to the U.S. Postal Service, the five most common street names in the United States are *Main*, *Maple*, *Second*, *Oak*, and *Park*. *Clinton* is the most common post office name in the country (twenty-six).

Tied for second place are *Franklin*, *Madison*, and *Washington* (twenty-five each). The lowest-number zip code (ZIP originally stood for Zone Improvement Plan) is 00501, a unique code for the Internal Revenue Service in Holtsville, New York. The highest-number zip code is 99950, in Ketchikan, Alaska.

Project Gutenberg

An e-book is a digitized version of a text that can be accessed and read as an electronic file on a computer device. The very first one—in the earliest days of what would become the World Wide Web—was created by Michael Hart, a founder of the Open Source Movement, which encourages the production of software that allows collaborative modification of online content. In 1971, he typed the Declaration of Independence into his computer at the University of Illinois and began Project Gutenberg. Its mission is simple: "To encourage the creation and distribution of eBooks." Since its founding, thousands of Project Gutenberg volunteers have typed or scanned more than thirty thousand works of fiction and nonfiction into the database; most are in the public domain and therefore have no copyright restrictions. Working with international partners and affiliated organizations, Project Gutenberg has made more than a hundred thousand works in a hundred languages—novels, poetry, sheet music, and reference books—accessible online in a variety of electronic formats.

In a 2009 interview with *Searcher* magazine, Hart said, "The Gutenberg Press was the very first example of mass production and Project Gutenberg is the first example of what I have called Neo-Mass Production which I hope will start up what I have called The Neo-Industrial Revolution."

> *So vast, so limitless in capacity is man's imagination to disperse and burn away the rubble-dross of fact and probability, leaving only truth and dream.*
>
> —William Faulkner (*Requiem for a Nun*, 1951)

The Implements of Communication

Pens were invented probably about six thousand years ago, when people first used a thin reed or straw to hold a small amount of ink (which was made from crushed vegetable matter or soot mixed with oil) so that it could be applied to a surface. Quill pens came next, which used goose or swan feathers, and there were also bronze or silver "reeds" in use in the ancient world, although they were not very common.

These pens were the primary type of writing instruments until steel nibs were invented in the nineteenth century. The fountain pen was a big advance, because it had a reservoir that could hold a supply of ink; earlier pens had to be dipped frequently into an inkwell or another container. The ballpoint—"a pen in which the point is a fine ball bearing that rotates against a supply of semi-solid ink in a cartridge"—was first patented in 1888 but was then used primarily by leather tanners to mark skins.

Much improved in the twentieth century, by the 1950s the ballpoint pen had become ubiquitous. Along with soft-tip and rollerball pens—and, of course, pencils—they are the main writing implements used throughout the world today.

Alternate Writing

In most writing systems, the symbols are written consistently from right to left, left to right, or vertically from top to bottom. Some forms of ancient writing, however, were in what is called the boustrophedon (*boo-stroh-FEE-don*) style, from the Greek term for "as the ox turns to plow the field." Here the lines are written in alternating directions: the first line goes from left to right, but then rather than beginning again at the left margin, the next line is written from right to left; then the next line is left to right, and so on. This saves a little time for the writer, although some practice is needed to read the backward script of the alternate lines. The term *boustrophedon* is still in use to describe something that goes back and forth or moves in a zig-zag manner—in robotics, mathematics, biochemistry, lawn mowing, and some types of printers. Town surveys and house numbering systems in some places use this method. In 2008, Evan Parker and the Transatlantic Art Ensemble released a CD called *Boustrophedon (In Six Furrows)*, in which, according to one reviewer, "Parker uses the back and forth analogy both in scales up and down and in the flow back and forth between the American and European musicians."

FOUR SCORE AND SEVEN YEARS AGO OUR FATHERS
BROUGHT FORTH ON THIS CONTINENT A NEW NATION,
CONCEIVED IN LIBERTY, AND DEDICATED TO THE
PROPOSITION THAT ALL MEN ARE CREATED EQUAL.

An example of boustrophedon writing

Unsyentifik, Unskolarli, Ilojikal Speling

Melvil Dewey (1851–1931) is revered (and reviled) by librarians and researchers for his attempt to classify all knowledge—past, present, and future—in a single subject-based numbering system. The Dewey Decimal System continues to be widely used throughout the world.

The father of modern librarianship was also a spelling reformer. He dropped the extraneous letters from *Melville* and for a while spelled his last name *Dui*. He wrote a description of his classification system as a method "that wud clas, arranje and index books and pamflets on shelvs." The Dewey Decimal System is owned by OCLC (Online Computer Library Center), which means that it is trademark protected and cannot be used without permission. The Library Hotel in New York learned this the hard way in 2003 when OCLC sued it for using Dewey numbers to name the hotel's floors and arrange a collection of books for guests (the case was settled out of court). There's an international board that oversees Dewey updates and the assigning of numbers to new works.

Alpha Bravo Charlie

With the advent of radio and telephone communications, many organizations—military, law enforcement, and aviation, for instance—realized that they needed some kind of phonetic alphabet to ensure an accurate understanding of individual letters, especially when transmission was unclear. The International Radiotelephony Spelling Alphabet, used by the North Atlantic Treaty Organization (NATO) and many others, assigns an acrophonic code word to each letter of the alphabet to increase intelligibility and clarity: *Alpha*, *Bravo*, *Charlie*, *Delta*, *Echo*, *Foxtrot*, *Golf*, and so on.

Nevertheless, several other systems have been used in various places and times. The British used *Emma* for *M* in the early days; they would say *Pip-Emma* to indicate *p.m.* or *Toc-Emma* for *trench mortar* (I'm sorry, that makes no sense to me).

Facts are counterrevolutionary.

—Eric Hoffer (*The Passionate State of Mind*, 1955)

The World Meteorological Organization adopted the U.S. military alphabet to name hurricanes in 1950 and used it for two years. The police departments in New York, Los Angeles (remember *Adam 12* on television in the 1970s?), and elsewhere have their own lists, primarily using men's names. In their lingo, the word *facts* would be *Frank-Adam-Charlie-Tom-Sam*. Another oddity: for *W*, NATO says *whiskey*; most other groups use *William*, but Italy and Spain use *Washington*.

Funny Papers on the Radio

In what could be considered a precursor to today's multimedia social networking phenomenon, Mayor Fiorello LaGuardia read the comics over municipal radio station WNYC to the children of New York City during the July 1945 newspaper deliverers' strike. The Library of Congress has included that broadcast in the National Recording Registry; here's an excerpt:

> Now, talking about newspapers. Well, I had a good story today in the newspapers, but with boys of the delivery union now on strike, you spoiled my story for me. . . . We just have time to read "Little Orphan Annie." Now, you know, poor little Annie the orphan is on trial for murder, and what a trial it is. All the nice society people, you know, all the nice society people that know so much about juvenile delinquency . . .

A Deadline for Real

Journalists know the meaning of *deadline*: you get your story in on time, or it's dead; it doesn't go on the air or in the paper (and if you miss too many deadlines, your career might be dead, too).

Originally, *deadline*'s meaning was even more literal. It was a term used in prisoner-of-war camps in the Civil War. A Confederate officer described one in 1864: "A railing round the inside of the stockade, and about twenty feet from it, constitutes the 'dead line,' beyond which the prisoners are not allowed to pass," or they could expect to be shot by the guards.

A Few Billion from the People

In the 2008 U.S. presidential campaign, $1,812,970,610 was raised by the twenty-seven candidates, most of it ($1.39 billion) from individual contributors. In the congressional races, 1,376 people running for the House of Representatives raised more than $978 million, and 168 Senate candidates took in $410 million.

The total amount of money collected (and mostly spent) in that election was $3.2 billion—equal to the amount that the United Nations budgeted for its entire peacekeeping operations in 2005–2006; or to the total value of the vehicle insurance claims settled in Louisiana and Mississippi in the first year after Hurricane Katrina; or to the price tag of the nuclear submarine USS *Jimmy Carter*.

The Cost per Vote

The most expensive self-financed political campaign in U.S. history was that of Michael Bloomberg when he ran for his third term as mayor of New York. He spent almost $110 million of his own money to win the election in November 2009, breaking the previous spending record, which was also his: he had shelled out more than $75 million in each of his mayoral runs, in 2001 and 2005.

In 2009, Hizzoner received about 585,000 votes, which means that he spent about $185 per vote, according to documents filed in January 2010. He won the election by a margin of 4.4 percent.

SOTU Loquaciousness

There is a requirement in the U.S. Constitution that the president "shall from time to time give to the Congress information on the State of the Union, and recommend to their Consideration such measures as he shall judge necessary and expedient." The State of the Union (SOTU) address was known as the Annual Message until the 1940s, and some presidents chose to send their addresses in writing rather than appearing in person. The House chamber is the normal setting for the speech, and the attendees, in addition to all the representatives and senators, include the Joint Chiefs of Staff, the Supreme Court justices, and the president's cabinet (with one secretary not attending, to preserve presidential succession in case of a disaster).

The longest SOTU address—at more than 27,000 words—was given by President William Taft in 1910 (you, like me, probably assumed the longest was one of Bill Clinton's). The shortest was President George Washington's first address in 1790, at about 1,000 words. In the nineteenth century, the average length was about 10,000 words (or approximately ninety minutes); that had been cut in half by the end of the twentieth century.

Franklin Roosevelt made twelve appearances before Congress (not all of them SOTU addresses). Zachary Taylor appeared only once, and William Henry Harrison and James Garfield delivered no addresses at all to Congress.

The first radio broadcast of a SOTU message was by Calvin Coolidge in 1923. Harry S. Truman's was the first on television (1947), and George W. Bush's was the first on a live webcast (2002). Since 1966, the television networks have offered the opposition party the opportunity to deliver a response.

Now what I want is, Facts. Teach these boys and girls nothing but Facts. Facts alone are wanted in life. Plant nothing else, and root out everything else. You can only form the minds of reasoning animals upon Facts: nothing else will ever be of service to them.

—Charles Dickens (*Hard Times*, 1854)

Initial Letters

A frequently asked question at many library desks: what's the difference between an acronym and an initialism? According to the *Acronyms, Initialisms and Abbreviations Dictionary*:

> Distinctions are not always made among the three terms used in the current title, nor are distinctions always necessary, since in many ways the definitions overlap. But the most commonly accepted, if somewhat simplified, explanations are as follows:
>
> An acronym is composed of the initial letters or parts of a compound term. It is usually read or spoken as a single word, rather than letter by letter. Examples include RADAR (Radio Detection and Ranging) and LASER (Light Amplification by Stimulated Emission of Radiation).
>
> An initialism is also composed of the initial letters or parts of a compound term, but is generally verbalized letter by letter, rather than as a single "word." Examples include PO (Post Office) and RPM (Revolutions per Minute).
>
> An abbreviation is a shortened form of a word or words that does not follow the formation of either of the above. Examples include Apr. (April), Ph.D. (Doctor of Philosophy), Bcstg. (Broadcasting), and Dr. (Doctor).

Little Old Ladies Laugh Out Loud

The initialism LOL isn't new; it was used by librarians (and probably many other people) way before computers, to describe a certain group of patrons: "little old ladies." Now standard Internet shorthand for "laughing out loud," it has equivalents in other languages too.

MDR in French (*mort de rire*) or Spanish (*muerto de risa*) means "die laughing." In Swedish, ASG is an abbreviation for *asgarva*, "big laugh." In Brazilian Portuguese, RS is used for *risos*, "laughs." The number five in Thailand is pronounced *ha*, so 555 works for LOL, "ha ha ha."

Please Don't BTQ

To *beg the question* (BTQ) has come to mean, "The question is begging to be asked" or even "Somebody, please raise this question!" But its original use was as a philosophical term: *petitio principii*, which would have been better translated as "laying claim to the principle."

There's even a Web site devoted to the phrase, in the hope of encouraging its proper use. (I think it's too late.) The site provides a business card that can be downloaded and used to explain the term: "[BTQ] is a form of logical fallacy in which an argument is assumed to be true without evidence other than the argument itself." Examples: Spinach is healthy because it's good for you. Lying is wrong because you shouldn't say things that aren't true.

My Favorite Punctuation

Commas bring clarity to written expression. Writing lacked any kind of punctuation—or even spaces between words—until the second century BCE, when Aristophanes of Byzantium (a librarian, of course) placed marks in lines of text to indicate pauses: short, medium, and long. The *media distinctio* was a comma, for a short pause.

His system was functional but not widely used. Alcuin, an English scholar and educator at the court of Charlemagne in the 780s, introduced some punctuation, but there was no standard system for another thousand years. I strongly believe in the use of the serial comma (also known as the Oxford or Harvard comma), because using a comma before the conjunction (*and*, *but*, *or*, *nor*) in a list of items makes it clear that the final two items are not a pair: "His favorite foods are haggis, pizza, chicken feet, and ice cream for dessert." If the final items are

Alcuin

paired, a comma is not required and would even be incorrect: "Her favorite foods are hot dogs, pizza, and peanut butter and jelly."

Avoiding ambiguity is always good. The *U.S. Government Style Manual* agrees.

The Department of Redundancies Department

A small sampling of everyday commonplace terms which, by consensus of opinion, are members of the Department of Redundancies Department:

self-censor yourself
please RSVP
2 a.m. in the morning
PIN number
SAT test
START treaty
LCD display
ATM machine
end result
basic fundamentals
free gift
closed fist
Rio Grande River
pair of twins
reason why
whether or not
hot water heater
unexpected surprise
past history
first began
enter into
prohibition against

Redundancy, pleonasm, tautologia: the use of more words than is necessary.

A Lot of Letters

Floccinaucinihilipilification, one of the longest words in the English language, means a judgment that something is worthless. Made up of four separate Latin terms for something that is trivial or without value, it was created in the eighteenth century by students at Eton from a list of terms in their Latin grammar book.

All the Others

The abbreviations *et al.* (Latin, *et alii* or *et aliae*) and *etc.* (Latin, *et cetera*) have the same basic meaning: and others, and the rest, and so on. The difference is that *et al.* should be used when referring to people, and *etc.* when referring to things. Also sometimes confused are *e.g.* and *i.e. Exempli gratia* (*e.g.*) means "for the sake of example," whereas *id est* (*i.e.*) means "that is."

Endangered Languages

Every two weeks, a language dies. When only a small number of fluent native speakers remains, a language is considered endangered. Half of the world's sixty-seven hundred languages are threatened with extinction as the elderly populations of a culture dwindle and the younger members do not learn to speak, read, or write the language.

Boa, the last native speaker of the Bo language of the Andaman Islands, died in January 2010; because her language is extinct, "a unique part of human society is now just a memory." Northern Australia, Central Siberia, and the Northwest Pacific Plateau are considered "language hotspots," where many dialects are dying. The languages with the most speakers are Mandarin Chinese, English, and Hindi.

> *The squirming facts exceed the squamous mind, If one may say so.*
>
> —Wallace Stevens ("Connoisseur of Chaos" in *Collected Poems*, 1990)

Euskera Spoken

The Basque language, spoken by the people of the Pyrenees region of Spain and France, is one of the world's more mysterious languages. Officially called Euskera (the name for the area is Euskal Herria, "land of Basque speakers"), its origin is utterly unknown. Linguists are in total disagreement on its relation to other languages, but it is definitely not Indo-European. Theories have been advanced that it's related to the languages of the Caucasus Mountains, or Uralic tongues (Hungarian and Finnish, for example), or even to the language of the Berbers of North Africa. Some Basques consider themselves and their language to be the direct descendants of the Cro-Magnon people of Paleolithic Europe.

Speaking the language was outlawed by Napoleon and then by Francisco Franco, but it persevered nonetheless. It's a collection of several dialects, and Batua is used as the standardized version. *Goenkale* ("Main Street") is a television soap opera in the Basque language that has aired in the region since 1995; it has helped to promote the use of Euskera, which is spoken by about six hundred thousand of the three million Basque people.

The Forest of Rhetoric

We all use figures of speech, and we even know the technical term for some of them: *pun*, *simile*, *paradox*, *hyperbole*. Too many of us, however, seem to forget that *irony* must contain or refer to the contrary or opposite of its obvious meaning; it is not mere coincidence. Here are a few figures of speech, from the *Silva Rhetoricae* (The Forest of Rhetoric), provided by Professor Gideon Burton at Brigham Young University:

antanaclasis: the repetition of a word or a phrase whose meaning changes
Vince Lombardi: "If you aren't fired with enthusiasm, you will be fired with enthusiasm."

antanagoge: giving a positive spin to something difficult

Unknown philosopher: "When life hands you lemons, make lemonade."

asyndeton: the omission of conjunctions between clauses
Julius Caesar: "*Veni, vidi, vici*" ("I came, I saw, I conquered.")

chiasmus: the repetition of ideas in inverted order
Iago: "Who dotes, yet doubts; suspects, yet strong loves."

epitrope: an ironic giving of permission
Dirty Harry: "Make my day."

litotes: a deliberate understatement
Holden Caulfield: "It isn't very serious. I have this tiny little tumor on the brain."

synecdoche: using a part to describe the whole, or vice versa
New car owner: "Listen, you've got to come take a look at my new set of wheels."

systrophe: listing many qualities without providing a definition
Hamlet: "What a piece of work is man, how noble in reason, how infinite in faculties, in form and moving, how express and admirable in action, how like an angel in apprehension . . ."

Mixed Metaphors

A metaphor is a comparison that is made by referring to one thing as another (and that doesn't use the words *like* or *as*; that would make it a simile). When two or more metaphors are combined incongruously or incorrectly, you get a mixed metaphor, which is often unintentionally hilarious. Here are a few howlers:

This house of cards will come home to roost.
Put it on the back burner and see who salutes.
A leopard can't change its stripes; a zebra can't change its spots.

The fickle finger of fate reared its ugly head.
Up a tree without a paddle.

The champion of mixed metaphors, perhaps, is Sir Boyle Roche (1736–1807), a member of the Irish House of Commons. Among his unusual rhetorical constructions were the following: "Mr Speaker, I smell a rat; I see him forming in the air and darkening the sky; but I will nip him in the bud," and "If we once permitted the villainous French masons to meddle with the buttresses and walls of our ancient constitution, they would never stop nor stay, until they had brought the foundation stones tumbling down about the ears of the nation." Some say that Roche was the inspiration for the character of Mrs. Malaprop in Richard Brinsley Sheridan's play *The Rivals*.

Sin versus Virtue

Ethics and Law

Sin against Virtue

Perhaps less well known than the seven deadly sins are the seven cardinal virtues. Here they are, paired with their respective sins:

Humility opposes pride.
Generosity opposes covetousness.
Chastity opposes lust.
Meekness opposes anger.
Temperance opposes gluttony.
Brotherly love opposes envy.
Diligence opposes sloth.

Other versions exist, from different times and cultures, and both groups are represented in art, literature, music, and even video games.

Green with What?

Am I the last person on earth who thinks that envy and jealousy are not synonyms? Envy is covetousness, the desire to obtain something one does not have. Jealousy is possessiveness, the desire to own or control someone or some object.

The First Charter of Human Rights

The Cyrus Cylinder is a clay cylinder on which is written, in Akkadian cuneiform script, an edict issued by Cyrus the Great (in Persian, Kourosh) upon his conquest of Babylon in 539 BCE. According to the British Museum, which holds the artifact in its collection, "This cylinder has sometimes been described as the 'first charter of human rights,' but it in fact reflects a long tradition in Mesopotamia where, from as early as the third millennium BC, kings began their reigns with declarations of reforms." The edict is often cited as the document that freed the Jews from Babylonian captivity, and although the Jewish people are not specifically named here, it was under Cyrus that they were released. The text says, "As for the population of Babylon [. . . , w]ho as if without div[ine intention] had endured a yoke not decreed for them, I soothed their weariness, I freed them from their bonds. . . . I collected together all of their people and returned them to their settlements." In 1971, when a replica of the cylinder was presented to the United Nations, Secretary-General U Thant said, "This proclamation reflects Cyrus' desire to establish peace in his vast empire[,] which he wisely understood could best be accomplished by allowing its varied peoples to keep their own customs and beliefs."

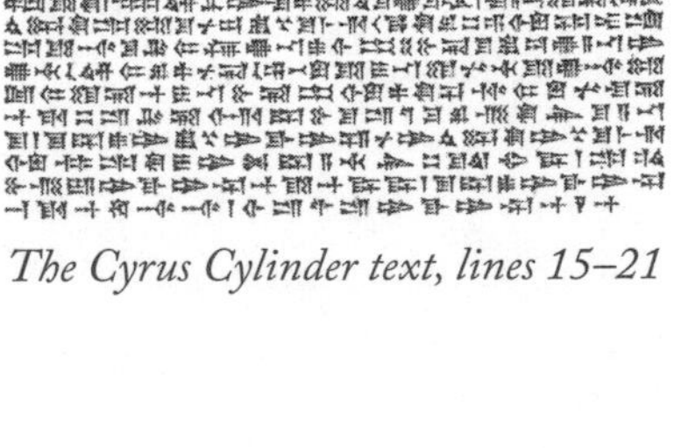

The Cyrus Cylinder text, lines 15–21

Curse You, Book Stealer

In medieval monasteries and libraries, before the invention of printing with movable type, the great works of the ancient Greek and Roman world were preserved by scribes who copied and recopied the texts from the exemplar, or master copy. The writing, proofreading, decorating, and binding took months of intense labor, so books were extremely expensive and were carefully guarded.

Books were chained to the tables in some libraries, to prevent theft. Notes were included in the text to remind the users of a book's fragility: "*Quisquis quem tetigerit, Sit illi lota manus*" ("Before touching this book, please wash your hands"); or "O reader, turn the leaves gently . . . for as the hailstorm ruins the harvest of the land[,] so does the unserviceable reader destroy the book."

Some libraries displayed anathemas: threats of excommunication, or worse, to warn the careless or malicious reader. Book curses go back to the earliest days of writing, but this example, written by a German scribe in 1172, is one of my favorites: "If anyone take away this book, let him die the death; let him be fried in a pan; let the falling sickness and fever seize him; let him be broken on the wheel, and hanged."

Let My People Go

Despite being almost universally banned, slavery still exists in the world. Between twelve and twenty-seven million people are enslaved today: held in forced or bonded labor, controlled by an employer, dehumanized or physically constrained, or denied freedom of movement.

> *The effectiveness of our memory banks is determined not by the total number of facts we take in, but the number we wish to reject.*
>
> —Jon Wynne-Tyson (*Food for a Future*, 1975)

According to the Central Intelligence Agency, "Approximately 800,000 people, mostly women and children, are trafficked annually across national borders, not including millions trafficked within their own countries; at least 80% of the victims are female and up to 50% are minors; 75% of all victims are trafficked into commercial sexual exploitation."

General Tubman of the Railroad

Harriet Tubman, the Moses of the Underground Railroad, was born in slavery on the eastern shore of Maryland around 1820. She worked very hard and suffered much abuse, including a head injury that caused health problems for the rest of her life. In 1849, angered by her owner's attempts to sell her and separate her from her family, Tubman escaped to Pennsylvania.

"I had reasoned this out in my mind," she said. "There was one of two things I had a right to, liberty or death; if I could not have one, I would have the other; for no man should take me alive; I should fight for my liberty as long as my strength lasted." Tubman was free, but she was alone and lonely for her relatives, so she returned to Maryland and began to help other slaves to escape—making at least fifteen trips in the next ten years. She was a "conductor" on the Underground Railroad, the secret network of abolitionists and free and emancipated blacks who aided fugitive slaves, hiding runaways in the woods and traveling with them at night until they reached the safety of the northern states or Canada.

Slave owners put a $40,000 bounty on Tubman's head. The militant abolitionist John Brown called her "General Tubman" and said that she was "one of the bravest persons on this continent." Frederick Douglass wrote to her, "Excepting John Brown . . . I know of no one who has willingly encountered more perils and hardships to serve

Time dissipates to shining ether the solid angularity of facts. No anchor, no cable, no fences avail to keep a fact a fact.

—Ralph Waldo Emerson ("History" in *Essays: First series,* 1841)

our enslaved people than you have." During the Civil War, Tubman was a cook, a nurse, and a Union spy; she even led a raid on plantations at the Combahee River in South Carolina in June 1863 that liberated hundreds of slaves. Later in her life, she worked with Susan B. Anthony in the fight for women's suffrage and spoke in favor of the cause. Tubman died in Auburn, New York, in 1913, and a plaque was placed on the courthouse to honor her. It says, in part:

> She braved every danger and overcame every obstacle. Withal she possessed extraordinary foresight and judgment so that she truthfully said—"On my Underground Railroad I nebber run my train off de track and I nebber los a passenger."

Harriet Tubman

From the Handbook of Robotics

The word *robot* comes from the Czech term for "work, labor, or drudgery." It was introduced in Karel Čapek's 1920 play *R.U.R.* (*Rossum's Universal Robots*). Isaac Asimov wrote dozens of stories and novels about robots, and he developed the Three Laws of Robotics to govern their behavior. (The first and third might not be bad guidelines for humans, either.) These are the laws:

1. A robot may not injure a human being or, through inaction, allow a human being to come to harm.
2. A robot must obey the orders given it by human beings, except where such orders would conflict with the First Law.
3. A robot must protect its own existence as long as such protection does not conflict with the First or Second Law.

Asimov cites the *Handbook of Robotics*, fifty-sixth edition, published in AD 2058, as his source. To explain his original idea about robots, Asimov later wrote: "One of the stock plots of science fiction was . . .

robots were created and destroyed their creator. . . . Knowledge has its dangers, yes, but is the response to be a retreat from knowledge? . . . Or is knowledge to be used as itself a barrier to the dangers it brings? . . . With all this in mind I began, in 1940, to write robot stories of my own—but robot stories of a new variety. Never, never, was one of my robots to turn stupidly on his creator for no purpose but to demonstrate, for one more weary time, the crime and punishment of Faust."

Who Can Be a Justice?

If you hope one day to be appointed to the Supreme Court of the United States (SCOTUS), you might be curious about the required qualifications. There are none. The Constitution is silent on this matter; there are no specifications of age, citizenship, or even legal experience:

> The judicial Power of the United States shall be vested in one supreme Court, and in such inferior Courts as the Congress may from time to time ordain and establish. The Judges, both of the supreme and inferior Courts, shall hold their Offices during good Behavior, and shall, at stated Times, receive for their Services a Compensation which shall not be diminished during their Continuance in Office.

In August 2010, Elena Kagan, a woman who is a great legal scholar and was dean of the Harvard University School of Law but has never been a judge, was confirmed to the court. The last non-judge to be confirmed to the Supreme Court was William H. Rehnquist in 1972.

The Secret Ballot

Election day in the United States, at least for the first century of our history, was usually a day of rowdy fun. Votes were cast by voice or some other nonwritten device (such as by raising your hand), by writing on any scrap of paper, or by using ballots that were supplied by the political parties or cut out of a newspaper.

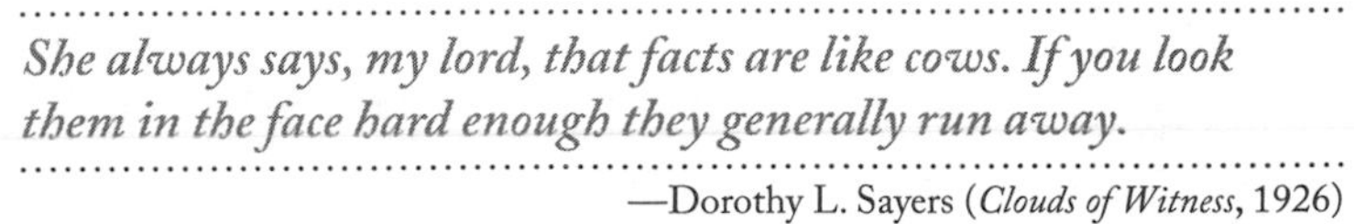

She always says, my lord, that facts are like cows. If you look them in the face hard enough they generally run away.

—Dorothy L. Sayers (*Clouds of Witness*, 1926)

In addition to the partying, there could be violence and even rioting at the polls. The lack of a secret ballot provided many opportunities for corruption, coercion, and intimidation, so the states began passing legislation to require official government-issued secret ballots by the late 1880s. Grover Cleveland was the first president elected by secret ballot, in 1892.

As Harvard University professor Jill Lepore wrote in the *New Yorker* in 2008, "By 1896, Americans in thirty-nine out of forty-five states cast secret, government-printed ballots. The turnout, nationwide? Eighty per cent, which was about what it had been since the eighteen-thirties. It has been falling, more or less steadily, ever since."

And Throw Away the Key

As with most statistics, it depends on who's counting and how, but according to the International Centre for Prison Studies at King's College, London, there are more than 9.8 million people who are being held for criminal activity in penal institutions around the world. These are the top five countries, in terms of incarceration rates (number of prisoners per 100,000 of the national population):

United States	753
St. Kitts and Nevis	660
Russian Federation	609
Rwanda	593
U.S. Virgin Islands	561

At the bottom of the list are Faeroe Islands, Tuvalu, Nauru, Nepal, and Timor-Leste (East Timor), which have fewer than 25 prisoners per 100,000.

At the end of December 2008, the U.S. Department of Justice reported that 1,610,446 people were imprisoned in the United States under federal or state jurisdiction in more than five thousand local, state, and federal jails, prisons, and penitentiaries. Males were imprisoned at a rate about fifteen times higher than females. About 34 percent of all sentenced prisoners were white, 38 percent were black, and 20 percent were Hispanic.

How Much Should I Pay Myself?

The Constitution of the United States directs that members of the House of Representatives and the Senate determine their own salaries. At the start of the first Congress, in March 1789, all representatives and senators were paid $6 per day while they were in session. Except for a brief period in 1815–1817, they maintained the per diem system until 1856, when salaries were raised to $3,000 a year.

The Ethics Reform Act of 1989 used a complicated formula that increased pay to $125,100 a year by 1991. In the 111th Congress (2009–2011), the salaries were $174,000 per year, with the leaders of each chamber receiving about $20,000 in additional compensation. The president currently earns $400,000, the vice president earns $227,300, and the chief justice receives $217,400 (a bit higher than the salaries of the associate justices).

Modus Mundi

The Science of Nature: Physics, Mathematics, Geography

I Seem to Be a Verb

R. Buckminster Fuller (1895–1983) was an engineer, a scientist, an architect, a philosopher, a poet, a mathematician, and one of the most creative thinkers of the twentieth century. He invented the geodesic dome (think of the Epcot Center at Disney World) and the dymaxion map, car, and house. He developed the concept of *design science*—applying the rigorous systematic study of our universe to solve human problems—and he believed that "technology had a redeeming humanitarian role." Affectionately known as Bucky to his legions of counterculture fans in the 1960s and 1970s, Fuller had a unique way of speaking and writing: in very long sentences full of compound words. He suggested that the words *in* and *out* should replace *up* and *down* and that *world-around* should replace *world-wide*, because the earth isn't flat.

"I live on Earth at present, and I don't know what I am," he wrote, attempting to understand his own existence. "I know that I am not a category. I am not a thing—a noun. I seem to be a verb, an evolutionary process—an integral function of the universe."

In 1959, Bucky was asked to describe, in a single unpunctuated sentence, what he did; he managed to do so in a hundred words. After many rewrites, by 1976 that sentence had expanded to three thousand words. Here are his concluding lines:

> And because the meaning of design is that all the parts are interconsiderately arranged in respect to one another and because all the generalized principles are omni-interaccommodative which is to say that none ever contradict any others the family of thus far scientifically discovered generalized principles constitutes a cosmic design to which human mind has the only known access other than that of the comprehensive absolutely mysterious intellectual integrity context of Universe itself.

The State of Plasma

We all learned that there are three states of matter—solid, liquid, and gas—but there is actually a fourth. Plasma is an ionized gas whose atoms have released electrons due to the influence of heat or another form of energy, which thus alters the electrical charge. Plasma's properties are significantly different from the other states of matter, but exactly how plasma behaves depends on the kinds of atoms that were ionized, the ratio of charged to noncharged particles, and the energy in those particles.

Plasma can be controlled by electric and magnetic fields, which enables it to be used in a variety of applications, from the sterilization of medical instruments to flat-screen televisions. Of the four states of matter, plasma is by far the most common, accounting for 99 percent of the visible universe.

"Plasma temperatures and densities range from relatively cool and tenuous (like aurora) to very hot and dense (like the central core of a star)," according to the Web site Plasmas International.

William Crookes, an English physicist, first identified plasma in 1879 and called it "radiant matter." In 1928, Irving Langmuir coined the term *plasma*: "the ionized gas contains ions and electrons in about equal numbers so that the resultant space charge is very small. We shall use the name plasma to describe this region containing balanced charges of ions and electrons."

I found a Web site that shows you "how to make a glowing ball of plasma in your microwave with a grape." I don't recommend that you try this at home; it looks very dangerous.

Elementary, My Dear Gell-Mann

Quarks are elementary particles, the building blocks of the atom; there are no known smaller parts in the nucleus. Quarks come in flavors—not cherry, lemon, or chocolate, but down, up, charm, strange, top (or truth), and bottom (or beauty).

Quarks combine with other quarks to form composite particles called hadrons (protons and neutrons, for example). Quarks have no measurable size; they're described as pointlike, and they differ from one another in mass and electrical charge.

Physicists Murray Gell-Mann and George Zweig separately developed the quark model in the early 1960s, before the existence of the particles had been proved. Gell-Mann explained the name this way: "In 1963, when I assigned the name 'quark' to the fundamental constituents of the nucleon, I had the sound first, without the spelling, which could have been 'kwork.' Then, in one of my occasional perusals of *Finnegan's Wake* by James Joyce, I came across the word 'quark' in the phrase 'Three quarks for Muster Mark' . . . the number three fitted perfectly the way quarks occur in nature" (the original model had three types of quarks). Gell-Mann received the Nobel Prize for Physics in 1969, "for his contributions and discoveries concerning the classification of elementary particles and their interactions."

Fullerenes and Buckyballs

Carbon, the element on which all life on earth is based, exists in more than a million compounds. When we hear the word, most of us probably think of the graphite in a pencil, or perhaps you recall Superman

It is of the highest importance in the art of detection to be able to recognise out of a number of facts which are incidental and which are vital.

—Sir Arthur Conan Doyle ("The Reigate Puzzle")

squeezing a lump of coal into a diamond. But there is another type of carbon, a group of molecules called *fullerenes*.

In its most common form—C_{60}, a molecule with sixty carbon atoms—a fullerene looks like a geodesic globe or a soccer ball, sort of a round hollow cage. It was named after R. Buckminster Fuller, the designer of the geodesic dome, who also inspired the nickname for the molecule: buckyball. Fullerenes with more than sixty atoms can come in different shapes: ellipsoids or cylinders, which are called nanotubes.

In 1996, three scientists—Robert F. Curl and Richard E. Smalley of Rice University in Houston and Sir Harold W. Kroto of the University of Sussex in England—were awarded the Nobel Prize in Chemistry for their discovery of the fullerene eleven years earlier. In presenting the award, Professor Lennart Eberson of the Royal Swedish Academy said, "A fullerene . . . has a closed, low-molecular structure that can be chemically processed and modified in an almost infinite number of ways . . . [, which] has implications for all the natural sciences. . . . The discovery of fullerenes has expanded our knowledge and changed our thinking in chemistry and physics. It has given us new hypotheses on the occurrence of carbon in the universe." Research into fullerenes is ongoing in a number of fields of nanotechnology: for use in solar power, monitoring systems, sporting goods, pharmaceuticals, and many medical applications, such as identifying cancer cells and targeting them for radiation. In 1997, the Texas legislature made "buckminsterfullerene" their official state molecule because "the almost unlimited potential of buckminsterfullerene in a wide range of applications portends a bright future for our state and its citizens."

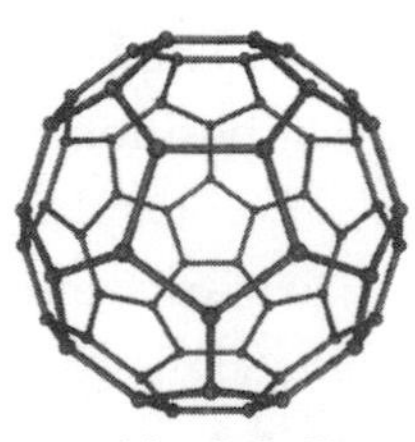

A buckyball

A Gas Can Be Noble

Noble gases are the elements in group 18 (formerly called group VIIIA) of the Periodic Table of the Elements; it's the last vertical column on the right of the chart: helium (He), neon (Ne), argon (Ar), krypton (Kr), xenon (Xe), and radon (Rn). These elements have also been referred to as *rare* or *inert gases*, but those designations are not quite accurate. Some of the noble gases are actually rather abundant in the atmosphere, and they aren't completely inert.

Since their atomic configuration is stable—the outer ring (valance shell) of electrons is full—the noble gases don't naturally interact with other elements. Some can be induced to form compounds under specialized conditions, however. The noble gases are monotomic, which means that they occur naturally as single atoms.

Why are they called *noble*? According to the *Encyclopedia Britannica*, "In chemistry and alchemy, the word *noble* has long signified the reluctance of metals, such as gold and platinum, to undergo chemical reaction; it applies in the same sense to the group of gases covered here." Noble gases are used in light sources, lasers, welding, refrigeration, and medicine.

The Seven Billion

The human population of the world was 6.8 billion at the end of 2009, and it will likely reach 7 billion before the end of 2011. Most of that growth will be in developing nations. The countries with the highest populations, according to the Population Reference Bureau, are China and India. By the year 2050, it's projected, they will switch places, and India will have the larger population (1.748 billion). The United States is in third place and is expected to stay in that position, growing from 308 million in 2009 to 439 million by midcentury.

The most densely populated country (number of people per square kilometer) is Monaco, since it is so tiny (it's even called a microstate): the entire population, about 33,000, lives in an area of about

I have no data yet. It is a capital mistake to theorise before one has data. Insensibly one begins to twist facts to suit theories, instead of theories to suit facts.

—Sir Arthur Conan Doyle ("A Scandal in Bohemia")

two square kilometers. After Monaco, Singapore, Bahrain, and Bangladesh have the highest population density. Mongolia, Western Sahara, Mauritania, Botswana, Namibia, Canada, French Guiana, Suriname, and Iceland have the lowest, with just two or three people per square kilometer.

Who They Are and What They Do

According to the CIA, about two-thirds of the 6.8 billion humans in the world are between the ages of 15 and 64; the median age is 28.4 years. Almost 50 percent live in urban environments, and more than half of us are Christian or Muslim. Our literacy rate (people over age fifteen who can read and write) is 82 percent, but "over two-thirds of the world's 785 million illiterate adults are found in only eight countries (Bangladesh, China, Egypt, Ethiopia, India, Indonesia, Nigeria, and Pakistan) and, of all the illiterate adults in the world, two-thirds are women." The world's per capita gross domestic product (GDP) is $10,500 (in 2008 U.S. dollars); Liechtenstein and Qatar have the highest GDP purchasing power per capita, and Zimbabwe has the lowest. The world's labor force comprises 3.2 billion people, who work in agriculture (40.5 percent), services (39 percent), and industry (20.5 percent).

Bulls and Bears on Wall Street

The first stock index was created by journalist Charles Dow in 1896. The Dow Jones Industrial Average was at first exactly that: a simple average of the prices of twelve important stocks. The first report, on May 26, 1896, was 40.94. The index broke 100 for the first time in 1920, went over 1,000 in 1972, and passed 10,000 in March 1999.

The Dow's highest point was 14,164.53—on October 9, 2007, just before the downward spiral that began a year later. After a low point in March 2009, the Dow again broke 10,000 on October 14, 2009. That day the traders on the floor of the New York Stock Exchange wore hats labeled DOW 10,000–2.0. The number and type of stocks indexed have changed several times over the years, and the mathematical formula is more complicated now.

A New York Minute

A "New York minute" is any very brief period of time. A nanosecond, in New York (according to Johnny Carson and others), is the amount of time that elapses before the driver in the car behind you honks the horn when the traffic light turns green. Everywhere else a nanosecond is one-billionth of a second (from the Greek *nanos* or the Latin *nanus*: "dwarf, very small").

How Many Cubic Dekameters in a Gill?

The metric system—officially, the International System of Units (abbreviated SI, for *Système international d'unités*)—is a decimal system of weights and measures based on the meter and the kilogram.

First suggested as early as the sixteenth century, the SI is now used almost universally throughout the world. Only three countries—Burma [Myanmar], Liberia, and the United States—have not adopted it. Although its use has been sanctioned in the United States since 1866, "it has been slow in displacing . . . the U.S. Customary System. The U.S. is the only industrialized nation that does not mainly use the metric system in its commercial and standards activities, but there is increasing acceptance in science, medicine, government, and many sectors of industry." Efforts to introduce the metric system in the United States go back to Thomas Jefferson and John Quincy Adams. There were several attempts by Congress to encourage (but not require) widespread use, and the U.S. Metric Association (USMA) has been promoting the system since 1916.

However, the USMA points out, "Conversions between unit systems are a poor way to learn the metric system, and conversion factors . . . can make the metric system look complicated." (That's certainly the way I remember it from elementary school.) Every four years, the General Conference on Weights and Measures meets to "ensure the propagation and improvement of the SI." In 1999, an incident demonstrated the serious repercussions of our failure to adopt the system fully when "NASA lost a $125 million Mars orbiter because one engineering team used metric units while another used English units for a key spacecraft operation."

China Was First

The four great inventions of Chinese technology are the magnetic compass (*zhinanzhen*, a needle pointing south); paper (*zhih*, a mat of fibers); printing (*yinshua*, a seal or a stamp and a brush); and gunpowder (*huoyao*, "fire drug"). As Chinese historian Deng Yinke points out, however:

> The four inventions do not necessarily summarize the achievements of science and technology in ancient China. The four inventions were regarded as the most important Chinese achievements in science and technology, simply because they had a prominent position in the exchanges between the East and the West and acted as a powerful dynamic in the development of capitalism in Europe. As a matter of fact, [the] ancient Chinese scored much more than the four major inventions: in farming, iron and copper metallurgy, exploitation of coal and petroleum, machinery, medicine, astronomy, mathematics, porcelain, silk, and wine-making. Many are at least as important as the four inventions, and some are even greater than the four.

There was a tribute to the four great inventions during the opening ceremonies of the 2008 Beijing Olympic Games. The Beijing

Social Facts and Public Opinion Survey Center found that it was "the most moving program to Beijingers . . . the four great inventions best displayed Chinese culture characteristics."

You Must See These Wonders

Described by the Greek historian Herodotus as *theamata*—must-see places—these were the Seven Wonders of the Ancient World:

- The Great Pyramid of Giza
- The Hanging Gardens of Babylon
- The Statue of Zeus at Olympia
- The Temple of Artemis at Ephesus
- The Mausoleum of Maussollos at Halicarnassus
- The Colossus of Rhodes
- The Pharos (Lighthouse) of Alexandria

Since only one of those (the Great Pyramid) is still standing, *USA Today* and ABC's *Good Morning America* convened a panel of experts in 2006 to select seven new wonders "that had been recently revealed, discovered or seen in a new light." They combined ancient and modern, man-made and natural wonders and came up with the following list:

- The Potala Palace in Lhasa, Tibet
- The Old City of Jerusalem
- The polar ice caps
- The Papahānaumokuākea Marine National Monument in Hawaii
- The Internet
- The Maya ruins in Yucatan, Mexico
- The Great Migration of Serengeti, the largest mass movement of land animals

In 1994, the American Society of Civil Engineers chose the "greatest civil engineering achievements of the 20th century" and designated them as the Seven Wonders of the Modern World:

- The Channel Tunnel, linking England and France
- The CN Tower, the tallest free-standing structure in the Americas
- The Empire State Building, currently the tallest building in New York
- The Golden Gate Bridge
- The Itaipu Dam, which spans the Parana River at the Brazil-Paraguay border
- The Netherlands North Sea Protection Works, a system of dams, floodgates, and barriers
- The Panama Canal

Other groups have chosen their own seven wonders—which include the Great Wall of China, the statue of Christ the Redeemer in Brazil, and the Taj Mahal—and have created other lists of natural, underwater, and industrial wonders.

The pyramid of Giza

Dreyfus and the Tour de France

Bicycle races in the nineteenth century were sponsored by newspapers as a gimmick to increase their circulation. The creation of the Tour de France was related, in part, to the Dreyfus Affair, in which a French army officer had been unjustly convicted of spying for Germany in a vicious anti-Semitic campaign. Captain Alfred Dreyfus was eventually completely exonerated.

Le Vélo, France's only daily sports newspaper, supported Dreyfus. Some anti-Dreyfus advertisers (who were also unhappy about high advertising rates) started a rival paper called *L'Auto*, and its editor and one of its reporters came up with the idea for a race around France to promote the new paper.

The first Tour de France, in 1903, was a clockwise circuit of the country, covering 2,428 kilometers in nineteen days. The route and distance have varied each year, but the cyclists (the pack of riders is called the *peloton*) usually race from 3,000 to 4,000 kilometers in about three weeks, and the finish line is always in Paris.

Just a Friendly Game

In most summers of the past century, the members of Congress have gathered to play a game of baseball—Democrats versus Republicans—to raise money for charities in Washington, D.C. The tradition was started in 1909 by Representative John Tener (R-PA), who had played professional baseball as a pitcher and an outfielder in the major and minor leagues, including a few seasons on the rosters in Baltimore and Chicago.

The *Boston Daily Globe* reported on the first game, "When they lined up at 4 o'clock the nine republicans were stalwart, grand old party men, while the democrats were of the pure Jeffersonian strain." The Dems beat the GOP, 26–16. The game was called in the seventh inning, according to the *Washington Post*, "partly as the result of an earnest request from the newspaper men in attendance, all of whom were completely exhausted as the result of their strenuous efforts to keep track of things." Until 1949, only members of the House participated; since then, "bicameral baseball" has been the norm, except for some years when no game was played. The Democrats have won thirty-three games, the Republicans forty-one, and there was a tie in 1983.

The program from the 1932 "Political World Series"

A Freak Pitch

The spitball was banned from major league baseball partly because Cleveland Indians shortstop Ray Chapman was beaned by a pitch and killed in August 1920, long before batting helmets were required. Yankees pitcher Carl Mays delivered the pitch, heard a loud crack, assumed that it was the ball hitting the bat, and fielded the grounder.

But Chapman had been hit in the temple, and his skull was fractured. He died the next day. Chapman was known as a great fielder and was batting over .300 that season.

News reports at the time didn't suggest that a spitball was the culprit; the question was whether Mays had beaned Chapman intentionally. Mays was notorious for throwing spitballs and other freak pitches, but he was exonerated by the New York district attorney's office. The presence of moisture (such as saliva, mud, tobacco juice, or hair cream) on a baseball changes the aerodynamics and can make it difficult for the batter to see the ball as it dances around on its approach to the plate. Perhaps that's why Chapman didn't duck. The spitball was outlawed that year, but some pitchers were "grandfathered in" and allowed to continue to throw it for the remainder of their careers.

Uniquely True-Going in Australia

Trugo is a game that was invented in the 1920s by Australian railway workers who were looking for something to do on their lunch breaks in the workshop. Using the measurements of a train car, they created an odd combination of lawn bowling and croquet that has remained popular and competitive around Melbourne for decades.

The players face away from the goal, place a ring (called the wheel) of hard black rubber on the ground between their legs, bend at the waist, and smack the wheel with a wooden mallet. It travels about ninety feet to the goal posts. A good shot between the posts is called a *true go*. Women play a slightly different version, GoTru, using a sidesweeping motion. The sport is dying out, however, because its aging club members are not being replaced by new enthusiasts.

Dying from the Heat

In the 1840s, Dr. John Gorrie was a Florida physician who was looking for a way to treat his malaria and yellow fever patients, or at least make them more comfortable. The discovery that mosquitoes carried those diseases was still years away, and Dr. Gorrie followed the current belief that the cause was noxious effluvium, or "bad air" (in Italian, *mal aria*). Figuring that cooling the air was the answer, he began developing a machine to do just that.

Here's how he explained the theory in an article for the *Apalachicola Commercial Advertiser*: "If the air were highly compressed, it would heat up by the energy of compression. If this compressed air were run through metal pipes cooled with water, and if this air cooled to the water temperature was expanded down to atmospheric pressure again, very low temperatures could be obtained, even low enough to freeze water in pans in a refrigerator box." Since this was in the days before electricity, the compressor would be powered by steam, water, or even horse. Gorrie patented his ice-making and air-cooling device in 1851, but his main financial backer died the same year. Gorrie was unable to find new investors and lost his old ones because his invention was being ridiculed in the press. He blamed the smear campaign on Frederic Tudor, known as the Ice King, who had made a fortune shipping insulated natural ice to warm climates.

Gorrie died destitute in 1855, and it would be another fifty years before true air-conditioning, using Gorrie's basic principles, was patented by Willis Haviland Carrier. A statue of John Gorrie, the father of refrigeration, was placed in National Statuary Hall at the U.S. Capitol in 1914.

From Senusret to Suez

The Egyptian pharaoh Senusret III excavated canals to support trade and warfare three thousand years ago, but today the Suez Canal (Qanat as-Suways) is an artificial sea-level waterway that allows passage between the Mediterranean Sea and the Red Sea across the isthmus of Suez in Egypt. It is actually a system of man-made channels that connect through several natural lakes. Since the levels of the

The facts: nothing matters but the facts: worship of the facts leads to everything, to happiness first of all and then to wealth.

—Edmond De Goncourt (*Pages from the Goncourt Journals*, 1962)

two seas are approximately the same, water flows freely, and the canal does not require locks.

The digging of the canal began in 1859, and ten years later, when it was completed, almost ninety-seven million cubic yards of sand and soil had been removed by 1.5 million workers (of whom about 120,000 lost their lives in the process). Subsequent dredging projects have increased the depth of the canal, one of the most important waterways in the world.

Can Queen Victoria Eat Cold Apple Pie?

The Seven Hills of Rome are not really hills as much as promontories, part of a volcanic ridge originating in the Alban Hills to the southeast of the city. Pyroclastic (composed of fragments) flows from ancient eruptions pushed a plateau of ash toward the Tiber River, changing its course. This gigantic lump of volcanic tuff (consolidated deposits of ash, pumice, and rock) was eventually eroded by streams and springs, creating the hills.

The seven hills are named Capitoline, Quirinal, Viminal, Esquiline, Caelian, Aventine, and Palatine, and they all lie east of the river. Some of them, particularly the Viminal, are barely noticeable today because of the huge amount of debris that has accumulated over the centuries, raising the street level as much as sixteen feet higher than it was in ancient times. Although there are other hills in Rome—the Vatican, the Janiculum, and the Pincian—they were not included because they didn't fall within the confines of the original city settlement. A popular mnemonic device for the names of the seven hills is "Can Queen Victoria Eat Cold Apple Pie?"

Squeezed into South Dakota

The entire region of New England, which is 71,992 square miles—Maine (35,385), New Hampshire (9,350), Vermont (9,614), Massachusetts (10,555), Connecticut (5,543), and Rhode Island (1,545)—could fit inside the state of South Dakota (77,116 square miles), with more than enough space to include Delaware (2,489 square miles), too.

What Ice Can Tell Us

The West Antarctic Ice Sheet (WAIS) Divide is a project of the National Science Foundation to study the climate history of the planet by drilling in Antarctica and collecting a deep ice core. "We're checking out history books made of ice," says chief scientist Kendrick Taylor. The NSF team is developing a detailed record of the presence of greenhouse gases in the last hundred thousand years and investigating the biology of deep ice.

In the same way that tree rings or soil sediment can provide information about the distant past, ice cores reveal details of temperature, precipitation, chemical composition, volcanic activity, and other climate indicators. The analysis of air bubbles trapped in ice cores has shown that increased levels of carbon dioxide are always accompanied by rising temperatures. An ice divide is the boundary between ice flows that are moving in different directions, and it's the most stable location for drilling ice cores. Similar projects have been conducted in Greenland, Peru, and Bolivia; on Mount Kilimanjaro; and in the Himalayas.

Salt and Ice

Salt melts ice because of the colligative property of freezing point depression. When salt molecules combine with water molecules, the freezing temperature of the water is lowered, and it becomes more difficult for ice to form. Other substances (sugar, alcohol, other kinds of salts) could be used instead of rock salt (halite), but rock salt is usually cheap and available. Ice is less dense than water, and that's why it forms on the top of rivers and lakes rather than on the bottom.

Ides, Kalends, and Nones

Beware the Ides of March, the soothsayer warned Julius Caesar. We should also beware thinking that all months have their ides on the fifteenth day. The Roman calendar, which was invented by the legendary Romulus and modified by Caesar, was a lunar calendar. The months were not divided into weeks (that's a much more recent concept). Instead, "day markers" or "signal days" based on the moon's position were used: kalends (the first day, at the first appearance of a crescent after the new moon), nones (the fifth or the seventh day, at the moon's first quarter), and ides (the thirteenth or the fifteenth day, at the full moon).

"Each day was numbered in a confusing system"—that is, according to how many days it fell before the kalends, the nones, or the ides. For instance, the Romans would refer to March 11 as "five ides," and this was as clear to any Roman as "March 11" is to us. Only the months of March, May, July, and October had their ides on the fifteenth.

As Time Goes By

Do you ever wonder how your computer knows what time it is? The ZoneInfo or TZ database, also known as the Olson Time Zone Database, is a public domain collection of code and data on local time rules—daylight saving, zone boundaries, and so on—that is used primarily by computer operating systems.

Logic might suggest that twenty-four hours in a day equals twenty-four time zones, starting with Greenwich Mean Time at 0 degrees longitude, each zone differing from the next by one hour. But it's not that simple; local customs and practicalities have resulted in irregular time zones, with some regions even having quarter- or half-hour variations. As the Time Service Department of the U.S. Naval Observatory points out, "Unfortunately, no U.S. Web page can provide official information on world time zones because nations are sovereign powers that can and do change their timekeeping systems as they see fit."

Time

I Can't See for Miles

If you're having trouble reading this entry, maybe you need eyeglasses. Spectacles have been around for more than seven hundred years, but we don't know who invented them. We do know that human eyes have a tendency to weaken over time and to be subject to disease or congenital defects. Thus humans have long searched for ways to compensate, to help the eyes focus light rays correctly.

In one of the earliest references to magnified reading, the Roman philosopher Seneca (4 BCE–65 CE), in his work *Questiones Naturales*, reports that "letters, however small and dim, are comparatively large and distinct when seen through a glass globe filled with water." About a thousand years later, the "reading stone" was developed. It was a glass half-globe, flat on one side and convex on the other, which could be placed on a book to magnify the text. The first mention in print of what we call eyeglasses was in 1289 in a manuscript titled *Traité de conduite de la famille*, by Sandra di Popozo, who writes of "glass lenses for spectacles recently invented, of great advantage to old people with weak vision."

The first time that eyeglasses were portrayed in a work of art was in 1352, in a fresco by Tomaso da Modena that depicted three monks, one of whom has glasses sitting on the bridge of his nose. A variety of eyeglasses then evolved, including the monocle, the lorgnette, and pince-nez ("nose pinchers"). The development of bifocals, which correct both near- and far-sightedness in one lens, is credited to Benjamin Franklin in the 1780s. Today there are innumerable styles of eyeglasses, as well as other ways of correcting eyesight, such as contact lenses and laser surgery.

Having gathered these facts, Watson, I smoked several pipes over them, trying to separate those which were crucial from others which were merely incidental.

—Sir Arthur Conan Doyle ("The Crooked Man")

A Sticky Syndrome

Before everything was digitized and put into computers, audio was recorded in analog format. The recording medium changed from wire to magnetic tape after World War II.

A few decades later, preservation problems emerged. Sounds and images on magnetic tape are subject to sticky shed syndrome, or stick-tion, "a condition resulting from the deterioration of the binder in magnetic tape that results in gummy residues on tape heads during playback." The polyester-urethane binding medium that holds the magnetic particles (which contain the actual content) to the base tape is unstable; over time it absorbs moisture, deteriorates, and becomes sticky. If you try to play back such a tape, you hear a screeching sound, and the content flakes away. It can damage the tape recorder as well as destroy the tape.

The solution, at least temporarily, is to bake the tape at a low temperature for many hours (various "recipes" differ on the details). Some audio engineers think that the molecules will rebind if the tapes are repeatedly baked, but according to the Library of Congress, "sticky tape damage is irreversible and reformatting should be given high priority." In other words, it's best if you transfer the audio to another medium—compact discs, for example, which is what we do at NPR with older tapes. But CDs won't last forever and no one knows what will come next.

Ugly Bags of Mostly Water

Zoology, Physiology, Medicine

All Pongidae

Although some humans might not like to admit it, it is true that *Homo sapiens* is a Great Ape, along with the gorilla, the bonobo, the chimpanzee, and the orangutan—we're all members of the family *Pongidae*. All people on earth, according to a 2009 analysis of the genomes of fifty-three populations, fall into just three genetic groups: Africans (descendants of the first humans in East Africa about two hundred thousand years ago); Eurasians (including Europe, the Middle East, and Southwest Asia); and East Asians (China, Japan, Southeast Asia, Oceania, and Native Americans). Population scientists were surprised to learn that each regional or ethnic group did not have a unique genetic signature, and there is actually little variation among them.

Take Me to Your Insect

A bee

The dominant life form on this planet, if we judge by numbers (and ignore the microscopic world), would be the class *Insecta*: Ten quintillion (that's a 10 followed by eighteen zeros) insects inhabit the earth at any given moment: flies, mosquitoes, beetles, cockroaches, bees, butterflies, moths, termites, lice, and others. At least one million species have been classified (and they represent approximately 80 percent of all organisms), but millions more are just waiting for us to name them.

A dragonfly

Spiders are not insects; they're a different subdivision—called arachnids—of the arthropods (invertebrate animals with segmented bodies and jointed appendages). Arachnids have eight legs, whereas insects have only six. Nor is *bug* a synonym for *insect*; it's a specific type of insect, the suborder *Heteroptera*, which includes stink bugs, bedbugs, and water striders.

A cockroach

Enlightened Beetles

Fireflies are also known as lightning bugs, but they are neither flies nor bugs; they're beetles (family *Lampyridae*). Their blinking lights are caused by bioluminescence, a chemical reaction that produces light but no heat, and the function of the light is to attract mates and ward off predators. Different species (there are about two thousand) have different flashing patterns. Growing from egg to larva to adult can take up to two years, but then the mature firefly's life span is only a couple of weeks.

Fireflies can be found on every continent except Antarctica, usually in warm humid regions. In the United States, lightning bugs are not often seen west of Texas. The Museum of Science in Boston runs a program called Firefly Watch to map sightings and to determine whether development and light pollution are causing fireflies to disappear from the landscape.

Thanks for the Topsoil

Earthworms—the "intestines of the earth," as Aristotle called them—"dramatically alter soil structure, water movement, nutrient dynamics, and plant growth," according to the U.S. Department of Agriculture. These segmented invertebrates have been around for half a billion years, but they have no eyes, ears, or lungs. They digest organic matter (such as dead leaves), soil, and even tiny stones, which are excreted as castings that enrich and aerate the soil.

Worms are pretty much responsible for all the rich soil on the planet. There can be as many as a million worms per acre in temperate regions. Some species are able to regenerate themselves: if one is cut in half, it can grow a new tail (but the pieces don't become two whole new worms).

Big Ugly Birds

The California condor has been described as a rat with a ten-foot wingspan and as the Elvis Presley of endangered species: "iconic . . . worshipped and despised. . . . And it's not really dead." These rescued-from-extinction predators—the largest flying bird in North America—have no voice boxes (but can hiss and grunt), can glide for miles without flapping their wings, and have primary feathers that can be up to twenty-four inches long.

Facts are becoming increasingly rubbery. There was a time when once a "fact" was discovered, it was immutable. Nowadays, "facts" are only true until someone proves otherwise.

—Amanda Credaro,
the Warrior Librarian
(http://warriorlibrarian.com/ROFL/quoteme.html#F)

Beautiful Little Butterflies

North American Monarch butterflies—proposed but not accepted as the national insect of the United States—migrate to Mexico every autumn to escape the winter freeze of the northeastern United States and Canada. No one butterfly of the hundreds of millions of monarchs makes the complete round-trip.

After flying up to two thousand miles to reach the mountains of central Mexico, the butterflies rest for five months, clustered in the oyamel fir trees. On the return trip in the spring, the monarchs mate, lay eggs, and die. Their progeny in the third or fourth generation begin the migration again the next fall.

A Monotreme Mammal

The platypus (*Ornithorhynchus anatinus*) is one of the world's two monotremes, or mammals that lay eggs (anteaters are the other). This duck-billed, flat-tailed, web-footed, toothless, semiaquatic furry creature lives along streams and rivers in eastern Australia. It eats insect larvae, frogs, fish eggs, and freshwater shrimp, which it finds through electrolocation: the ability to detect electric fields generated by movement in the water. Despite also being one of the few venomous mammals, the platypus was considered cute enough to be one of the mascots of the Sydney Olympics in 2000.

A platypus

A Horse of a Different Color

The seahorse (the genus *Hippocampus*) is unique among animal species: the male seahorse becomes pregnant. The female deposits eggs in his brood pouch, and he fertilizes and gestates the babies (called *fry*) until they're ready to be released (gestation time is only about two weeks). Seahorses are monogamous, and a pair swims together with their tails entwined in a courtship dance. Instead of scales, they have thin bony plates. They're poor swimmers and use their tiny fins for maneuvering rather than for speedy travel.

Seahorses and their cousins, pipefish, are used in traditional Chinese medicine to treat many conditions, from skin problems to heart disease to impotence. They are protected under the Endangered Species Act and the Convention on International Trade in Endangered Species. In 2009, a pygmy seahorse—the smallest known, at about half an inch long—made the top ten new species list of the International Institute for Species Exploration at Arizona State University.

A seahorse

American Dromedaries

Camels once roamed the American southwest. Part of an ill-fated experiment by the U.S. Army, the Camel Corps began in 1855 under Jefferson Davis, who was then secretary of war and would soon become president of the Confederacy. Horses and mules had difficulty in the arid regions between Texas and California, so camels seemed to be the obvious solution.

Thirty-three camels were purchased in Egypt and shipped to Camp Verde in Texas in 1856, and another forty-four arrived the next year. Although the soldiers did not like the temperamental and smelly beasts, the animals proved to be effective at carrying heavy loads long distances with less need for food and water than horses or mules would have.

As the Civil War loomed, optimistic plans were put aside, and the experiment ended. The camels were all but forgotten. Part of the herd was auctioned off in 1863, the rest in 1865. Some were released into the desert, where they (or their descendants) were still sighted in the early 1900s.

Grunting Cows

Yaks (*Bos mutus* and *Bos grunniens*) are shaggy-haired bovines designed for high elevations: their hearts and lungs are larger than those of sea-level cattle, and they have sturdy short legs with broad hooves that make them sure-footed on mountain terrain. Yaks live on the treeless uplands of the Tibetan Plateau, eat grass and lichens, and do not thrive at lower altitudes.

There are wild yaks, which are black, and domestic breeds, which are smaller and usually white—about twelve million total, mostly domestic. In the snow, wild yaks travel in single file, each one stepping in the hoofprints of the leader. The species name *grunniens* means "grunting"; yaks don't moo like other cows.

Domesticated probably more than two thousand years ago in Tibet, today the animals provide milk, fiber, meat, transportation, fuel (dung), and entertainment; yak racing is a popular sport at traditional festivals in Tibet and Mongolia.

Crossbred Dogs

Coyotes (*Canis latrans*) are wild dogs, so they can breed with domestic dogs, producing either a coydog (the offspring of a male coyote and a female dog) or a dogote (the offspring of a male dog and a female coyote). Such hybrids are rare, especially since the wild coyote population is declining.

Birds of War

The carrier or homing pigeon (*Columba livia*) is any variety of pigeon that is domesticated and trained to deliver information. The first such recorded use would be the dove sent out from Noah's ark, which returned with an olive branch. "The Pharaohs of Egypt used carrier pigeons . . . but the Roman Empire first recognized the military possibilities," according to French Army officer and pigeon historian Jean-Pierre Fauvez. In 732, Charles Martel announced his victory over the Arabs at Poitiers via pigeon: "Saracens defeated." Charlemagne raised carrier pigeons, and Genghis Khan had a bird-based relay post system in Asia and eastern Europe in the eleventh century. At the Siege of Paris in 1870, in World War I, and in World

The history of his present majesty, is a history of unremitting injuries and usurpations . . . all of which have in direct object the establishment of an absolute tyranny over these states. To prove this, let facts be submitted to a candid world, for the truth of which we pledge a faith yet unsullied by falsehood.

—Thomas Jefferson (Declaration of Independence, 1776)

War II, pigeons carried messages where no other means of communication was possible. The Germans even strapped cameras to them—photographer pigeons—before aerial reconnaissance planes were invented.

A British group, the People's Dispensary for Sick Animals, created the Dickin Medal in 1943 to honor animals in war; thirty-two pigeons received the medal for their valiant service in World War II. The medal "is a large, bronze medallion bearing the words FOR GALLANTRY and WE ALSO SERVE all within a laurel wreath." The French Army still had a hundred carrier pigeons in 1985, even though its last military use of the birds had been in the Algerian War in the 1950s. The Army of Switzerland had not been engaged in a foreign war for almost five hundred years, yet it did not retire its final group of pigeons—the world's last military pigeon service—until 1996.

Ugly Bags of Mostly Water

Every living thing on earth is made primarily of water. A tomato is about 95 percent H_2O. Human beings are approximately 65 percent water (a character on *Star Trek: The Next Generation* referred to us as "ugly bags of mostly water"), and men are sloshier than women. We can live without food for about thirty days, but without water we would last only a week. Americans use more than 175 gallons of water a day per person.

Water is the only substance to be found in solid, liquid, and gaseous states in normal earth conditions. "Because of nature's water cycle," the *World Book Encyclopedia* tells us, "there is as much water on the earth today as there ever was—or ever will be. Water changes only from one form to another, and moves from one place to another. The water you bathed in last night might have flowed in Russia's Volga River last year. Or perhaps Alexander the Great drank it more than 2,000 years ago."

The Chemistry of Humans

The human body is made of chemical elements, much of it in the form of water. Here's the list:

1. Oxygen: 65%
2. Carbon: 18%
3. Hydrogen: 10%
4. Nitrogen: 3%
5. Calcium: 1.5%
6. Phosphorus: 1%
7. Potassium: 0.25%
8. Sulfur: 0.25%
9. Sodium: 0.15%
10. Chlorine: 0.15%
11. Magnesium: 0.05%
12. Iron, fluorine, zinc, copper, iodine, selenium, chromium, manganese, molybdenum, and cobalt: about 0.5%, total
13. Lithium, strontium, aluminum, silicon, lead, vanadium, arsenic, and bromine: trace amounts

How the Nose Knows

Olfaction, the sense of smell, works this way (to put it simply): Molecules evaporate from a substance and float into your nostrils, then receptor cells at the top of the nasal cavity are stimulated and send an impulse along the olfactory nerves to the olfactory bulbs in the brain. The forebrain interprets the information and identifies the odor.

Humans can recognize about ten thousand different odors. We can smell only those substances that are "volatile" (that release molecules), however; that's why roses have a scent but gold does not. Human olfactory bulbs are much smaller than those in dogs, which should come as no surprise. When you have a cold, you can't smell anything because your swollen mucous membranes limit the movement of air to the smell receptors. The ability to smell deteriorates with age—doesn't everything?

An electronic nose is being developed, and this may be able to replace sniffer dogs to detect dangerous or contraband substances. It can also be used to monitor air quality, identify spoiled food, or even detect the presence of cancer or other diseases. Companies are also working on olfactory perception–altering technologies to block bad odors. Gawker, a gossip news Web site, has an interactive New York City subway smells map, where you can report and track odors—good and bad—at individual subway stations.

Cleanliness Was Next to Impossible

In colonial America, personal hygiene was not a high priority. In farms, villages, and cities, dirt and disease were prevalent; soap and clean water were not reliably available, and there was no cultural impetus to be clean. The lack of indoor plumbing made washing anything difficult and tedious.

Although Francis Bacon had pointed out in 1605 that "cleannesse of bodie was ever esteemed to proceed from a due reverence to God," it wasn't until the nineteenth century that American reformers attempted to make the issue a moral one ("Cleanliness is next to Godliness"). Technology—municipal sewer systems, water heaters, and commercially available soap—brought improved hygiene. During the Civil War, the realization that more soldiers were killed by disease than battle led to better sanitation.

There were serious health problems (cholera and typhoid) in the growing industrialized cities of the early twentieth century, and cleanliness campaigns emerged. In 1914, the New York State Department of Health told mothers that children should be bathed once daily. "During the mid-1960s, however," writes Suellen Hoy, "as more married women (traditionally the quintessential agents of cleanliness) entered the workforce, they spent less time at housecleaning, and most husbands chose not to take up the slack."

Hygeia, goddess of health and cleanliness

Scrubbing Bubbles

Soap is a surfactant (a surface active agent) whose molecules grab dirt from a surface and hold on to it so it can be washed away. The soap-making process, saponification, uses animal or vegetable fats (beef tallow, palm oil, or olive oil) plus alkali (lye) to form bars, granules, flakes, or viscous liquids.

There are recipes and references to soaplike substances in ancient documents, but the true origin of soap is uncertain. The soap industry became well established in the first millennium CE. Soap in colonial America was homemade from potash and animal fat; it was harsh and foul smelling.

Detergents, which use synthetic ingredients and a more complicated chemical process, were developed for industrial use around the time of World War I, spurred by the shortage of animal fats. Fine soaps are superfatted, which means that they have a higher ratio of fat to alkali (which increases the moisturizing quality), and they are then purified and finished. Antibacterial metal powders, scouring agents, and perfume can also be added to soap. Some states have banned the use of phosphates in detergents because they are harmful to the environment.

Wine as Ancient Health Food

Patrick McGovern, an archaeochemist at the University of Pennsylvania's Museum of Archaeology and Anthropology, has studied the residue in wine jars from Egypt in the fourth millennium BCE and has found that "ancient Egyptians settled on adding herbs and other ingredients that had marked medicinal effects," probably including tree resins, mint, coriander, sage, and senna, which flavored and preserved the wine and also provided health benefits.

McGovern's findings seem to correspond to information found in later Egyptian medical papyri, which contain recipes for herbs and resins dissolved in wine and other beverages; these were thought to relieve pain, act as laxatives or diuretics, or even serve as aphrodisiacs. As Hippocrates, the father of medicine, said, "Wine is fit for man in a wonderful way provided that it is taken with good sense by the sick as well as the healthy."

For this reason poetry is something more scientific and serious than history, because poetry tends to give general truths while history gives particular facts.

—Aristotle (*Poetics*)

Ah-Choo!

The common cold is caused by a rhinovirus (and about two hundred other viruses) that brings about a runny nose, sneezing, and scratchiness in your throat. "Everyone knows the first signs of a cold, probably the most common illness known. People in the United States suffer 1 billion colds each year," by some estimates. According to the Centers for Disease Control and Prevention, twenty-two million school days are lost annually in the United States due to the common cold. It's been around for a long time, too: ancient Egypt had hieroglyphs to indicate cold symptoms, and Hippocrates described it in the fifth century BCE. Benjamin Franklin figured out how the disease is transmitted by observing that "people often catch cold from one another when shut up together in small close rooms, coaches, etc. and when sitting near and conversing so as to breathe in each other's transpiration." Chicken soup has been considered an excellent remedy for at least a thousand years. But there is no cure; chicken soup, herbal teas, antihistamines, and decongestants can only relieve the symptoms. Zinc, in nasal sprays or lozenges, seems to shorten the duration of a cold.

The Deadliest Virus

Ebola hemorrhagic fever—caused by the Ebola virus, one of the deadliest pathogens known to science—was first identified in 1976 and is named for the Ebola River in the Democratic Republic of Congo (then called Zaire). The first cases were reported in a hospital in the town of Yambuku, where more than three hundred people were infected, most of whom died.

The investigators from the U.S. Centers for Disease Control had the task of naming the new virus. "Although Yambuku would seem to suggest itself," some CDC researchers wrote, "Karl [Johnson of the CDC] didn't think it sounded quite right, perhaps because he didn't want to stigmatize the town any further. After studying a map of the area, he noticed a river that ran close to Yambuku . . . the name of the river was Ebola." Although Ebola is actually rarely found in humans, epidemiologists are concerned about future outbreaks of the virus, because its mortality rate is as high as 90 percent, and there is no cure. "Death comes from a combination of dehydration, massive hemorrhaging, and shock," a news report explains, "which results from this massive release of [very toxic] cytokines." Cytokines are proteins released by the infected cells.

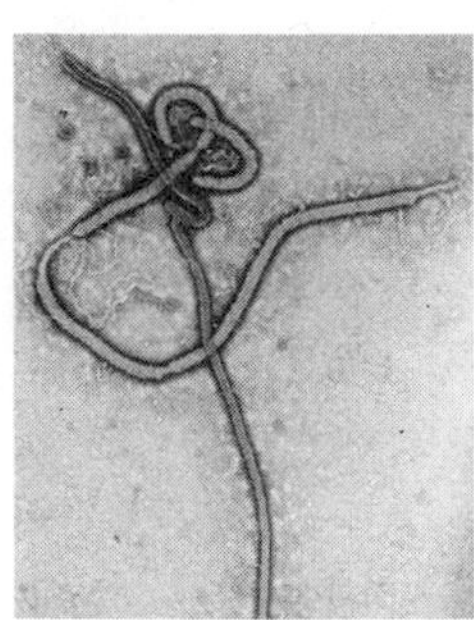

Ebola virus

Lather, Rinse, Repeat

The United States currently has one of the highest frequency rates of hair washing in the world. "Several hair specialists recommend the shampooing of the hair as often as every two weeks," the *New York Times* advised in 1908, "but from a month to six weeks should be a better interval if the hair is in fairly good condition." Nevertheless, Americans now shampoo an average of four or five times a week, which is twice as often as some Europeans.

Such frequent shampooing might not be good for your hair, says Columbia University dermatologist Michelle Hanjani. Hair is protected by a coating of lipids (fatty molecules) and by the sebaceous glands in the scalp, which release oil. Too much washing removes the protection and causes the hair to become dry. "If you wash your hair every day, you're removing the sebum," explains Hanjani. "Then the oil glands compensate by producing more oil." More oil picks up more dirt, your hair doesn't look clean, and you wash it again. Lather, rinse, repeat.

Plasticized Hair

According to the Web site General Chemistry Online, "Hairspray is a solution of long, chainlike molecules (called polymers) in a very volatile solvent. Spraying deposits a stiff layer of the polymer on your hair after the solvent evaporates." The original solvents were made from chlorofluorocarbons, but when they were discovered to be damaging the environment, they were replaced with alcohol and hydrocarbons, which are flammable. The polymers can include the same material that is used to glue layers of plywood together. In 2008, a "spray-on new species" of bacteria, *Microbacterium hatanonis*, was discovered in hairspray; further testing is required to determine if the bacteria are harmful to humans. Hairspray has been associated with birth defects in boys whose mothers were exposed to it during pregnancy and with liver cancer in hairdressers and barbers.

Zzzzzzz

Do you find yourself getting tired while working, reading, or doing any daily task? Then take a nap! It will do you a world of good. Most Americans don't get the recommended eight hours of sleep per night, and some of the negative consequences of that can be ameliorated by napping during the day. Some wise cultures build naps (siestas) into the workday, especially in tropical regions.

Even north of the tropics, many Mediterranean cultures have this practice. In Italy and France, for instance, businesses normally close for an hour or two right after lunch. That period coincides with our normal biological rhythms. Humans have an internal alerting signal that fights the desire to sleep as the day goes on, but there is a lull in that signal in the early afternoon. Taking a short nap then can act as a restorative, providing increased alertness and reducing the possibility of accidents and mistakes.

Our sleep patterns change as we age. Newborns sleep sixteen to twenty hours a day, but sporadically; only after three or four months do they start to settle into a pattern of longer sleeping periods at night. Through childhood, the amount of sleep we get gradually decreases, so that by the time we're adults, we need about "eight sweet hours of shut-eye," according to one NASA study. Some elderly people cannot sleep in a single consolidated block during the night, so napping during the day becomes more essential for them. There are many famous nappers, including Ronald Reagan, Napoleon, Albert Einstein, Thomas Edison, and Winston Churchill, who had this to say about napping: "Don't think you will be doing less work because you sleep during the day. That's a foolish notion held by people who have no imagination." A ten- to thirty-minute rest seems to be optimal; longer naps can leave you feeling groggy (that's called sleep inertia). A NASA study on military pilots and astronauts found that a forty-minute nap improved performance by 34 percent.

Calculus: Mouth, Not Math

That sticky, invisible biofilm (a colony of microorganisms) that forms daily on your teeth is called *plaque*. If it's allowed to harden, it's called *tartar* or *calculus*. Plaque contains bacteria, which turn sugars and starches from food into an acid that causes tooth demineralization (dissolving of the enamel) and leads to tooth decay (cavities, or caries). Calculus irritates the gums, which brings about gingivitis (inflammation); if left untreated, this can develop into the more serious periodontal disease.

The bacteria that live in the human mouth are not normally harmful, but if they are not removed by brushing, they can build up into a thick layer. Then the bacteria nearest the tooth surface begin to metabolize food with anaerobic respiration (without oxygen); the waste products of that process are very acidic.

Daily brushing, flossing, and use of mouthwash are the primary preventative methods. Dentists can remove plaque in a process called scaling; if gum disease is present, root planing is utilized.

Face Bugs

Did you know that you have tiny parasites living on your face? There are two species of eyelash mites—*Demodex folliculorum* and *D. brevis*—that infest just about all of us. They live in the hair follicles and sebaceous glands at the ends of our eyelashes or eyebrows, and they eat dead skin cells and oil. We're not aware of their presence because they are infinitesimal—about a hundredth of an inch long.

Mites have semitransparent, scaly bodies with eight legs and minuscule claws. Female mites remain snug in their little homes, but the males walk around at night, looking for mates. Yes, they mate and lay eggs, live and die, and eat—all right there on your skin—but their digestion is so efficient that they don't produce waste material.

Demodex ("lard worm") can be transferred from one person to another by close facial contact. If too many of these microscopic arachnids collect in one follicle, they can cause itchiness or inflammation, called demodicosis, but they are mostly harmless and perhaps even beneficial.

The Wild Blue Yonder and What's Below

Astronomy, Meteorology, Botany, Mineralogy, Chemistry

Solar Circle

Possibly the first solar observatory in the world (at least until some archaeologist finds an older one), the Goseck Circle is an enclosure outside the town of Goseck, Germany, near Leipzig. About 250 feet wide, the 7,000-year-old site "consisted of four concentric circles—a mound, a ditch, and two wooden palisades . . . with three sets of gates." It was used to worship celestial objects, such as constellations, and predict the summer and winter solstices, two thousand years before the Egyptians built their first pyramids.

After aerial photographs revealed the presence of circular ridges beneath a farmer's field, archaeologists began excavating the site in

2002 and found hundreds of well-preserved objects: flints, wooden tools, and bits of pottery. Local officials built a reconstruction of the site in 2005, placing more than two thousand hand-carved oak posts to re-create an authentic Neolithic appearance. According to *Archaeology*, "When the site was finally opened on December 21, just in time for the winter solstice, more than 2,000 people gathered to watch a pale winter sun blaze its last rays on the southeastern gate of the enclosure," just as it had in 4600 BCE.

Goseck is frequently called a *henge*, but by some definitions, a henge is a site in Britain or Ireland that includes standing stones. No evidence of stones has been found at the Goseck Circle.

The First Sky Map

In 1999, not far from the Goseck Circle, treasure hunters discovered the Nebra Sky Disk, a flat bronze plate, twelve inches in diameter, with a beautiful green patina and images of the sun, the moon, and the stars in gold leaf. Since it was not excavated with the proper archaeological techniques, its lack of provenance caused some to doubt its authenticity.

However, the dating of objects associated with the disk indicates that it was created circa 1600 BCE, and the copper has been identified as being from the Austrian Alps. The plate also contains golden arcs that accurately represent the angular distance of the sun, between its rising and setting points at the summer and winter solstices, at that precise location in central Europe in the Bronze Age.

The Nebra Sky Disk was an agricultural marker that could be used to calculate the times for planting and harvesting—and some scholars think that its markings are based on observations made at Goseck. According to Professor Miranda Aldhouse-Green of Cardiff University, "These symbols are part of a complex European-wide belief system . . . people looked at the heavens . . . worshipped the

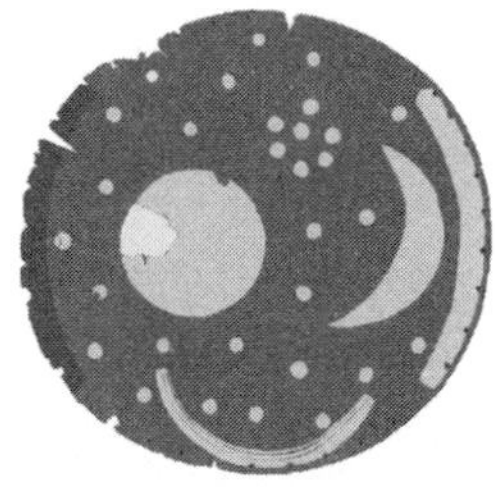

The Nebra Sky Disk

sun, the moon, aligned their monuments on the sunrise or the moonrise. . . . Nebra has brought these symbols together [and] tells us for the first time perhaps what people were really seeing, perceiving and believing."

The Wild Blue Yonder

The first scientist to explain why the sky is blue was John Tyndall (1820–1893), an Anglo-Irish physicist who worked in a number of disciplines, including atmospherics, geology, and mathematics (he was also a mountain climber and a poet). In 1859, he pointed out that the earth's atmosphere contains microscopic particles of dust that act like prisms and scatter sunlight as it passes through the air. Since the light at the blue end of the spectrum is scattered more than the light at the red end, a clear sky appears blue. This phenomenon became known as the Tyndall Effect.

Tyndall was also well known as a science educator, a role he took very seriously: "I do not know a higher, nobler, more blessed calling, than that of the man who . . . converts the knowledge he imparts into a lever, to lift, exercise, and strengthen the growing minds committed to his care." Tyndall had a knack for explaining difficult principles in straightforward language, and he wrote a number of tutorials, such as *Heat* (1863), *Sound* (1867), and *Light* (1873), for nonscientific audiences. His books stayed in print for decades.

A strong supporter of Charles Darwin, Tyndall tangled with the Catholic Church over the separation of religion and science. In an 1874 address before the British Association for the Advancement of Science, he said: "All religious theories, schemes and systems, which embrace notions of cosmogony, or which otherwise reach into the domain of science, must, in so far as they do this, submit to the control of science, and relinquish all thought of controlling it."

Don't let adverse facts stand in the way of a good decision.

—Colin Powell (*My American Journey*, 1995)

We Are Not Alone

In the early years of the twentieth century, most astronomers believed that the Milky Way was the only galaxy in the universe and that the fuzzy nebulae they observed around it were just nearby clouds of dust and gas. In 1924, Edwin Hubble (1889–1953), working with the powerful telescope at Mount Wilson Observatory, was able to calculate that the Andromeda nebula is actually at least one million light years away from us and must therefore be a separate galaxy. He invented "the idea of the universe . . . discovered the cosmos, and in doing so founded the science of cosmology." Continuing to observe, photograph, measure, and analyze objects in deep space, he developed Hubble's Law, which states that "the velocity at which a galaxy or any other distant object appears to be receding from us is proportional to its distance." The universe is expanding, he realized, and this was the evidence that proved the Big Bang theory of creation and allowed Albert Einstein to complete his general theory of relativity. Subsequent research has shown that the universe is even larger and older than what Hubble found, but he is considered a pioneer of science on a level with Galileo and Newton. NASA named its space-based observatory, launched in 1990, in his honor. The Hubble Space Telescope has collected hundreds of thousands of images and, according to NASA, "has revolutionized astronomy by providing unprecedented deep and clear views of the Universe." In a lecture published in 1954, Hubble described his work by saying, "Equipped with his five senses, man explores the universe around him and calls the adventure Science."

Space Fireflies

John Glenn, the first American to orbit the earth (February 20, 1962), saw something outside the window of *Friendship 7* that he couldn't explain. Here is his account from the mission transcript: "I am in a big mass of some very small particles that are brilliantly lit up like they're luminescent. I never saw anything like it . . . they look like little stars.

A whole shower of them coming by. They swirl around the capsule and go in front of the window and they're all brilliantly lighted." In the same transcript, Glenn later described them as "the color of a very bright firefly, a light yellowish green color" and said that he had thought of the "lost Air Force needles [see "Space Junk," below] that are some place in space, but they were not anything that looked like that at all." Scott Carpenter also saw the "fireflies" during his Mercury flight three months later.

NASA Flight Director Gene Kranz explained the phenomenon this way: "The 'fireflies' reported on Glenn's and Carpenter's missions were simply frozen droplets of water from the evaporators used to cool the cabin and space suits. They were most noticeable at sunrise on each orbit."

Space Junk

On February 6, 1971, astronaut Alan Shepard famously hit some golf balls during his walk on the moon. Although he claimed that one went "for miles and miles," it actually still rests on the moon's surface today and did not achieve escape velocity. Even though there are no golf balls in lunar orbit, there is plenty of orbital debris or space junk circling the earth. Spent rockets and dead satellites, Ed White's glove, flecks of paint, crystallized urine, and other detritus make up 94 percent of the stuff that floats around the earth along with operational satellites. (The glove stayed in orbit only about a month.)

There are also remnants of Project Needles (official name: Project West Ford), a 1960s plan to orbit tiny strips of metal to be used as antennae in a worldwide communication system. (These are the "lost Air Force needles" referred to by Glenn, above.)

In early 2009, the International Space Station had a close call with a piece of micrometeoroid orbital debris. According to NASA, approximately nineteen thousand objects larger than ten centimeters in diameter are known to exist; there are also an estimated five hundred thousand particles between one and ten centimeters and tens of millions of particles smaller than one centimeter.

No facts are to me sacred; none are profane; I simply experiment, an endless seeker with no Past at my back.

—Ralph Waldo Emerson ("Circles" in *Essays: First Series*, 1841)

The space agency points out that although "collisions with even a small piece of debris will involve considerable energy," NASA has a surveillance network to monitor debris during space shuttle missions, and the shuttle can be maneuvered away from an object if the chance of collision exceeds one in ten thousand, which occurs about once every year or two. The International Space Station is well shielded and can withstand the impact of debris as large as a centimeter in diameter.

Balanced in Space

Lagrange (*la-GRAHNZH*) or Lagrangian points, named in honor of the eighteenth-century French mathematician who theorized their existence, are "five special points in the vicinity of two orbiting masses where a third, smaller mass can orbit at a fixed distance from the larger masses. . . . [T]he Lagrange Points mark positions where the gravitational pull of the two large masses precisely equals the centripetal force required to rotate with them." In other words, at a Lagrange point, a small body (such as a probe or another space vehicle) can maintain its position between two large bodies (such as the earth and the sun) while expending very little energy. The Trojan Asteroids are groups of natural satellites that are trapped in Lagrange points near Mars and Jupiter. The phenomenon has some very practical applications. Since 2001, the Wilkinson Microwave Anisotropy Probe (WMAP), residing at a Lagrange point between the sun and the earth, has been measuring cosmic radiation: "producing our new Standard Model of Cosmology . . . WMAP definitively determined the age of the universe to be 13.73 billion years old." NASA scientists have mapped a "freeway in space," possible flight paths among Lagrange points where spacecraft can travel without using much fuel; this would make the exploration of Mars or the rest of the solar system significantly easier and less expensive. The James Webb Space

Telescope (scheduled for launch in 2014) will observe distant galaxies from Lagrange Point 2 between the sun and the earth, about a million miles away.

A Thing High Up

Meteors, or shooting stars, are chunks of space rocks (primarily bits of asteroids or comets) that are "heated to incandescence by the friction of the air." Before they enter the earth's atmosphere and catch on fire, they're called *meteoroids*, and if they don't completely vaporize but instead hit the ground, they're *meteorites*.

Every day, tons and tons of rocks fall to the earth. Most of them are very tiny, dustlike particles, but larger meteorites have left their mark on the planet: more than a hundred impact craters have been found around the globe, and the meteorite that struck Chicxulub in the Yucatan Peninsula sixty-five million years ago may have caused the extinction of the dinosaurs and other species. The word *meteor* comes from the Greek term for "a thing high up" or "celestial phenomena."

A meteor

The Costliest, Deadliest, and Most Intense

During Hurricane Katrina (2005), many librarians learned that searching for information on the *worst* storm is not a good strategy—the correct terms are *costliest*, *deadliest*, and *most intense*. Katrina caused the most damage: $84.6 billion has been spent on cleanup and repairs. Before Katrina, the costliest was 1992's Hurricane Andrew, at $48 billion (adjusted for inflation). Five of the ten costliest hurricanes occurred in 2004 and 2005.

The unnamed storm that hit Galveston, Texas, in 1900 killed between eight thousand and twelve thousand people, so it is by far the deadliest hurricane to hit the United States.

The most intense storms—category five at landfall, with winds greater than 155 miles per hour—were the 1935 Florida Keys hurricane, Camille (1969), and Andrew. Katrina was a category-three storm when it hit New Orleans.

The Same, Only Different

What's the difference between a hurricane and a typhoon? Location, location, location. The generic term for both is *tropical cyclone*, a "non-frontal synoptic scale low-pressure system over tropical or sub-tropical waters with organized convection (i.e.[,] thunderstorm activity) and definite cyclonic surface wind circulation." When a storm occurs in the North Atlantic Ocean, the Northeast Pacific Ocean east of the international dateline, or the South Pacific Ocean east of longitude 160 East, it's called a *hurricane*. It's a typhoon if it is in the Northwest Pacific Ocean west of the international dateline. Meteorologists make some finer distinctions, however. If the storm develops in the Southwest Pacific Ocean west of 160 East longitude or in the Southeast Indian Ocean east of 90 East longitude, it's a *severe tropical cyclone*. In the North Indian Ocean it's a *severe cyclonic storm*, and in the Southwest Indian Ocean it is called simply a *tropical cyclone*.

All the above must have sustained winds greater than seventy-four miles per hour to qualify. When the winds are between thirty-nine and seventy-four miles per hour, the phenomenon is called a *tropical storm*; with winds less than thirty-nine miles per hour, it's merely a *tropical depression*.

Hurricane clouds from overhead

The Great London Fog

In December 1952, a killer smog spread across and around London in one of the worst environmental disasters ever recorded. For four days, a dirty blanket of pollution and fog paralyzed the area. Cold, damp air had become trapped below a layer of warmer air (a temperature inversion). This mixed with pollutants from coal fires and auto exhaust to create what the BBC called a "toxic darkness."

One survivor recalled, "It had a yellow tinge and a strong, strong smell, strongly of sulphur. . . . Even in daylight, it was a ghastly yellow colour." Almost all transportation was shut down, stranding commuters and travelers; cultural and sports events had to be canceled; muggings increased; and cows suffocated in the fields. "The association between health and air pollution during the episode was evident as a strong rise in air pollution levels was immediately followed by sharp increases in mortality and morbidity," an environmental journal reported. At least four thousand people, and perhaps as many as twelve thousand, died as a result (direct or indirect) of the fog. Public outrage led to the introduction of Britain's Clean Air legislation in 1956.

Plastic Soup

There are islands floating in the world's oceans that are composed solely of marine debris. According to the National Oceanic and Atmospheric Administration, "Marine debris is any persistent solid material that is manufactured or processed and directly or indirectly, intentionally or unintentionally, disposed of or abandoned into the marine environment." Media reports on these garbage patches sometimes make it sound as if they are huge collections of solid trash visible from above, but they're actually made up primarily of small pieces of nonbiodegradable plastic just below the surface of the water, like a "plastic soup." Garbage becomes trapped in ocean gyres, areas where strong currents and light winds create a slow whirlpool.

The Hawaiian Trash Vortex, for example, is twice the size of Texas and reaches almost to Japan, and it's growing. It was discovered by Charles Moore while he was sailing near the islands in 1999: "In the week it took to cross, no matter what time of day I looked, plastic debris was floating everywhere: bottles, bottle caps, wrappers, fragments." Moore then founded the Algalita Marine Research Foundation and became an environmental activist. "It's a swirling plastic cesspool," he said, "a dispersed congregation of our debris from civilization." He also noted, "If it's calm it sort of looks like a giant salt shaker has sprinkled bits of plastic onto the surface of the ocean." These bits of plastic cause the deaths of sea birds, turtles, and other creatures that ingest the particles. Plastic that has absorbed toxic substances enters the food chain this way and can thus pose a health risk to humans. Scientific research on the extent, the content, and possible solutions of the problem is ongoing, but reducing our use of plastic is probably the only way to prevent continued environmental hazards from these great garbage vortexes.

The Measure of Great Rivers

What is the longest river in the United States, the Missouri or the Mississippi? You might think that this is an easy question to answer; surely our government has measured our rivers. However, the length of a river isn't so easily determined—it meanders, it changes course, it's dammed or dredged; at precisely which points do you start and end the measuring?

Different sources have different opinions on the longest U.S. river; it all depends on whom you ask and when. The Missouri was calculated at 2,540 miles long, but after channelization (engineered changes), it's now about 2,315 miles, making it shorter than the Mississippi, which is frequently listed at 2,350 miles. As the National Park Service points out, the Mississippi is "constantly changing. . . . The staff at Itasca State Park, the Mississippi's headwaters, say the Mississippi is 2,552 miles long. The U.S. Geological Survey has published a number of 2,300 miles, the EPA [Environmental Protection Agency] says it is 2,320 miles long, and the Mississippi National River and Recreation

Both the myths of religion and the laws of science, it is now becoming apparent, are not so much descriptions of facts as symbolic expressions of cosmic truths.

—René Dubos (*A God Within*, 1972)

Area maintains its length at 2,350 miles." Since the Missouri is a tributary of the Mississippi, we can lump them together into one system. The National Park Service says that "compared to other world rivers, the Mississippi-Missouri River combination ranks fourth in length at approximately 3,902 miles," after the Nile (4,135 miles), the Amazon (3,980 miles), and the Yangtze (3,917 miles).

Other sources disagree on either the ranking or the precise measurements. Describing the Missouri River, also known as the Big Muddy, someone—possibly Mark Twain—said, "It's too thick to drink and too thin to plow." About the Mississippi, Twain said that it "cannot be tamed, curbed or confined . . . you cannot bar its path with an obstruction which it will not tear down, dance over and laugh at. The Mississippi River will always have its own way; no engineering skill can persuade it to do otherwise."

Minuscule Blooms

The tiniest flowering plants on earth are the watermeal and the mud midget, members of the duckweed genus (*Wolffia*). They have no stems, roots, or true leaves, and they rarely produce flowers and fruit; they float on or just beneath the surface of slow-moving water. They've been described as looking like one candy sprinkle or bits of cornmeal, and they weigh only as much as two grains of salt.

Duckweeds quickly remove minerals and organic nutrients from water, so they are used in sewage and wastewater treatment. Since they have as much protein as soybeans, with high concentrations of essential amino acids, duckweeds provide food for fish and livestock and can be used for human sustenance as well.

Giant Meat Flowers

Rafflesia arnoldii is the world's largest flower: it measures up to three feet in diameter and weighs as much as fifteen pounds. Bright red-orange in color, *arnoldii* and other species are found in Indonesia, the Malay Peninsula, and the Philippines. "More bizarre than beautiful," according to one scientist who studies them, *Rafflesia* is a parasite, with no visible leaves, roots, or stem. It attaches itself to a host plant with threadlike outgrowths (called *haustoria*) to absorb nutrients. To attract pollinating insects, the flower produces an awful stench like that of rotting flesh (which explains its local names, "meat flower" and "corpse flower").

Rafflesia arnoldii

Ancient Evergreens

One of the world's oldest and most majestic trees, the alerce is a national monument in Chile. Also called *lahuan* (the native name) or the Patagonian cypress, it is the Southern Hemisphere's equivalent of the ancient redwood of the Pacific Northwest. The alerce tree can reach a diameter of thirteen feet and "can live for more than 3,000 years, making it the second-longest living organism on Earth." Charles Darwin saw alerce specimens that were 130 feet tall, and he named the tree *Fitzroya cupressoides* in honor of Robert FitzRoy, the captain of the HMS *Beagle*. According to a Web site on conifers, "The reddish brown wood is lightweight, durable, easily worked on account of its straight grain and was formerly much used for shingles, furniture, cooperage, masts, and spars. However, all logging of this extraordinary tree (sometimes called the Sequoia of South America) was officially stopped in 1976." Alerce can be found in southern Argentina (in the Parque Nacional Los Alerces) and in Chile, especially in Parque Pumalín, a national reserve created in 1991 by an American, Douglas Tompkins, who purchased thousands of acres of temperate evergreen rain forest to preserve it from exploitation.

Herbal Remedies Used Up

Silphium, or giant fennel (in Greek, *silphion*; a species of the genus *Ferula*) was successfully used for birth control by the ancients all around the Mediterranean. The juice of the plant had additional medicinal uses—for cough, indigestion, and seizures—and was so popular that it was even depicted on coins. Grown only around Cyrene (today's Libya) on the coast of North Africa, silphium was difficult to cultivate, and it became extinct by the first century CE, probably from overuse.

Silphium (pictured on a coin)

Pliny the Elder considered silphium, which is also called laser, to be "among the most precious gifts presented to us by Nature." The Roman satirist Juvenal said, two thousand years ago, "We have so many sure-fire drugs for inducing sterility," but he was concerned about the same moral issues of contraception and abortion that continue to be debated today.

Killer Weed

People have a long history with nicotine use and addiction. Originating in Mesoamerica, the tobacco plant (*Nicotiana*) was probably first smoked in Peru about two thousand years ago. The Aztecs considered the goddess Cihuacoatl to be the incarnation of tobacco. Shamans used tobacco for its psychoactive properties; and it was "snuffed, chewed, drunk, inhaled or swallowed as smoke, dripped in the nose, eaten as a concentrated paste, and even taken as an enema." When Columbus first came to the islands of the Caribbean, the "Indians" gave him pungent dried leaves, which he discarded. But soon two of his crew reported observing the natives rolling up tobacco leaves, setting them afire, and "drinking" the smoke. It was said to stave off hunger and thirst, provide energy, and alleviate pain.

In 1586, an English visitor to the region noted the effects of smoking: "Their bodies are notably preserved in health, & know not many greevous diseases wherewithal wee in England are oftentimes afflicted." Its use spread rapidly; within a century of Columbus's voyages, "tobacco was either grown or consumed in most of the known world." Eighteenth-century physicians used tobacco-smoke enemas to revive drowning victims, and resuscitation kits, which included tobacco enemas, were made available at various points along the Thames.

As the World Health Organization pointed out in a 2002 report about tobacco use, "Only the mode of delivery has changed. In the 18th century, snuff held sway; the 19th century was the age of the cigar; the 20th century saw the rise of the manufactured cigarette, and with it a greatly increased number of smokers. At the beginning of the 21st century about one third of adults in the world, including increasing numbers of women, used tobacco."

The Wine of the Bean

Qahwah or kahve, java, joe, tar, brain juice, or mud—all names for coffee—originated, according to legend, when a goatherd (usually named Khaldi) noticed his flock cavorting energetically near a bush with red berries. He sampled the berries and discovered their stimulating properties. At a nearby monastery, the monks figured out how to roast the berries and brew them, and they found that the resulting beverage gave them an exquisite ability to concentrate at prayers.

Originally grown in Ethiopia, coffee is now also cultivated throughout Latin America and the Caribbean, Hawaii, India, Sumatra, and other parts of Africa. According to the U.S. Department of Agriculture (USDA), Americans consumed 9.6 pounds (or 22.7 gallons) of coffee per person in 2007, down from a high point of 19.6 pounds (46.4 gallons) per person in 1946. As coffee consumption has declined, soft drinks—especially carbonated beverages—have taken the place of the "wine of the bean."

The Drink of the Gods

Mate (*MAH-tay*) is a caffeinated tea that is enormously popular in South America, where it is known as the "drink of the gods" and is a multimillion-dollar industry with huge exports to the Middle East and the United States. Mate is common in Chile, Bolivia, and Brazil, and it is the national beverage of Argentina, Paraguay, and Uruguay.

Made from yerba mate (*Ilex paraguariensis*), an evergreen plant of the holly family, which is indigenous to South America, the tea was probably first used by the Guarani people (nomads who lived in the pampas) before the arrival of the colonial powers. The drink's proponents claim many health benefits in addition to the kick from caffeine, including anti-inflammatory and antioxidant properties.

Rich in vitamins and minerals, mate has been called a "liquid vegetable," but some scientific studies show a possible increased risk of cancer among those who consume large quantities. Mate is a social drink, with specific rituals for imbibing.

To brew the tea, the preparer (*cebador*) chops the leaves and twigs of yerba mate and puts them into a calabash gourd, which is then tipped and shaken so that the heavier bits fall to the side. Cold water is poured into the gourd, and once that is absorbed, a metal straw known as a bombilla is inserted to filter out the bits of leaves. Then hot water (but not boiling water, which would make the drink bitter) is added.

The gourd is then shared by a group: each person drinks and then passes it back to the *cebador*, who refills it with water and presents it to the next person. Green or dried leaves each produce a different beverage. One user has described the taste as "a combination of lightly smoked wood, weak coffee, and flavored hay."

Fruit or Vegetable?

Watermelon (*Citrullus lanatus*) is one of the more popular fruits in the United States. However, it's also considered a vegetable because it's a member of the gourd family (Cucurbitaceae), along with cucumbers and squashes. Nutritionally, watermelons are low in calories and high in vitamin C, beta carotene, and lycopene.

Probably originating in southern Africa, watermelons were first cultivated along the Nile five thousand years ago; watermelon seeds were placed in the tomb of King Tut as a nourishing snack for him in the afterlife. A Japanese farmer has developed cube-shaped watermelons, which are easier to pack and store but rather pricey.

The USDA's Agricultural Research Service is looking at using rinds and juice from rejected watermelons (those that are too scarred or weird-looking for the market) to make biofuels. In April 2007, the Oklahoma legislature chose the watermelon as the official state vegetable (it already had a state fruit—the strawberry—and also considered okra for the state veggie). The sponsors of the bill, State Representative Joe Dorman and State Senator Don Barrington, have participated—and done well—in watermelon seed-spitting competitions.

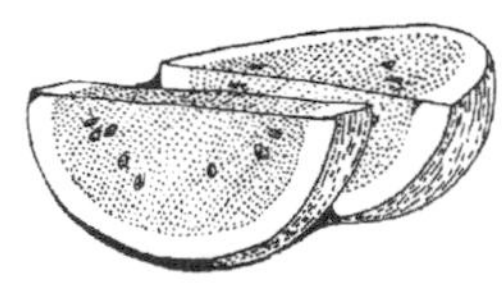

Watermelon

Pink and White Petals

A gift of 3,020 cherry trees from the people of Japan in 1912 eventually led to the Cherry Blossom Festival, which draws thousands of tourists to Washington, D.C., every spring. Although the original donation of trees was infested with insects and had to be destroyed, they were replaced by twelve varieties of flowering cherries, which were planted along the Tidal Basin, around East Potomac Park, and on the grounds of the White House. Yoshino and Kwanzan are now the dominant varieties.

Glistening Ice Plants

Members of the fig-marigold or carpetweed family (*Aizoaceae*), ice plants are succulents: plants that store water in their roots, stems, or leaves. Despite the name, they live in dry, not cold, regions; many are indigenous to South Africa. Ice plants have "glistening, hairlike parts" that resemble ice crystals from a distance. They are low, mat-forming, fast-growing plants with brilliantly colored flowers that have been recommended for erosion control; they're used extensively along roadways in California, for example.

Ice plants are considered invasive species, competing with threatened or endangered plants: Their "main impacts are smothering, reduced regeneration of native flora and changes to soil pH and nutrient regimes." Cousins of the ice plant include sea figs, or beach apples, and lithops, also known as pebble plants or living stones, because that's exactly what they look like.

The Tiniest Park

The smallest public park in the world is in Portland, Oregon. Less than two feet in diameter, the park began when journalist Dick Fagan returned from World War II and noticed a hole for a light post in the median of the roadway near his office. A pole was never placed, so Fagan planted flowers, then began writing about it in his *Oregon Journal* column. He claimed that the park was home to "the only leprechaun colony west of Ireland." Mill Ends Park was formally designated a municipal park in 1976, and it has hosted all kinds of unusual exhibitions and events throughout the years, including the temporary installation of a tiny swimming pool for butterflies.

An Uncommon Park

Boston Common (not Commons) is the oldest public park in the nation. Purchased from the city's first settler, William Blackstone, by the citizens of Boston in 1634, the land was soon made a community park and was originally used as a military training ground and a cow pasture. There were public hangings there—and burials, too, when the Central Burying Ground became part of Boston Common in 1839.

Boston Common has been the site of many historic events: the British staged troops there before heading out to Lexington and Concord in 1775; George Washington inspected his troops there a year later; antislavery protests were held there in the 1860s; the first U.S. subway system opened at the Park Street station in 1897; and both Martin Luther King Jr. and Pope John Paul II spoke to crowds of people on the Common.

Facts are more powerful than arguments.

—Thomas Paine (letter to Abbé Raynal, 1792, in *The Life and Writings of Thomas Paine*, 1908)

Consuming Minerals

A mineral is a "naturally occurring inorganic element or compound having an orderly internal structure and characteristic chemical composition, crystal form, and physical properties." Sand, gold, sulfur, and turquoise are all minerals; rocks are aggregates of minerals.

According to the Minerals Information Institute, each of us in the United States uses about forty-eight thousand pounds of minerals per year, and at today's level of consumption, the average newborn infant will need the following as a lifetime supply:

854 pounds of lead
776 pounds of zinc
1,319 pounds of copper
32,980 pounds of iron
21,418 pounds of clay
31,040 pounds of salt
1.71 million pounds of stone, sand, and gravel
72,994 pounds of cement

A Barrel of Energy

One barrel of crude oil contains 42 gallons. When refined, it yields approximately 19.6 gallons of motor gasoline. The remainder of the barrel produces distillate fuel oil, residual fuel oil, jet fuel, and other products (ink, crayons, tires, deodorant, and heart valves). That 42 gallons of oil will release six million British Thermal Units (one BTU is the amount of energy required to raise the temperature of one pint of water one degree Fahrenheit; it's equal to one match tip). A typical American uses about one million BTUs every day.

The amount of petroleum products consumed in the United States is not tracked as such by the Department of Energy; rather, it counts "product supplied." Its system "measures the disappearance of petroleum products from primary sources; [this] approximately represents consumption of petroleum products." We used 3,290,057,000 barrels (more than 137 billion gallons) in 2008.

Oil Futures

The world's proven petroleum reserves—"those quantities of petroleum which, by analysis of geological and engineering data, can be estimated with a high degree of confidence to be commercially recoverable from a given date forward, from known reservoirs and under current economic conditions"—total about 1.343 trillion barrels. Saudi Arabia, Canada, Iran, Iraq, and Kuwait have the top five, with almost 800 billion barrels among them. The United States is twelfth on the list, with about 21 billion barrels, and there are many countries—including Iceland, Slovenia, Nepal, Panama, and Ireland—that have no petroleum reserves at all.

An oil well

Sweet Medicines

Coal tar is the viscous black liquid that results from the carbonization of coal—that is, "the heating of coal in the absence of air, at temperatures ranging from about 1,650° to 2,200° F." Many commercially important products are derived from coal tar. Saccharin, the world's first artificial, calorie-free sweetener, was developed by scientists working on coal tar derivatives in the late 1870s. Today, products made from coal tar are used to treat psoriasis, eczema, dandruff, head lice, and other skin conditions. These keratoplastic drugs work "by causing the skin to shed dead cells from its top layer and slow down the growth of skin cells." You can rub coal tar into your skin, but you can also slather it on your roof: coal tar–based products are used for waterproofing, as well as for dyes, explosives, paints, and insulation.

What's in Your Food?

As the USDA Food Safety and Inspection Service (FSIS) points out, "People have been using food additives for thousands of years. Today about 2,800 substances are used as food additives. Salt, sugar, and corn syrup are by far the most widely used additives in food in this country." The Food and Drug Administration defines an additive as "any substance used to provide a technical effect in foods. . . . Additives are used for flavor and appeal, food preparation and processing, freshness, and safety." Here are a few examples of the many types of natural or chemical compounds that are added to food: flavoring agents (benzyl isobutyl carbinol); sweeteners (isomol or lactitol); fumigants (ethylene oxide, to control insects); humectants (potassium polymetaphosphate, for moisture retention); sequestrants (sodium dihydrogen phosphate, to improve stability); and texturizers (acetylated monoglycerides, which affect appearance or feel).

The first use of additives may have been by Stone Age cooks who smoked meat or soaked fish in seawater to improve its flavor.

PART THREE

ON IMAGINATION, POETRY, AND ART

Imagination, from which comes Poetry: Poetry has for its object imaginary individual beings, which are the imitation of historical beings . . . it is no less true to say of a painter that he is a poet, than to say of a poet that he is a painter, and of a sculptor or an engraver that he is a painter in relief or in depth, than of a musician that he is a painter through his sounds. The poet, the musician, the painter, the sculptor, [the architect], etc., imitate and counterfeit nature. . . . Such is the poetical part of human knowledge, which one can relate to imagination.

—JEAN LE ROND D'ALEMBERT

Perfect Circles

Sacred and Profane Art: Painting, Sculpture, Architecture

The Start of Art

Art began about forty thousand years ago in the Paleolithic era, as modern humans were replacing the Neanderthals in Europe. Deep inside caves, they began painting and incising, marking the environment for religious or hunting rituals or other magical purposes. These original artists were not primitive in terms of fundamental techniques—they knew how to draw and paint, vividly and with sophistication. In *A History of Western Art*, John Sewell explains that they "reached a level of skill which must be described as superb. . . . Paleolithic painting stands as irrefutable proof that the history of art is by no means equivalent to an upward evolution of technique. . . . One cannot paint better; he can only paint differently." Hidden for millennia, cave paintings were discovered in the nineteenth and twentieth centuries in Spain and France, and there are also sites in Africa, Asia, the Americas, and Australia from various prehistoric periods. In 1940, four teenagers who were searching for a lost dog stumbled into a network of caves in Lascaux, in the Dordogne region of southern France. There they discovered a large number of painted images of animals—horses, bison, deer, and wolves, among others—plus some abstract designs, but no vegetation, and only one human figure was depicted. The rush of spectators damaged the caves, which were closed to the public in 1963. A replica with very accurate reproductions of the artwork was opened nearby twenty years later.

At Lascaux, Altamira, Chauvet, and elsewhere, cave paintings and rock carvings provide "the earliest unequivocal evidence of the human capacity to interpret and give meaning to our surroundings. Through these early achievements in representation and abstraction, we see a newfound mastery of the environment and a revolutionary accomplishment in the intellectual development of humankind."

What Is Art?

Philosophers have long considered art: its definition, scope, and meaning in society. From the ancients to the twenty-first century, there has been little consensus, and the debate is unlikely to be resolved.

The esteemed American philosopher Paul Weiss wrote this about the nature of art in 1961: "Art enables men to learn basic truths about themselves and the world, and this by attending, not to the world or themselves, but to what they can create. Works of art are made with the help of emotion. And it takes emotion to appreciate them properly. . . . [Art] is quite different from craftsmanship, no matter how splendid; it is not at all a form of play, no matter how ingenious and enjoyable this may be. Unlike these it demands a fresh and unmistakable act of creativity, terminating in the production of a self-sufficient excellence. . . . The outcome of the act of creation is a work of art. . . . Art makes a great difference to man primarily because it is revelatory of the domain of existence which lies beyond him and it."

The Goddesses of Inspiration

The Nine Muses (Mousai) of Greek mythology were goddesses who inspired the creation of art, literature, and science; they are usually identified as the daughters of Zeus and Mnemosyne, the goddess of memory. The Muses dwelled on Mount Olympus with Apollo and, like him, remained perpetually young and beautiful.

These are the Nine Muses, as described in *A Dictionary of Greek and Roman Biography and Mythology* in 1867:

> Calliope, the Muse of epic poetry, appears with a tablet and stylus, and sometimes with a roll of paper;
> Clio, the Muse of history, appears in a sitting position, with an open roll of paper, or an open chest of books;
> Euterpe, the Muse of lyric poetry, with a flute;
> Melpomene, the Muse of tragedy, with a tragic mask, the club of Heracles, or a sword; her head is surrounded with vine leaves, and she wears the cothurnus [high, laced boots];
> Terpsichore, the Muse of choral dance and song, appears with the lyre and the plectrum [pick];
> Erato, the Muse of erotic poetry, sometimes, also, has the lyre;
> Polymnia, or Polyhymnia, the Muse of the sublime hymn, usually appears without any attribute, in a pensive or meditating attitude;
> Urania, the Muse of astronomy, with a staff pointing to a globe;
> Thalia, the Muse of comedy and of merry or idyllic poetry, appears with the comic mask, a shepherd's staff, or a wreath of ivy.

Euterpe

Too Much Excitement

If your pulse quickens and you feel dizzy or confused while on a whirlwind tour of Europe's art museums, you may be manifesting Stendhal syndrome, a psychosomatic condition named for the nineteenth-century French writer Marie-Henri Beyle (Stendhal was one of his pseudonyms).

He found himself overwhelmed by the intense beauty of the art and the architecture of Florence, Italy. "I was in a sort of ecstasy," he said, "from the idea of being in Florence, close to the great men whose tombs I had seen. . . . I had palpitations of the heart . . . I walked with the fear of falling." Fyodor Dostoevsky is said to have suffered an incidence of Stendhal syndrome as he gazed ecstatically at Holbein's *Dead Christ* in a Swiss museum.

A Perfect Circle

Giotto di Bondone was the thirteenth-century Florentine artist who is called the father of modern painting. He rescued it from the flat iconic images of Byzantine art and introduced naturalistic, truly human figures. There's a charming story about him in *Lives of the Most Eminent Painters, Sculptors and Architects*, written in 1550 by the world's first art critic and historian, Giorgio Vasari. The pope, hearing of Giotto's brilliance, sent an envoy to request a sample of his work, and here's what happened:

> Giotto . . . took a paper, and on that, with a brush dipped in red, holding his arm fast against his side . . . with a turn of the hand he made a circle, so true in proportion and circumference that to behold it was a marvel. This done, he smiled and said to the courtier: "Here is your drawing." He, thinking he was being derided, said: "Am I to have no other drawing but this?" "Tis enough and to spare," answered Giotto.

The pope recognized the exquisite talent revealed by Giotto's O and brought him to Rome to create paintings of the life of Christ for the old St. Peter's Basilica.

We are not afraid to entrust the American people with unpleasant facts, foreign ideas, alien philosophies, and competitive values. For a nation that is afraid to let its people judge the truth and falsehood in an open market is a nation that is afraid of its people.

—John F. Kennedy
(speech on the 20th anniversary
of the Voice of America,
February 1962)

In a Man's World

Artemisia Gentileschi was one of the very few female painters in the early Baroque period. Born in Rome in 1593, she showed amazing talent as a child and was producing significant paintings while still a teenager. Trained by her father, Orazio, an early follower of Michelangelo Merisi da Caravaggio, Gentileschi was the first woman admitted to the Accademia del Disegno in Florence.

Most of what we know of her life comes from the transcript of the trial of her teacher, Agostino Tassi, who was accused of raping her, promising marriage, and then reneging. She was vilified, personally and artistically; Tassi was convicted but suffered only minor consequences. Gentileschi then traveled with her father and painted in several cities of Italy and at the court of Charles I in England.

When other women were creating portraits and small religious paintings, Gentileschi preferred to focus on heroic women and historical events: *Judith Slaying Holofernes* (two versions); *Susannah and the Elders*; *The Penitent Magdalen*. Ignored or dismissed by critics for centuries (called a "lascivious and precocious girl" by art historians Rudolf and Margot Wittkower in 1963), feminist historians rediscovered Artemisia Gentileschi in the late twentieth century, and she has recently been depicted in a novel, a play, and a film, in addition to a number of museum exhibitions.

Done with Mirrors

The camera obscura (literally, "dark chamber") is an optical apparatus that casts an upside-down image. In its simplest form it is a box or a room with a pinhole in one side. As light from outside travels through the pinhole, it is inverted, and the image is projected onto the far side of the box or the room.

The principle behind this device, the forerunner of the modern camera, was first described by the Chinese philosopher Mo-Tzu (470–390 BCE). The first actual camera obscura was probably built by the Arab scientist Abu Ali al-Hasan ibn al-Haytham (known in the West as Alhazen) around 1000 CE.

The Web Gallery of Art explains the camera obscura this way: "For centuries the technique was used for viewing eclipses of the Sun without endangering the eyes and, by the 16th century, as an aid to drawing; the subject was posed outside and the image reflected on a piece of drawing paper for the artist to trace. Portable versions were built, followed by smaller and even pocket models; the interior of the box was painted black and the image reflected by an angled mirror so that it could be viewed right side up." Artist David Hockney proposed in 2001 that many famed artists—including Caravaggio, Jean Ingres, and Jan Vermeer—used a camera obscura to help them create realistic images. The idea was at first dismissed, but more and more art critics have been persuaded that Hockney is correct.

British art historian Philip Steadman analyzed Vermeer's work, especially the angles of the room portrayed in many of his paintings, and came to the conclusion that he did use a camera obscura to obtain his superrealistic images. However, Steadman made clear that he considered Vermeer a great artist who used the device as an aid to his work, not as a substitute for talent.

The Madman of Arles

Dutch Postimpressionist painter Vincent van Gogh sold only one or two paintings in his lifetime, even though his work is now auctioned for tens of millions of dollars. Did he really cut off his own ear? Most versions of his life story say that it was an act of self-mutilation caused by madness. But recently, two German scholars examined correspondence and police records and concluded that the ear was sliced off with a sword by Paul Gauguin, van Gogh's close friend and fellow painter, as they argued on a street in Arles. To protect the friendship, the historians claim, van Gogh remained silent. The curator of the van Gogh Museum in Amsterdam is skeptical, however.

Maori *Moko*

Humans, also known as "naked apes," have always attempted to decorate their bodies. Skin can be painted, dyed, pierced, cut, or burned to produce temporary or permanent embellishments. The original people of New Zealand, the Maori, were known for their complex skin art, called *Tā moko*. This is not traditional tattooing, because the skin is carved rather than punctured. Using a very sharp, narrow chisel made from bone, shark tooth, or stone, the artist made deep incisions in the flesh and applied the pigments.

Moko is a mark of status and rank for men; it indicates their accomplishments and tribal connections and also documents the fact that they could withstand such a painful ordeal. Some women also received *moko*, outlining their lips in blue or decorating just their chins. Christian missionaries in the nineteenth century found the practice vulgar and discouraged it, so it mostly died out.

Maori moko

In recent decades, however, there has been a resurgence of *moko*, along with a general revival of Maori language and culture. The Maori warrior Netana Whakaari of Waimana said in 1921, "You may be robbed of all that you cherish. But of your *moko*, you cannot be deprived, except by death. It will be your ornament and your companion until your final day."

Seduction of the Innocent

Fredric Wertham was a respected psychologist in the 1930s and the 1940s who concentrated on the effects of the environment and a person's social background on psychological problems. He was also an ardent opponent of segregation who helped to establish a psychiatric clinic in Harlem, and his work on racial discrimination was used to support the case of *Brown v. Board of Education*. But he achieved real fame when he went after comic books, which he considered unwholesome and psychologically damaging to children. Many comics at that time were indeed gory, sexist, and sadistic.

Concerned about the impact of violence in the media, Wertham wrote some articles against comics in the late 1940s and then published a major book, *Seduction of the Innocent*, in 1954. It focused on crime and horror comics and used much anecdotal evidence to show that comics encouraged criminal behavior in children. He testified at the televised hearings of Estes Kefauver's Senate Subcommittee to Investigate Juvenile Delinquency, which gave his theories even more prominence.

Frightened by potential government censorship, the comics industry developed the Comics Code Authority to censor itself; this was a severely restrictive set of rules that was probably harsher than anything the government would have imposed. Hundreds of comics folded, and one company, EC Comics, dropped all its horror titles and focused solely on its humor magazine, *Mad*. Wertham always claimed that he was not in favor of censorship; he opposed the Comics Code and later in life wrote a book extolling the virtues of comics fandom.

Everyone a Rembrandt

The United States of the 1950s has the reputation of having been staid, unimaginative, and acquiescent. Those were the words that critics used to disparage a craze that swept the nation during that decade: paint by number.

Developed in 1951 by Dan Robbins and Max S. Klein of the Palmer Paint Company, Craft Master Paint by Number kits were a way for anyone, artistically talented or not, to produce a "work of art." Each kit contained paints, brushes, and a canvas or a board with an image etched in light blue. The image was broken up into different numbered spaces, each number corresponding to a paint color.

Robbins first suggested using abstract art, but it turned out that Americans preferred representational images: landscapes, animals, historical sites. Many people found it an easy and painless way of participating in a creative endeavor, despite the critics who bemoaned the mindless conformity of the hobby.

One writer to *American Artist* magazine grumbled, "I don't know what America is coming to when thousands of people, many of them adults, are willing to be regimented into brushing paint on a jig-saw miscellany of dictated shapes and all by rote. Can't you rescue some of these souls—or should I say 'morons'?"

But critics couldn't stop the groundswell. Palmer had sold some twelve million kits by 1954, and it was estimated that more "number pictures" than traditional art hung on U.S. living room walls. (For those who found painting too messy, there were the Venus Paradise Coloring sets that used pencils in dozens of brilliant hues.)

By the end of the 1950s, paint by number was popular enough to be parodied by pop artists such as Andy Warhol, and it became part of the national lexicon as a term for mindless mass culture. The popularity of the hobby faded in the 1960s, but it didn't disappear. Kits are still available today, and a number of museums and galleries have had exhibitions of paint-by-number art.

No Straight Lines

Austrian painter, designer, and architect Friedensreich Hundertwasser (1928–2000) based his aesthetic philosophy on the hope that art could create harmony between humans and nature. His work was unique and idiosyncratic, full of undulating lines, irregular forms, contrasting bright colors, and much ornamentation.

In his 1958 treatise, *Mouldiness Manifesto: Against Rationalism in Architecture*, Hundertwasser explained why he despised contemporary functional building style: "The straight line is godless and immoral. The straight line is not a creative line, but it is an imitating line. In it there lives no God and no human spirit, but the mass-created, brainless ant addicted to comfort." The spiral was Hundertwasser's signature symbol.

In the mid-1980s, he designed a residential housing block in Vienna whose organic elements perfectly expressed his artistic ideas: crooked, brightly colored walls; uneven floors; oddly shaped windows with trees growing from them; onion domes, pillars, balconies, and statues.

"Even now, I am still struck by the beauty of it all each time I come home," one resident told the Associated Press in 2005. "Art must be precious, must create values and not destroy them," Hundertwasser said. "Everything is so infinitely simple, so infinitely beautiful."

Nourished by Marble Dust

Michelangelo Buonarroti—extraordinary painter (the Sistine Chapel), sculptor (*David*), and architect (St. Peter's Basilica)—did not love the act of painting; he signed his correspondence "Michelangelo, Scultore." Nursed by a stonecutter's wife in Settignano, "he breathed the dust of sculpture from his birth," a historian of the Renaissance writes, and Michelangelo told Giorgio Vasari that "if I have anything of the good in my brain, it came to me from being born in the subtle air . . . of Arezzo, even as I also sucked in with my nurse's milk the chisel and hammer with which I make my figures." Michelangelo was able to see the form in a block of marble, and he simply removed the excess to "free" the figure and allow it to emerge. When he did paint (or was forced to by Pope Julius II), he preferred to work in fresco rather than easel-painting, and he once said that "oil-painting was a woman's art or [a] slack and slothful technique."

The Greatest Rivalry

Leonardo da Vinci was twenty-three years older than Michelangelo, but that didn't prevent these two geniuses of the Italian Renaissance from becoming rivals; biographer Giorgio Vasari said there was "very great disdain" between them. Their philosophies, temperaments, and personalities were completely different. One biographer provided this comparison: "Leonardo was elegant, Michelangelo slovenly; Leonardo well-mannered, Michelangelo anti-social; Leonardo famous for his generosity and grace, Michelangelo for his obsessive secrecy and terrible temper. Michelangelo also finished his commissions, something Leonardo often failed to do." And Michelangelo taunted Leonardo publicly about that, on at least one occasion. Whereas Michelangelo considered himself primarily a sculptor who could also paint, Leonardo's strength was painting, yet he also did some sculpting.

But that doesn't mean he liked it. In his notebook *A Treatise on Painting*, Leonardo said:

> The sculptor in creating his work does so by the strength of his arm by which he consumes the marble, or other obdurate material in which his subject is enclosed: and this is done by the most mechanical exercise, often accompanied by a great sweat which mixes with the marble dust and forms a kind of mud daubed all over his face. The marble dust flours him all over so that he looks like a baker; his back is covered with a snowstorm of chips, and his house is made filthy by the flecks and dust of stone. The exact reverse is true of the painter . . . [who] sits before his work, perfectly at ease and well dressed, and moves a very light brush dipped in a delicate color; and he adorns himself with whatever clothes he pleases. His house is clean and filled with charming pictures; and often he is accompanied by music or by the reading of various and beautiful works which, since they are not mixed with the sound of the hammer or other noises, are heard with the greatest pleasure.

Cultural Vandalism

The Elgin Marbles (usually pronounced with a soft *g* in the United States, but always with a hard *g* in Britain) are a collection of sculptures and architectural remnants from the Acropolis in Athens that are now in the British Museum.

Thomas Bruce, the seventh Earl of Elgin, was the British ambassador to the Ottoman Empire from 1799 to 1803. A lover of antiquities and ancient history, Lord Elgin was concerned that the already damaged Acropolis was in danger of further deterioration under Greece's indifferent Turkish rulers. Possibly with their permission, he removed tons of statues and other objects and shipped them to England; the British Museum acquired them in 1816.

The Karyatid Porch on the Parthenon

Even at that time, there was much controversy over his acquisition; Lord Byron was among many who joined the outcry against Elgin. The dispute between the Greek and the British governments has continued, passionately, up to the present. The British Museum describes its Parthenon collection as containing: "roughly half of what now survives: 247 feet of the original 524 feet of frieze; 15 of 92 metopes; 17 figures from the pediments, and various other pieces of architecture. It also includes objects from other buildings on the Acropolis: the Erechtheion, the Propylaia, and the Temple of Athena Nike." The term *elginism* has been coined to describe any act of cultural vandalism.

Carving a Mountain

"To protect and preserve the culture, tradition and living heritage of North American Indians," sculptor Korczak Ziolkowski and Lakota Chief Henry Standing Bear began work on the Crazy Horse Memorial in 1948. Their plan was to carve an image of the great Lakota warrior on Thunderhead Mountain in the Black Hills of South Dakota. The location is near Mount Rushmore, where Ziolkowski had earlier been an assistant to sculptor Gutzon Borglum.

When the Crazy Horse Memorial is completed (and no one can say when that might be) the monument will be 641 feet long and 563 feet high. The face of Crazy Horse, measuring 87.5 feet, was completed in 1998. Through the years, millions of tons of rock have been blasted away. The project is controversial among some Native Americans, who believe that it desecrates holy ground.

Ziolkowski died in 1982 and is buried at the base of the mountain; his wife and children continue the project and museum, and more than a million people visit each year.

The Art of Packaging

Christo and Jeanne-Claude—Christo Vladimirov Javacheff and Jeanne-Claude Denat de Guillebon—a husband and wife team of environmental artists, created dozens of installations in urban and rural landscapes. Their work is about packaging and wrapping; as a 1970 biographer explained, "In a materialistic age, their art is a profound comment on the chronic expectations and frustrations aroused by the increasing number of consumer products that are 'enhanced' through packaging." They have wrapped the Reichstag in Berlin and the Pont Neuf in Paris with silver and gold fabric, planted thousands of giant umbrellas in Japan and California, and surrounded islands in Biscayne Bay with pink polypropylene. In 2005, they installed more than seventy-five hundred gates on the paths of Central Park in New York, with hanging saffron-colored nylon panels. The five million people who visited during the sixteen days of the exhibition found "a golden river appearing and disappearing through the bare branches of the trees and highlighting the shape of the meandering footpaths." All their works are ephemeral. Jeanne-Claude, who died in November 2009, spoke in an interview in 2002 about "the quality of love and tenderness that we human beings have for what does not last. . . . The fact that the work does not remain creates an urgency to see it." Christo told the same interviewer, "Our work is a scream of freedom."

Brunelleschi's Dome

The great dome that sits atop the cathedral of Santa Maria del Fiore in Florence, Italy, is an architectural engineering marvel. At 143 feet in diameter, it's still the largest dome in the world. Filippo Brunelleschi (1377–1446), the man responsible for designing it, was not a famous architect at the time but had trained as a goldsmith, a clockmaker, and a sculptor.

The cathedral had already been under construction for more than a century, open to the elements and with no clear plan for erecting the dome that the original designer had imagined, when Florence held a competition in 1418 to finally find a workable design. Brunelleschi and his great rival, Lorenzo Ghiberti, were jointly made architects in chief, but eventually Brunelleschi emerged as the sole master builder (*Capomaestro*). Great domes had been built in the past, particularly on the Pantheon in Rome, which Brunelleschi studied closely in preparing his design. But the techniques of ancient Roman vaulting—the recipe for concrete, for example—had been lost, making the task particularly daunting.

Brunelleschi's plan called for "an inner hemispherical dome . . . within [the] octagonal drum. A second, ovoid brick dome was to be placed on top, and nine sandstone rings would then hold the structure together, like a barrel," and without the buttresses that had been standard supporting elements in Gothic cathedrals.

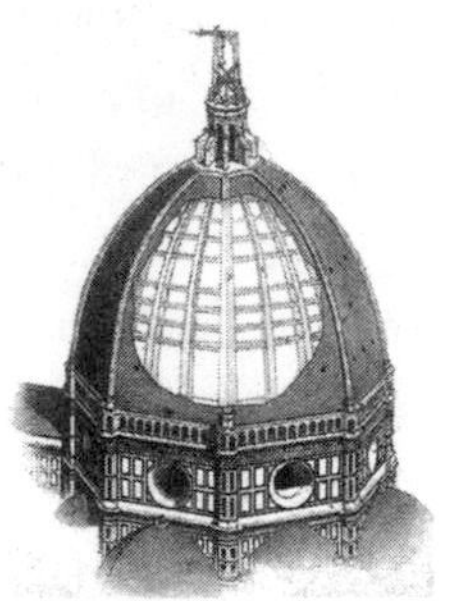

Brunelleschi's dome

The dome was also constructed without centering—that is, without a scaffolding to support the bricks and sandstone that would make up the dome. To complete the task, Brunelleschi invented a number of ingenious hoists and cranes to lift more than seventy million pounds of material (including four million bricks) hundreds of feet into the air. It took twenty-eight years to complete the dome, but Brunelleschi succeeded and was hailed as a genius and one of the greatest architects of all time.

Mimetic Architecture

There is something about human beings that makes us want to construct buildings that look like something other than buildings, such as giant animals, coffeepots, baskets, or milk bottles. The "oldest functioning example of mimetic architecture, [and] also our oldest zoomorphic structure," according to *Buildings in Disguise*, is Lucy the Elephant, a former hotel in Margate, New Jersey.

James W. Lafferty, an engineer and a real estate developer, patented a design for elephant-shaped buildings, and he erected a hotel in 1881 that later became known as Lucy. He opened a grander hotel, the Elephantine Colossus, at Coney Island three years later. A third pachyderm structure, called the Light of Asia, was built from Lafferty's plans and used as a concession stand in South Cape May.

The two hotels were a gimmick to help Lafferty develop beach lots, but he overextended himself and had to sell both properties. The Elephantine Colossus burned down in 1896, and Lucy eventually became a tavern (called the Elephant Cafe). By the 1960s, Lucy was dilapidated and in need of major repairs. It was donated to the city of Margate; the local civic association raised funds to restore it and move it to a beachfront site, and Lucy became a National Historic Landmark in 1976.

Here are a few other examples of U.S. mimetic architecture:

- Dinny the Apatosaurus, a gift shop in Cabazon, California
- Peachoid, a water tower in Gaffney, South Carolina
- Longaberger Company, a basket-shaped corporate headquarters in Newark, Ohio
- Big Musky, a leaping muskellunge—the shrine to anglers at the National Fresh Water Fishing Hall of Fame in Hayward, Wisconsin

Scary Waterspouts

Gargoyles and grotesques are architectural elements that protrude from buildings. While grotesques are purely decorative, gargoyles are functional: they are waterspouts. The term *gargoyle*, which sounds like *gargle* or *gurgle*, evolved from words for the throat, the gullet, or the windpipe.

Neither one is just a feature of medieval cathedrals; carved figures have been used to decorate and to divert rain from ancient temples, Gothic Revival colleges, and modern office buildings. The Greeks favored lion heads, the Chrysler Building in New York has automobile hood ornaments and eagles, and the Washington National Cathedral features the head of Darth Vader.

A gargoyle

Grotesques are also known as chimeras, a mythological term for a monstrous creature made from the parts of several animals. (The *Iliad* refers to "that savage monster . . . she had the head of a lion and the tail of a serpent, while her body was that of a goat, and she breathed forth flames of fire.") Their frightening appearance is said to ward off evil spirits.

A Secret Spire

Arguably the most beautiful skyscraper in the world, the Chrysler Building, completed in 1930, is universally admired by both architects and everyday New Yorkers. Its steel-plated crown of radiating sunbursts is an icon of New York art deco style.

The building was originally commissioned by developer William J. Reynolds, who hired architect William Van Alen. Reynolds considered the initial design too expensive and sold it to Walter P. Chrysler, the chairman of the Chrysler Corporation. There was serious competition at the time to construct the world's tallest building, and Chrysler wanted his building to be bold, forward looking and, most important, tall. He had Van Alen redesign the building, adding to its original 807 feet and also creating wonderful ornamentation based on features of Chrysler automobiles.

When ground was broken for the skyscraper in 1928, another building under construction in Manhattan was also aiming for the tallest building title: the Bank of Manhattan Trust Building at 40 Wall Street. Those plans were revised so that it would be two feet taller than the Chrysler Building, and when construction was completed, the building at 40 Wall Street was the tallest—but not for long.

William Van Alen had devised a covert plan to add a spire to the top of the Chrysler Building. Assembled secretly inside the building, the seven-story-tall spire was hoisted into position in only ninety minutes, suddenly elevating the Chrysler Building to the height of 1,047 feet, the tallest in the world. That lasted only a few months however, until it was surpassed by the Empire State Building.

Rhapsodies in Bloom

Music Theory and Practice

An Audible Sign of Life

The human voice was the first musical instrument. Before we spoke, we sang, imitating the sounds of nature. "In the beginning was the voice," says a language historian. "Voice is sounding breath, the audible sign of life." Like speaking, singing is produced when air from the lungs passes over the vocal cords. Vibrating air creates sound. "The technique of singing depends ultimately on the coordination of the various anatomical mechanisms in order to produce a propulsion of sound in a steady flow," according to *Encylopedia Britannica*. There are six vocal ranges: soprano, mezzo-soprano, contralto (or alto), tenor, baritone, and bass.

The German composer Richard Wagner said, "The human voice is really the foundation of all music; and whatever the development of the musical art, however bold the composer's combinations, however brilliant the virtuoso's execution, in the end they must always return to the standard set by vocal music."

The Sound of Music

Any musical note has four properties: pitch, dynamics, duration, and timbre (*TAM-ber*). Pitch is the relative highness or lowness of a tone and is determined by the frequency of the vibrations that the tone produces. Faster vibrations create higher tones. On a piano, the upper strings are the shortest and vibrate the fastest, thus producing higher notes. The lower strings are the longest and vibrate the slowest, producing the bass notes.

Dynamics refers to the relative loudness or softness and has to do with the amplitude of the vibrations. A piano key struck hard will produce more amplitude, and therefore a louder tone, than one struck lightly.

Duration is the length of time a tone persists. A piano tone begins when the string is struck by a hammer, and it ends when the vibrations fade out.

Medieval music notation

Timbre refers to tone "color": the quality given to a sound by its overtones. The timbre can be bright, dark, mournful, rich, mellow, and so on. It's what makes a French horn sound different from a clarinet or one person's voice different from another's, and it is the most subjective of the four properties.

Music of the Winds

There is one musical instrument that is not played by human action; neither hand nor breath creates the music, and it's not electronic, either. The aeolian harp (from Aeolus, the Greek god of the winds) is a stringed instrument that is sounded by natural wind, producing beautifully ethereal harmonic tones.

The harp is placed in a window or in any location where the wind can pass over the strings. According to Grove Music Online, the basic structure of a wind harp is usually four to twelve strings stretched over one or two hardwood bridges, with some device to concentrate the wind on the strings. The exact means by which aeolian tones are generated is still not fully understood.

Eeee-Oooo-Eeee

There is a musical device that is played by a performer who does not make physical contact with the instrument. The theremin was invented in 1920 by Russian physicist Lev Sergeivich Termen, known in the west as Léon Théremin. It was one of the very first electronic instruments.

The theremin consists of a box with two protruding antennae, one horizontal and one vertical, and a speaker, from which electronic tones emanate. The antennae are connected to oscillators that control pitch and volume. You play a theremin by moving your hands around the antennae, producing notes that vary in frequency and amplitude. In performance it looks a bit like someone conducting an imaginary orchestra. Since it's not possible to precisely control the placement of the hands, it is notoriously difficult to play the theremin well.

There have been a number of concert thereminists over the years, including Clara Rockmore and Lydia Kavina, who were protégés of Léon Théremin himself. The instrument also inspired a number of electronic enthusiasts, such as the young Robert Moog, who began building his own theremin in the 1950s while he was still a high school student. Moog says that his fascination with the theremin led directly to the development of his famed eponymous synthesizer.

The theremin has been used in many film scores, including *Spellbound* and *The Day the Earth Stood Still*, but not in the movie that many people associate with it: *Forbidden Planet* (it used a different type of electronic tonalities). The popularity of the theremin declined when more flexible electronic instruments were developed, but it is still available today through Robert Moog's company, Big Briar, Inc.

The Sibyl of the Rhine

In the Middle Ages, when women—especially women in religious orders—were practically invisible, Hildegard of Bingen was a notable exception. A Benedictine abbess in Germany, she was a prolific composer as well as a visionary, a theologian, a naturalist, and an author.

Born in 1098, Hildegard is one of the few composers of that era with a biography written during her lifetime. When she was in her early forties, she had a vision that inspired her life's work; she described it in her book, *Scivias*: "I heard the voice from Heaven, saying to me, 'Speak therefore of these wonders, and, being so taught, write them and speak' . . . and a fiery light accompanied by lightning came down from heaven. It flowed through my brain and glowed in my chest." Her music, considered unique in comparison to standard medieval composition, is contained in two large works, the *Ordo Virtutum* ("The Play of the Virtues") and *Symphonia Armonie Celestium Revelationum* ("Symphony of the Harmony of Celestial Revelations"). She wrote plainchant, the style of the time, which has a single melodic line. Her music is not plain, however; sometimes it demands a two-octave vocal range, and it often contains elaborate flourishes. In a letter to the prelates of Mainz, she pointed out that music calls to mind "that divine melody of praise which Adam, in company with the angels, enjoyed in God before his fall."

Papa Bach

He is number one on most lists of great composers—"he vitalized the polyphonic music of the past with the passion and humanity of his own spirit . . . he is the culminating figure of Baroque music . . . his mastery of the techniques of composition has never been equaled"—but

> *Facts which at first seem improbable will, even on scant explanation, drop the cloak which has hidden them and stand forth in naked and simple beauty.*
>
> —Galileo (*Dialogues Concerning Two New Sciences,* 1638)

Johann Sebastian Bach was not so celebrated a composer in his own lifetime. He was known more as an organist, a choirmaster, and a teacher. Bach's works, especially in the last decades of his life, were considered a bit old-fashioned: Baroque style was waning, and Classical was the new thing.

Part of a multigenerational musical family, Bach had twenty children (about half of whom survived childhood), and several of them became prominent musicians themselves. Though a devout Lutheran, Bach wrote the *Mass in B Minor* (considered by many to be the greatest classical musical composition) for the Elector of Saxony, his Catholic boss.

When "Old Bach" died in 1750, there was no grand funeral or crowded grave site. Other composers knew and revered his work, but it was infrequently performed. Bach's reputation with the public was revived in large part due to Felix Mendelssohn, who in 1829 conducted the *St. Matthew Passion* in Berlin to excellent reviews. Interest in and acclaim for Bach's compositions has grown ever since.

Teaching Little Fingers to Play

One of the most feared names to any student of piano is Carl Czerny. Born in 1791 in Vienna, he is best remembered for his pedagogic works, such as *The School of Velocity* and *The Art of Finger Dexterity*, which have tied uncounted numbers of young fingers into knots.

A child prodigy, Czerny was introduced to Beethoven in 1800 and played for him the composer's own *Pathétique Sonata*. Beethoven took him on as a pupil and worked with him for three years. Although he performed in public occasionally as a youth, Czerny soon gave up performing to concentrate on teaching, his true vocation. Franz Liszt was Czerny's most famous pupil, but he taught many important artists, including Theodor Leschetitzky, who became one of the world's greatest piano instructors. Leschetitzky taught Artur Schnabel, who taught Leon Fleischer, who taught Yefim Bronfman—continuing, to our day, a direct line from the most authentic interpretation of Beethoven's works.

Czerny never married and had no siblings, but he did keep a houseful of cats. Late in life Czerny was visited by Frederic Chopin, and the two played together privately. Chopin may not have been a fan of Czerny's music, but he liked the man personally, saying, "Czerny was warmer than any of his compositions."

A Self-Playing Instrument

In the mid-1800s, the piano became an almost essential part of any U.S. household that could afford one. But not everyone learned to play well, so a device was developed that allowed piano music to be played mechanically: the player piano.

Although the concept had been around since the 1870s, the first successful piano player, the pianola, was developed by Edwin Votey in 1895. It was a separate external cabinet with protruding wooden "fingers" that was pushed up to the piano and pressed the keys. Foot treadles operated a complex system of bellows, pneumatic tubes, and paper rolls with holes punched in them to indicate the notes to be played.

True player pianos, which incorporated the pianola mechanism into the piano itself, were developed at about the same time. Although the device played the notes, a human player—the pianolist—still had to move various levers to control the dynamics of tempo, volume, and sustain.

Player pianos were extremely popular in the first decades of the twentieth century, but many people thought they sounded too mechanical. The development of the reproducing piano changed that. Considerably more complicated than a player piano, the reproducing piano was powered by electricity and had mechanisms that could control dynamics through extra holes punched in the rolls, thus making the piano sound very close to the way a real performer would play.

A player piano

The Welte-Mignon, the first reproducing piano, was introduced around the turn of the twentieth century, followed shortly by the Ampico and the Duo-Art, made by the Aeolian Company. Most major pianists of the day made reproducing rolls, including Edvard Grieg, Alexander Scriabin, and Sergei Rachmaninov in the classical genre, along with Fats Waller, Scott Joplin, and George Gershwin in jazz and popular music. Gershwin's reproducing piano roll of his *Rhapsody in Blue* was actually a two-piano version, with Gershwin performing both parts, and was a top seller.

Rhapsody in Blue

The amazing American pianist and composer George Gershwin (1898–1937) began his musical career at the age of fifteen, when he quit school and became a "song plugger" for Jerome H. Remick and Company in New York. Song pluggers were pianists who performed in music stores, playing whatever sheet music patrons requested.

Gershwin soon began to write his own tunes, and at seventeen started making piano rolls for both the Standard Music Roll Company and the Aeolian Company. His first hit, thanks to Al Jolson's recording in 1920, was "Swanee," cowritten with lyricist Irving Caesar.

Four years later, Gershwin hit the true big-time with a jazz-and-classical experiment he called *Rhapsody in Blue*. Bandleader Paul Whiteman had asked Gershwin to compose a concerto for a jazz concert he planned to hold at Aeolian Hall in New York. Gershwin wasn't sure he would have the time, but he didn't say no. In January 1924, a notice in the *New York Tribune* said that Gershwin was writing the concerto, so he decided that he'd better get started—the concert was only five weeks away.

On a trip to Boston, he said, the idea came to him: "It was on the train, with its steely rhythms, its rattle-ty bang that is often so stimulating to a composer. . . . I frequently hear music in the very heart of noise. And then I suddenly heard—and even saw on paper—the complete construction of the rhapsody from beginning to end. . . . I hear it as a sort of musical kaleidoscope of America—of our vast melting pot, of our unduplicated national pep, of our blues, our metropolitan madness. By the time I reached Boston I had a definite plot of the piece, as distinguished from its actual substance." Three weeks later, the work was finished and Gershwin delivered it to Ferde Grofé, Paul Whiteman's arranger. Grofé finished the orchestration just eight days before the concert. February 12, 1924, was a long night for the attendees at Aeolian Hall. There were twenty-six performances that night, the ventilation system had broken down, and the audience was getting restive by the time Gershwin came out.

But as soon as the *Rhapsody* opened with its unforgettable clarinet glissando, the mood instantly changed. British music producer Rodney Greenberg described the concert: "By the end of Gershwin's rhapsody, it was clear that the originality of its invention, its unconventional yet convincing structure, its brilliantly effective piano part, its attractive tunes coloured by Grofé's masterful instrumentation, and its sheer verve had all combined to save the day. The applause was almost frenzied." Gershwin was instantly catapulted into the upper ranks of American composers. It is estimated that *Rhapsody in Blue*, through sales of sheet music, recordings, and piano rolls, earned Gershwin a quarter of a million dollars in the decade after its premiere.

Musical Embellishments

Many people probably think that a piece of classical music is fixed and unchangeable, fully notated so that any performer will play exactly what the composer intended. That is true in many cases, but it was not always that way. Cadenzas are embellishments, ornaments to a piece of music, and they were originally intended to be improvised by the performer. The word *cadenza* comes from "cadence," a passage at the close of a piece.

In the Baroque era, an opera singer would improvise a short bit at the end of an aria with some vocal gymnastics. Eventually, cadenzas grew in length and migrated to other forms, especially the concerto, in which the orchestra would become silent, leaving the soloist room to expand on the themes of the work. Beethoven's Violin Concerto (in D major; Opus 61) is a good example, with many different performers creating personal improvisations near the end of the first and third movements.

These were show-off moments, when performers displayed their virtuosity and mastery of their instrument. The quality of cadenzas varied with the quality of the performer, of course, and over time that led composers to write out preferred cadenzas. This caused the improvisational form to decline during the nineteenth century. Today, more and more musicians are attempting to bring back the improvised cadenza.

Yankee Doodle Boy

In the early years of the twentieth century, there were few Americans more famous than George M. Cohan (1878–1942), known as the Man Who Owned Broadway. As an actor and a singer, dancer, songwriter, director, producer, and theater owner, he was the country's first show-business superstar. Cohan was the quintessential born-in-a-trunk child of the theater. His parents, Jeremiah and Helen (known as Jerry and Nellie) were vaudevillians, touring the country on the B. F. Keith circuit.

George began playing violin in pit bands but soon graduated to the stage, along with his older sister, Josie. The family became the extremely successful Four Cohans. A rambunctious, abrasive, and extraordinarily talented child, George began to write catchy tunes and one-act plays, and when he was seventeen his father put him in charge of the family act. American musical theater up to that point had been dominated by the light operas of Europeans such as Gilbert and Sullivan, and it had not yet developed its own identity.

When the Four Cohans came to Broadway, that was destined to change. George M. Cohan's first big smash was *Little Johnny Jones* in 1904, which contained the hit tunes "Yankee Doodle Boy" and "Give My Regards to Broadway." It set the tone for all of Cohan's work: patriotic, brash, and fast-paced, with clever songs, vibrant dancing, and wisecracking dialogue.

Dozens of hits soon followed, including *Forty-five Minutes from Broadway*; *George Washington, Jr.*; *The Yankee Prince*; and the semi-autobiographical *The Man Who Owns Broadway.* With the outbreak of World War I, his tune "Over There" became an unofficial anthem that cemented his fame. After the war, a more jaded United States began to view Cohan's brand of patriotism as naive and overly sentimental, but he continued to produce, even though the shows' runs became shorter.

In 1933, Cohan tried his hand in Hollywood, starring in *The Phantom President.* It was not a success, and the experience soured him on films. Four years later, he starred on Broadway as President Franklin Roosevelt in *I'd Rather Be Right*, which was a big hit. He last performed in *The Return of the Vagabond* in 1940, before stomach cancer ended his stage career.

Cohan's life story was given the full big-screen treatment in 1942, in *Yankee Doodle Dandy*, starring an incredible James Cagney. Cohan got to see the movie (his comment: "My God, what an act to follow!") before his death on November 5, 1942. His statue now stands in New York's Times Square.

The Subtle Beauty of the Guitar

Famed classical guitarist Andrés Segovia (1893–1987) often said that one of his goals in life was to "rescue" the guitar from folk music and elevate it to the concert stage. By the force of his talent and personality, he did indeed bring the instrument to heights it had never before achieved, and earned the title of father of the classical guitar.

Born in Linares, Spain, Segovia showed an early affinity for music. His parents tried to steer him toward piano or cello, but Segovia developed an attraction to the guitar that turned into a lifelong passion. Largely self-taught, Segovia had his professional debut at age sixteen, and he continued to perform well into his nineties. Along the way he increased the repertoire of his instrument by transcribing many works—most famously, the Chaconne (concluding part) of Bach's *Partita No. 2* in D minor—and by commissioning such composers as Manuel Ponce and Heitor Villa-Lobos to write for the guitar.

As a teacher he intimidated many young students during his numerous master classes, but his roster of pupils contains many well-known names: Christopher Parkening, Julian Bream, Oscar Ghiglia, and dozens of others. After World War II, Segovia championed the use of nylon strings, which gave the guitar a more even, consistent tone. In concert, he could silence a fidgety audience with a simple stare, then mesmerize them with his romantic and expressive playing.

Reflecting on his life in his autobiography, Segovia said, "I pride myself only in having been a daring, tireless prober of the subtle beauty of the guitar, in conquering for it the love of millions in the world ahead."

A guitar

A Music Hall on Goat Hill

Everyone knows how to get to Carnegie (*KAR-neh-gee*) Hall: practice, practice, practice. But first the hall had to be built. A friendship between the young conductor Walter Damrosch and wealthy industrialist Andrew Carnegie (*kar-NAY-gee*) led to the formation of a company in 1889 to design and construct a much-needed music venue for New York City. Land was acquired in a "suburban" uptown area—Seventh Avenue and Fifty-seventh Street (which was then unpaved)—on the edge of Goat Hill near Central Park.

On May 5, 1891, the music hall opened with three performance spaces: the main auditorium (seating almost three thousand) plus recital and chamber music halls. The first performance was Beethoven's *Leonore Overture No. 3*, conducted by Damrosch, followed by Peter Ilych Tchaikovsky conducting his *Marche Solennelle*. The next day, the *New York Times* said, "The audience which assembled to assist at the baptism by sound of the new house was large, brilliant of appearance, and enthusiastic." Carnegie Hall was intended to be a venue for all types of music, and its first jazz concert was James Reese Europe's

Clef Club Orchestra in 1912. Folk, pop, and rock stars (starting with the Beatles in 1964) have filled the seats throughout the decades. And it's not only music that is hosted there: Carnegie Hall lecturers have included Jack London on communism and Margaret Sanger on birth control, and Mark Twain and Booker T. Washington appeared together in 1906 to raise funds for the Tuskegee Institute.

The hall was almost demolished for an ugly skyscraper in 1960, but violinist Isaac Stern led the efforts to save and eventually restore the beautiful and acoustically superb concert hall.

The Wordless Chorus

Vocalise (*voh-kah-LEEZ*)—"song without words"—is any musical composition in which the melody is sung using vowels or nonsense syllables rather than lyrics. These pieces were originally used primarily as training exercises for singers, but starting in the early twentieth century, major composers wrote vocalise works for concert performances: Gabriel Fauré, Maurice Ravel, Sergei Rachmaninov.

Scat singing, a sort of jazz equivalent, was popularized by Jelly Roll Morton, Cab Calloway, and Louis Armstrong (some say he invented it when he dropped a lyric sheet during a recording session, but that's unlikely). It continued to develop and expand throughout the years. Ella Fitzgerald, Sarah Vaughan, the Swingle Singers, Betty Carter, Al Jarreau, and Bobby McFerrin "have shown that this vocal art can strike out in directions of its own, independent of developments in instrumental jazz or avant-garde music." Vocalise has become popular with film score composers, too; a lovely example is the score for the movie *Glory* (1989), written by James Horner.

The Mother of Gospel

Mahalia Jackson, the first queen of gospel music, was born in New Orleans in 1911; her grandparents had been slaves. During the Great Migration of African Americans out of the South in the 1920s, she moved to Chicago, where she met composer Thomas A. Dorsey, the father of gospel. He became her advisor and accompanist, and they toured together for more than a decade.

Jackson's rich, powerful contralto voice helped to bring gospel music to an international audience. She was devoted to religious music and performed it exclusively, resisting the efforts of friends and family to persuade her to sing popular tunes. "I'll never give up gospel songs for the blues," she said. "Blues are the songs of despair, but gospel songs are the songs of hope."

She sang at the White House and at Carnegie Hall and toured the world. Jackson was a strongly committed supporter of the civil rights movement; at the request of her close friend Dr. Martin Luther King Jr., she performed at the 1963 March on Washington. When Dr. King was assassinated five years later, Jackson sang his favorite hymn, "Precious Lord, Take My Hand," at the funeral; Aretha Franklin then sang it for her when she passed away in 1972.

President Richard Nixon released this statement at the time of Mahalia Jackson's death: "All her years she poured out her soul in song and her heart in service to her people. Millions of ears will miss the sound of the great rich voice 'making a joyful noise unto the Lord,' as she liked to call her work—yet her life story itself sings the Gospel message of freedom, and will not cease to do so."

Radio Perennials

In 1925, the very early days of the new medium of radio, a program called *The WSM Barn Dance* aired in Nashville. Two years later, the name was changed to *The Grand Ole Opry*, and it went on to become the longest-running live radio program in the United States. It has had a number of hosts over the decades, beginning with George D. Hay.

The longest-running radio program with a single host is *Folksong Festival* on WNYC-AM, New York City's public radio station. Oscar Brand, a folksinger and the curator of the Songwriters Hall of Fame, began the show in December 1945 and is still hosting it every Saturday night.

Both shows have been platforms for a wide range of folk and country music talent over the decades.

In the Jungle, the Mighty Jungle

"The Lion Sleeps Tonight" is one of the more enduring pop songs of the last century, and it has a rather convoluted history. In the 1930s in Johannesburg, South Africa, Solomon Linda and some of his friends—kitchen and factory workers—began singing a cappella on weekends. They recorded a song called "Mbube," which means "the lion" in the Zulu language; it was a simple chant overlaid with Linda's soaring falsetto, and it became a local hit.

Eventually the producers sent it and other records to the United States with the hope that someone might be interested in distributing it. Folklorist and musicologist Alan Lomax was working for Decca Records at the time and found the pile of recordings from Africa. He brought them to his friend Pete Seeger, then a struggling folk music performer, who liked "Mbube" and arranged it for his group, the Weavers.

In transcribing the chant, Seeger thought the word *uyimbube* sounded like *wimoweh*, so that's what he named his version. The Weavers released the song, and it made it to No. 6 on the charts. Other groups (too many performers to list here) recorded cover versions. Then George David Weiss, Hugo Peretti, and Luigi Creatore rearranged the tune and added lyrics, and their version was recorded by the Tokens, a doo-wop group from Brooklyn. It was a monster hit. Over time the song has become part of international pop culture, especially after it was used in *The Lion King* (in both the movie and stage versions).

Solomon Linda, the originator of the song, never saw any royalties and died penniless in October 1962, one year after the Tokens released their megahit. In 2006, Linda's daughters settled a royalties lawsuit with the publisher. "In the jungle, the mighty jungle, the lion sleeps tonight."

Rock Launched

The song that introduced rock 'n' roll to the world was a failure on its initial release. "Rock around the Clock," by Bill Haley and His

Comets, was recorded in 1954 on the Decca label, but the group had already been performing the song on stage.

Written by Max Freedman and James E. Myers (under the pseudonym Jimmy DeKnight), "Rock around the Clock" was the B side of an odd rhythm-and-blues tune called "Thirteen Women" (about a postapocalyptic world with only thirteen women and one man). A modest seventy-five thousand copies were sold, and both tunes faded into obscurity.

Then came the MGM movie *Blackboard Jungle* in 1955. The producer was looking for a song to capture the spirit of teen rebellion, and "Rock around the Clock" fit the bill. It ran during the opening credits; with that exposure, the song took off, and rock 'n' roll entered the musical mainstream.

The song was later used as the theme for the television sitcom *Happy Days* in its first season. Although sales figures are difficult to confirm, it is generally believed that "Rock around the Clock" sold twenty-five million copies, making it one of the top-selling singles of all time.

Egyptian Surfer Girl

Lots of popular songs have interesting antecedents, but few are more unusual than the surf music classic "Misirlou," recorded and popularized by Dick Dale and His Del-Tones in 1962 and revived for the movie *Pulp Fiction*. The name of the composer is lost to history, but the song seems to have originated as a dance tune in the urban folk style called *rembetiko* (or *rebetiko*); it is claimed by both Greek and Turkish communities, and it's popular from Iran to Morocco.

The first recording was probably made by a Greek bandleader around 1930. That was followed by many others, including Woody Herman, Pete Seeger, Xavier Cugat, the Klezmer Conservatory Band, and Kronos Quartet, in styles ranging from folk to jazz to doo-wop to easy listening. It's been used in commercials, video games, and other movies. Dick Dale, whose father was Lebanese, remembered hearing the tune played on the oud (a Middle Eastern lute) in his childhood.

An oud

At a performance in California, a young boy asked Dale if he could play a whole song using only one string of the guitar, and an intensely speeded-up version of "Misirlou" is what Dale came up with. The word *misirlou* (or *miserlou* or *mousourlou*) means "Egyptian girl."

When Did He Leave the Building?

Elvis Presley's last concert was in Indianapolis at the Market Square Arena on June 26, 1977, and the last song he played was "Can't Help Falling in Love." But who first said, "Ladies and gentlemen, Elvis has left the building"?

I have found at least three people who may have originated or popularized the phrase: Frank Page, Horace Lee Logan, and Al Dvorin. Either Page or Logan was probably first, because they had been announcers on the radio program *Louisiana Hayride*, which introduced Elvis to the world in 1954. Dvorin claimed that he came up with the phrase at a concert in Minneapolis. A couple of members of Presley's band recalled a promoter named Oscar Davis, but I can't find any documentation for his use of the phrase. (See what I mean about facts?)

He Chose Poorly

Dick Rowe of Decca Recording Company rejected the Beatles after they auditioned for the label on January 1, 1962: "We don't like their sound and guitar groups are on the way out." Instead, Decca signed the other group Rowe heard that day: Brian Poole and the Tremeloes.

Feel the Music

Evelyn Glennie is the world's first full-time solo percussionist, and she also happens to be profoundly deaf, which means that she can hear some sounds, but the quality is very poor, especially with the spoken word.

Out of frustration with interviewers who misunderstood her and her music and focused only on her deafness, Glennie wrote "Hearing Essay" to "set the record straight." In it she explained, "Sound is simply vibrating air which the ear picks up and converts to electrical signals, which are then interpreted by the brain. The sense of hearing is not the only sense that can do this[;] touch can do this too. . . . For some reason we tend to make a distinction between hearing a sound and feeling a vibration, [when] in reality they are the same thing. . . . There is one other element to the equation[:] sight. We can also see items move and vibrate. If I see a drum head or cymbal vibrate or even see the leaves of a tree moving in the wind[,] then subconsciously my brain creates a corresponding sound." Glennie feels different vibrations in different parts of her body, and she performs without shoes so that she can "hear" the instruments through her feet. Glennie has won many awards, from Scotswoman of the Decade to the Order of the British Empire, and she's in the Percussive Arts Society's Hall of Fame. Also a motivational speaker, a teacher, and a collector of percussion instruments, Glennie has written her autobiography and was the subject of a documentary, *Touch the Sound*, in 2004.

According to *Contemporary Musicians*, "She is a master of common percussion instruments from around the world—marimba, xylophone, timpani, chimes, congas, steel pan, djembes, bodhrans, daiko drums, and many more. She creates instruments herself, like an adapted car muffler she strikes with triangle beaters. She also has made music on common items such as a hospital bed, camera, wheel hub, garbage can lid, flower pot, and starting gun." Glennie would like the world to "please, enjoy the music and forget the rest."

Your Brain on Jazz

Scientists at Johns Hopkins University and the National Institute on Deafness and Other Communication Disorders tried an interesting experiment in 2008. They wanted to observe in real time what happens in the brains of jazz musicians when they improvise or compose spontaneously, so they put six pianists in a "brain scanner," a functional magnetic resonance imaging machine.

Using special keyboards, the musicians performed several improvised exercises. Scientists Charles Limb and Allen Braun then analyzed the musicians' brain activity and found that: "Changes in prefrontal activity during improvisation were accompanied by widespread activation of neocortical sensorimotor areas (that mediate the organization and execution of musical performance) as well as deactivation of limbic structures (that regulate motivation and emotional tone)."

In other words, the musicians' brains showed dampening in the areas that control inhibition and augmented activity in the regions of self-expression while they produced music that had never been heard before.

Love Songs and Lost Words

Literature, Drama, Narrative

Little Songs of Love

A sonnet (from an Italian word for "little song") is a form of lyric poetry that consists of fourteen lines of iambic pentameter. There are two main types of sonnets: Petrarchan or Italian, and Shakespearean or English; the differences are in the structure and in the rhyme schemes or patterns. Iambic pentameter is the meter, or rhythmic structure, of the poem; each line contains ten syllables, alternating unstressed and stressed syllables (da-DUM da-DUM da-DUM da-DUM da-DUM).

The sonnet was invented in Sicily in the twelfth century and then spread to the rest of Italy, where Francesco Petrarca (known as Petrarch, the father of humanism) became closely associated with the form. He wrote his *Canzioniere* ("songbook"), a vernacular Italian collection of sonnets and other poems in praise of his unattainable love, Laura.

Two English poets, Thomas Wyatt and Henry Howard, introduced the sonnet form to their country; in the late 1500s, the works of William Shakespeare, Edmund Spenser, and Philip Sidney made the love sonnet very popular. Many poets have written sonnets, from Dante and John Milton to William Wordsworth and, among the most famous, Elizabeth Barrett Browning, who counted the ways she loved Robert Browning in *Sonnets from the Portuguese.*

Lost Words of the Bard

The plays of William Shakespeare are well known to millions, but few of us have ever heard of two that he might have written: *Love's Labours Won* and *Cardenio* (or *Cardenno*). Contemporary records show that the King's Men, Shakespeare's company, performed *Cardenio*, a play based on a character in Miguel de Cervantes' *Don Quixote*, in 1613. The sequel to *Love's Labours Lost* appears on a list in 1603, but some scholars think that rather than being a sequel, *Love's Labours Won* may just be an alternative title for a known play. No manuscript or published copy is believed to exist for either work.

Shakespeare and Cervantes both died on April 23, 1616, but since England and Spain used different calendars at that time, their deaths were actually ten days apart. In 1995, UNESCO selected April 23 as World Book and Copyright Day, in their honor, "to promote reading, publishing and the protection of intellectual property."

William Shakespeare

Fairy-Tale Finders

The Brothers Grimm—Jacob (1785–1863) and Wilhelm (1786–1859)—were German scholars and librarians who devoted their lives to collecting and studying the literature of their nation. They spent decades searching for traditional folktales; they published many collections of them and were widely recognized and praised for their work.

"Cinderella," "Snow White," "Sleeping Beauty," "Little Red Riding Hood," and "The Frog King" are among their most well-known and well-loved stories. All their tales were intended "to demonstrate the virtues of an opportunistic protagonist who learns to take advantage of gifts and magic power to succeed in life . . . and they all comply with the phallocratic impulses and forces of the emerging middle-class societies of Western culture," according to *The Oxford Companion to Fairy Tales. Kinder- und Hausmärchen* (Children's and Household Tales) was issued more than a dozen times between 1812 and 1864, and some editions were illustrated by a third brother, Ludwig. The Grimms also published significant works on German law, language, and customs.

Some Light on the Subject

In the *limelight* is where you'll find people who are famous. The principle of limelight was discovered in the 1820s by a young British scientist and inventor named Goldsworthy Gurney. He had already developed an oxyhydrogen blowtorch and experimented with it on various substances. He found that when a lump of quicklime—calcium oxide—was burned, it gave off a brilliant white light.

That idea was soon developed by others into a new form of illumination for lighthouses, for surveying, and especially for the theater. Up to that point, candles, lanterns, and gaslight were used to provide overall stage lighting, but none of them could be focused into a beam.

Limelights changed that, beginning in the 1830s. Their intense light could be narrowed and used to highlight an individual actor; thus they became the first spotlights. Painted glass slides could also be placed in front of a limelight to provide different kinds of color effects. Each light required constant monitoring from an operator to make adjustments as the block of lime burned down.

Limelights were replaced by electric lighting in the late nineteenth century, but the term has remained in popular usage.

Depend upon it there comes a time when for every addition of knowledge you forget something that you knew before. It is of the highest importance, therefore, not to have useless facts elbowing out the useful ones.

—Sir Arthur Conan Doyle (*A Study in Scarlet*)

A Real Detective

Sherlock Holmes, the world's first consulting detective and arguably the most famous fictional character in English literature, was introduced to the world by Sir Arthur Conan Doyle in 1887 with the publication of the novel *A Study in Scarlet*. Forty years later, the final Sherlock Holmes story, "The Adventure of Shoscombe Old Place," appeared in *Strand* magazine.

In those intervening four decades, Sherlock Holmes and his colleague, Dr. John H. Watson, had become immensely popular around the globe, with millions breathlessly waiting for the next story to be published. When Conan Doyle killed off Holmes in "The Final Problem," published in 1893, the public outcry was so great that the author felt compelled to revive the detective, which he did eight years later.

Holmes's address, 221B Baker Street in London, has become almost as famous as the detective himself. The Sherlock Holmes Museum, the first to be dedicated to a fictional character, now resides on Baker Street, and it still receives letters sent to the famous detective at that address. A representative of the museum said that staff members respond to those letters, and, especially if the correspondent is a young child, they might answer in the person of Holmes himself so as not to spoil the illusion.

Holmes and Watson

A 2008 poll conducted for the British cable channel UKTV Gold found that although large numbers of Britons think that Winston Churchill (23 percent) and Richard the Lionhearted (47 percent) were fictional characters, a whopping 58 percent believe that Sherlock Holmes was real. Of course, true Sherlockians know that Holmes left his rooms at 221B, retired to the Sussex Downs to raise bees, and has kept out of the public eye.

Unreal Books

It's pretty safe to say that all librarians love books. There are, however, two kinds of books that make many librarians crazy: ghost books and fictitious books.

Ghost books, or bibliographical ghosts, are not works about spirits from beyond; rather, they are works "recorded in bibliographies, catalogs, or other sources, of whose actual existence there is no conclusive evidence." Sometimes a publisher announces a new book, and it's included in lists of forthcoming works or mentioned in periodicals. However, the book is never issued, for some reason, but its apparent existence means that people will want to read it and will ask their librarians or bookstores to locate a copy.

A twentieth-century example of a ghost book was titled *Poetics* and was supposedly written by the poet and literary critic John Crowe Ransom. "Announced in 1942 by the publisher New Directions, it was never published but found its way into *Cumulative Book Index* and was cited in a biographical essay in *Contemporary Authors* in 1962 and in the *Dictionary of Literary Biography* in 1986." Fictitious books, also called invisible or imaginary books, are those that exist only in the pages of other works. For example: the *Necronomicon*, a nonexistent book on magic, appears in stories by H. P. Lovecraft, and several works by T. S. Garp are included in John Irving's *The World According to Garp*.

Science fiction writer Dean Koontz quotes poems from *The Book of Counted Sorrows* in several of his novels. Readers asked for it at the public library, and librarians spent hours searching for it; both groups pestered Koontz until he eventually admitted that there was no such book. (However, he did publish an e-book collection of his poems under that title in 2001.)

The Father of Film

Charlie Chaplin called David Wark Griffith "the teacher of us all," and Lillian Gish named him the father of film. Griffith originally wanted to be a playwright, but when one of his first plays flopped, he moved into acting and then directing in the new medium of motion pictures. From 1908 to 1913, Griffith worked for the American Mutoscope and Biograph Company, directing hundreds of films, primarily one-reelers, and perfecting techniques that became the grammar of film.

Early motion pictures were still attached to the static concepts of the stage. Griffith broke free of that, developing new camera movement and angles, close-ups, and lighting and editing techniques that influenced generations of filmmakers. He left Biograph to develop longer feature films, and in 1915 he directed the film that would change the course of cinema, ensure his reputation, and also ensnare him in controversy: *The Birth of a Nation.*

This story of the Civil War and Reconstruction was the first blockbuster, and despite its unprecedented three-hour length, it was a smash at the box office. Its combination of intimate human scenes and large-scale spectacle enthralled the public, but it also engendered a harsh backlash for its depiction of slavery as a benign institution and the Ku Klux Klan as heroes of the South.

There were protests against the film for its promotion of white supremacy, and many groups, especially the NAACP, unsuccessfully attempted to have it banned. Griffith, the son of a Confederate Army colonel, was shocked at the reaction, and his next film took a different direction, focusing on universal brotherhood. *Intolerance* (1916) was Griffith's most complex film, interweaving four stories set in different historical periods. These two films "established the motion picture as a medium capable of artistic excellence and historical significance." In the next decade, Griffith produced some fine films, but his work began to be perceived as passé, and soon the directing jobs dried up. D. W. Griffith died in 1948, having spent his last fifteen years mostly unemployed. Still, his contribution to the history of film prompted critic James Agee to write, "To watch his work is like being witness to the beginning of melody, or the first conscious use of the lever or the wheel; the emergence, coordination, and first eloquence of language; the birth of an art: and to realize that this is all the work of one man."

A Noble Actor

Noble Johnson was one of early Hollywood's more successful African American actors. Born in 1881, he began working in silent films in 1914, playing a variety of roles, including Native American and Arab as well as black characters. He was also an entrepreneur who started his own film company, the Lincoln Motion Picture Company, which made films for black audiences. Its first feature was *The Realization of a Negro's Ambition* in 1916.

Johnson reinvested his earnings as an actor to keep his company going for four years, until the demands of his acting career caused him to resign. Oscar Micheaux, usually credited as the first African American filmmaker, actually started his company a few years after Johnson's.

A highly respected character actor, Noble Johnson appeared in numerous films, including these silent movies: *Intolerance*; *20,000 Leagues under the Sea*; *The Ten Commandments*; *The Thief of Baghdad*; and *The King of Kings*. In talkies: *Moby Dick* (1930)—he was Queequeg to John Barrymore's Ahab—and *The Mummy*. Perhaps his most famous character was the native chief in the original *King Kong*.

One of his last roles was Chief Red Shirt in John Ford's 1949 classic *She Wore a Yellow Ribbon*. He retired from the film business in 1950 and died in 1978.

'Twas Not Beauty Killed the Beast

The two creators of *King Kong*, Merian Cooper and Ernest Schoedsack, made an uncredited appearance in their famous 1933 film (and for true fans, that is the only version that matters). When Kong is atop the Empire State Building, swatting at the airplanes that are attacking him, Cooper and Schoedsack can be seen flying in one of the Curtiss biplanes. Cooper is the pilot (he had said, "We should kill the sonofabitch ourselves") and Schoedsack is the gunner, making the final strafing run that killed the beast that made them rich.

Four Universal Frankensteins

Four actors portrayed Mary Wollstonecraft Shelley's famed Frankenstein monster in the series of movies from Universal Studios, "the foremost producers of horror films in Hollywood" in the 1930s and 1940s. (Note: Frankenstein is not the name of the monster, it's the name of the scientist who fabricated him; in the book, he named his creation Adam.) There were two early silent-film adaptations, but the monster didn't reach his stiff-legged stride until 1931, when the studio released *Frankenstein*, directed by James Whale and starring a little-known British actor, Boris Karloff, as the monster. Karloff, adorned in Jack Pierce's fabulous iconic makeup, made the role his own and played the part in two subsequent Universal movies: 1935's *Bride of Frankenstein*, directed again by Whale and considered the best film of the series, and *Son of Frankenstein* (1939).

After that, Karloff thought he had exhausted the role's possibilities, and the monster was portrayed by Lon Chaney Jr. in the next film, *Ghost of Frankenstein* (1942). Chaney had successfully portrayed the lead character in *The Wolf Man* for Universal in 1941, but he was out of his element here, and his beefy face was too unlike Karloff's gaunt features for audience acceptance.

For 1943's *Frankenstein Meets the Wolf Man*, Chaney returned to the Wolf Man role while the monster was played by the man who had turned down the role in the original film: Bela Lugosi. It was not a success. Lugosi was old, and his Hungarian-accented voice provoked laughs with test audiences, so all his dialogue was eliminated, which gave the film an odd, incoherent feel.

But the franchise was still making some money, so Universal continued with *House of Frankenstein* in 1944. Karloff returned to the series, but not as the monster. Instead he portrayed a scientist who had once been an assistant to Dr. Frankenstein. The monster was played by Glenn Strange, who was previously known for cowboy roles. He was tall and thin like Karloff, and his monster was well enough received to continue with two more films: *House of Dracula* (1945), and the final entry in the franchise, *Abbott and Costello Meet Frankenstein* (1948).

Universal Studios revived the franchise in 2004 with *Van Helsing*, but the Frankenstein monster no longer sported Pierce's well-known makeup.

Yak's Greatest Stunt

Yakima Canutt (his real name was Enos Edward Canutt) was one of the greatest stuntmen in Hollywood history, and he developed many techniques and safety devices that are still in use today. He is best remembered for a stunt he performed in John Ford's 1939 classic, *Stagecoach*, starring John Wayne.

Canutt, who had started out as a rodeo rider, had initially done what he called the "transfer stunt" in an earlier film. In *Stagecoach*, he portrayed an Indian who jumps from his galloping steed onto the coach horses. The John Wayne character then shoots him, he falls between the horses, and the stagecoach rolls over him.

Canutt perfected the trick (or gag, in stuntman parlance) later that year in the Republic Pictures' serial, *Zorro's Fighting Legion*. This time, as Zorro, he leaped onto the stagecoach's horse team, dropped between the fast-moving horses, did a backflip, and then pulled himself beneath the stagecoach. He emerged in the back, where he climbed up the rear of the coach and wrestled with the driver.

Steven Spielberg copied the stunt to perfection in his 1981 film, *Raiders of the Lost Ark*, substituting a Nazi truck for the stagecoach (with the stunt performed by Terry Leonard).

A Chilly Reception for Boris

Doktor Zhivago, the masterpiece of Russian writer Boris Pasternak, was published in 1957—but in Italy, not in the Soviet Union, by publisher and radical activist Giangiacomo Feltrinelli. Pasternak had submitted the work to the Soviet periodical *Novy Mir*, and he received a ten-thousand-word rejection that came down to this: the novel demonstrated a lack of acceptance of the socialist revolution. Even fellow writers branded him a traitor.

Pasternak was awarded the Nobel Prize for Literature in 1958 ("for his important achievement both in contemporary lyrical poetry and in the field of the great Russian epic tradition"), but he refused to accept it because he feared he would not be permitted to return to Russia if he traveled abroad to receive the award.

Pasternak died in 1960. The novel was finally published in the USSR almost thirty years later, and his son accepted his Nobel Prize in 1989.

Fear on Trial

Texas storyteller John Henry Faulk (1913–1990) was making a good name for himself in the post–World War II United States. After working at a variety of radio stations, he landed the *John Henry Faulk Show* on CBS in 1951.

But it was the era of the blacklist, and Faulk ran into trouble. He belonged to the American Federation of Television and Radio Artists, which he and some other union members thought was too closely connected to Aware, Inc., a for-profit right-wing group that searched for supposed links to communism. Aware's founder had earlier been involved in the publication of *Red Channels*, a 1950 report on the alleged communist influence in radio and television, which outed such dangerous commies as Aaron Copland, Arthur Miller, Judy Holliday, and Edward G. Robinson.

Faulk was unfairly branded a communist by Aware in 1957 and lost his radio show. But supported by CBS newsman Edward R. Murrow, he fought back, hired attorney Louis Nizer, and sued Aware for libel. After five years of delay engineered by Aware's lawyers (including Roy Cohn, the controversial counsel for Senator Joseph McCarthy's committee hearings), Faulk won his case and was awarded $3.5 million, the largest judgment ever granted in a libel suit up to that point. Later reduced to $500,000, it was eaten up by lawyer fees and other debts.

Still, the case was one of the nails in the coffin of the blacklist. Faulk wrote about his experiences in the book *Fear on Trial*, and folksinger Phil Ochs composed a song about it called "The Ballad of John Henry Faulk."

A Naked Literary Hoax

Popular *Newsday* columnist Mike McGrady, chagrined at the state of contemporary American novels, decided in 1966 to write a deliberately bad potboiler with a thin plot but lots of sex. He sent a memo to other *Newsday* writers, inviting them to contribute a chapter for *Naked Came the Stranger*: "As one of *Newsday*'s truly outstanding literary talents you are hereby officially invited to become the co-author of a best-selling novel. There will be an unremitting emphasis on sex. Also, true excellence in writing will be quickly blue-penciled into oblivion."

He recruited his sister-in-law, Billie Young, to portray the fictional author, named Penelope Ashe, in meetings and publicity shots. The book was published in 1969 and was successful, but some of the authors felt guilty about making money from such bad writing and soon leaked the story to the media.

The publicity catapulted the book to the *New York Times* bestseller list for a week. The success of the parody inspired similar efforts, including *Naked Came the Manatee* and *Naked Came the Sasquatch*. McGrady wrote about the hoax in his own book, *How to Write Dirty Books for Fun and Profit*. In 1975 *Naked Came the Stranger* was made into an X-rated film starring Darby Lloyd Rains.

Facts are meaningless. You could use facts to prove anything that's even remotely true. Facts, shmacts.

—Homer Simpson
in "Lisa the Skeptic" (*The Simpsons*, November 23, 1997)

Moral Fiction

In 1978, the novelist John C. Gardner published a book-length essay called *On Moral Fiction*, which presented his view of the purpose of art. He believed that "true art is moral: it seeks to improve life, not debase it. It seeks to hold off, at least for a while, the twilight of the gods and us. . . . That art which tends toward destruction, the art of nihilists, cynics, and merdistes, is not properly art at all. Art is essentially serious and beneficial, a game played against chaos and death, and entropy." It was a serious creed, and Gardner worked hard to live up to it in his own writing. But the book caused a firestorm in literary circles, primarily because Gardner did not hold back in his criticism of his contemporaries—Thomas Pynchon, John Updike, Donald Barthelme—whom he accused of not producing moral art.

The controversy brought Gardner a strange sort of fame, with an appearance on *The Dick Cavett Show* and a cover story in the *New York Times* magazine, but it also hurt him professionally. Gardner felt that lingering ill will from the book brought unfair criticism to his later works. At the very least, it made the purpose of art part of mainstream literary conversation again. Unfortunately, Gardner's part in that conversation ended in 1982, when he was killed in a motorcycle accident.

Banned in the U.S.A.

Since 1982, the last week of September has been designated Banned Books Week by the American Library Association (ALA) and other book-loving organizations. Among the works that have been challenged or banned for offensive language or sexual references throughout the years are such classics as *The Great Gatsby*, *The Grapes of Wrath*, *To Kill a Mockingbird*, and *The Catcher in the Rye*.

From 1995 to 2008, the ALA recorded 7,470 examples of books being banned or challenged in school or public libraries: 44 percent of the complaints were about sexuality, 24 percent were about language, 12 percent objected to violence, and 12 percent found problems with the book's religious, political, or so-called antifamily views. The most frequently challenged authors in the twenty-first century include Judy Blume, J. K. Rowling, Stephen King, Toni Morrison, and Mark Twain.

The definition of a challenge, according to the ALA, is "an attempt to remove or restrict materials, based upon the objections of a person or group. A banning is the removal of those materials. . . . Due to the commitment of librarians, teachers, parents, students, and other concerned citizens, most challenges are unsuccessful and most materials are retained in the school curriculum or library collection."

In Conclusion

We often see lists of the greatest opening lines in fiction. Closing lines also appeal to me; they give you your final moments with a book, that feeling of sadness because you cannot live in this story's universe any longer. These lines grab you or make you sigh, and they guarantee that you'll remember the book forever. Here are some worth recalling:

The Great Gatsby: "So we beat on, boats against the current, borne back ceaselessly into the past."

The Good Earth: "'Rest assured, our father, rest assured. The land is not to be sold.' But over the old man's head they looked at each other and smiled."

Native Son: "He still held on to the bars. Then he smiled a faint, wry, bitter smile. He heard the ring of steel against steel as a far door clanged shut."

The Dead: "His soul swooned slowly as he heard the snow falling faintly through the universe and faintly falling, like the descent of their last end, upon all the living and the dead."

Middlemarch: "But the effect of her being on those around her was incalculably diffusive, for the growing good of the world is partly dependent on unhistoric acts, and that things are not so ill with you and me as they might have been is half owing to the number who lived faithfully a hidden life and rest in unvisited tombs."

Andersonville: "He went past abandoned earthworks, abandoned camps, going directly to his plantation and into the future, and toward challenges waiting there. When he had nearly reached the lane, birds rose before him like an omen."

The Dharma Bums: "Then I added 'Blah,' with a little grin, because I knew that shack and that mountain would understand what that meant, and turned and went on down the trail back to this world."

Angela's Ashes: "I stand on the deck with the Wireless Officer looking at the lights of America twinkling. He says, 'My God, that was a lovely night, Frank. Isn't this a great country altogether?' 'Tis.'"

The Pearl: "And the pearl lay on the floor of the sea. A Crab scampering over the bottom raised a little cloud of sand, and when it settled the pearl was gone. And the music of the pearl drifted to a whisper and disappeared."

David Copperfield: "O Agnes, O my soul, so may thy face be by me when I close my life indeed; so may I, when realities are melting from me like the shadows which I now dismiss, still find thee near me, pointing upward!"

Still Life with Woodpecker: "But I can and will remind you of two of the most important facts I know: (1) Everything is part of it. (2) It's never too late to have a happy childhood."

The World According to Garp: "In the world according to her father, Jenny Garp knew, we must have energy. Her famous grandmother, Jenny Fields, once thought of us as Externals, Vital Organs, Absentees, and Goners. But in the world according to Garp, we are all terminal cases." (Author John Irving has said that he always writes the last lines first.)

Acknowledgments

It is proper and polite to acknowledge people who are helpful, and it's always a good idea to thank everyone who assists or supports you in a project; then, if it doesn't turn out well, at least they will commiserate and maybe share your guilt.

I must begin with Robert Malesky, without whom I can't do much of anything. He was my research assistant, proofreader, graphics wrangler, grocery shopper, housecleaner, and most sincere supporter, and he made it possible for me to complete this difficult assignment without either tearing out all my hair or turning into a useless slug. For more than forty years, he's been my dear heart and favorite person, and I cannot thank him enough.

At John Wiley & Sons, my editor, Stephen Power (this was all his idea), and editorial assistant, Ellen B. Wright, have been truly invaluable to this first-time author, and a pleasure to work with. And production editor Rachel Meyers held my hand through computer conflicts, guided me through the intricacies of *The Chicago Manual of Style*, and saved me from some terrible mistakes.

The first thing you learn as a news librarian is to turn to the experts whenever possible; it's somebody's job to know the fact you want. I turned to the New-York Historical Society, Graceland, the Egyptian government, the Great Lakes Historical Society, the American Jewish Committee archives, and Oklahoma state senator Don Barrington and state representative Joe Dorman. I appreciate their assistance. Special thanks to the academics who were willing to help me with details or let me borrow from their work: Edith W. Clowes, Slavic Languages and Literature, University of Kansas; Charles F. Hutchinson, Office of Arid Land Studies, University of Arizona; Orley R. "Chip" Taylor, University of Kansas and Monarch Watch; Gideon Burton, Forest of Rhetoric, Brigham Young University; Adam Jones, Texas A&M University.

My language advisors include Gul Tuysuz, Matina Kourkoutas, Lionel Wharton, Lawrence R. Schehr, Sylvia Poggioli, Anthony Kuhn, and Doualy Xaykaothao. Thanks also to Sister Mary Walter, CSJ, who taught me Latin long ago (which has proved to be the most practical and continually useful thing I learned in high school).

Current and former NPR friends and colleagues provided good suggestions or helped to save me from embarrassment: Scott Simon, Ken Rudin, Alex Chadwick, John Nielsen, Daniel Schorr, Ned Wharton, Kimberly Adams (and her grandmother, Marion North Alexander), David Kestenbaum, Rich Rarey, Davar Ardalan (and her parents, Laleh Bakhtiar and Nader Ardalan), and Walter Ray Watson.

The NPR staff librarians who shouldered my portion of the work for six months deserve my deepest appreciation (and I promise them parts in the movie version): Mary Glendinning, Katie Daugert, Barbara van Woerkom, and Jo Ella Straley (and also Elizabeth Allin and Barbie Keiser, who helped out). Our supervisor, Laura Soto-Barra, has been completely supportive from the beginning and was sometimes more enthusiastic than I was.

Because they rarely receive the recognition they deserve, I want to mention our broadcast librarians, who archive, preserve, and protect the programs and handle all things audio and visual: Beth Howard, Denise Chen, Maureen Clements, Hannah Sommers, Lauren Sin, Janel White, and Robert Goldstein, and our transcript coordinators, Dorothy Hickson (who was also my advisor on Goth matters) and Laura Jeffrey.

Finally, I must remember my absent friends—Robert Montiegel, Joseph P. Williman, Fred Calland, and Anne Marie Marans—whose creativity, brilliance, and generosity inspire me every day to do my best work.

Notes and Sources

I read books, articles, and Web pages for each fact included in this book: at least two sources for each, and in many cases, several more. I also consulted journalists, academics, and other professional experts. The sources listed for each fact are the ones that tell the best story or cover the most detail. In the case of online resources, I have included links to reputable sites. But, like you, I hate getting long URLs in print that I then have to type into my browser, often needing a few attempts until I get it right. So if you go to my Web site, http://www.allfactsconsidered.com, you will find the complete list of source links in clickable form. The books and articles cited here are available at your local public libraries or through their online services. In each case, you can read more about it, and I hope you will. (The not-so-hidden agenda of any librarian is to get you to read.)

All links were accessed on January 1, 2010.

Introduction

2 *"wholly imaginary"* Steven Biel, "Parson Weems Fights Fascists," *Common-Place* 6, no. 4 (July 2006). http://www.common-place.org/vol-06/no-04/biel/

2 *"has never been proven"* Randolph Schmid, "George Washington's Boyhood Home Discovered: No Sign of Cherry Tree or Hatchet," Associated Press, July 2, 2008.

3 *"the dignity of a work of art"* André Breton and Paul Eluard, eds. *Dictionnaire abrégé du Surréalisme* (Paris: Galerie Beaux-Arts, 1938), 23. The following definition of *ready-made* is attributed to Marcel Duchamp: *objet usuel promu à la dignité d'objet d'art par le simple choix de l'artiste* ("an ordinary object elevated to the dignity of a work of art by the mere choice of the artist").

4 *"general distribution of"* Jean Le Rond d'Alembert, *Preliminary Discourse to the Encyclopedia of Diderot*, trans. Richard N. Schwab (Chicago: Univ. of Chicago Press, 1995), 143.

4 *"which communicated the idea"* Robert Darnton, "Philosophers Trim the Tree of Knowledge: The Epistemological Strategy of the Encyclopédie." In *The Great Cat Massacre and Other Episodes in French Cultural History* (New York: Basic Books, 1984), 194.

Diderot, Denis, and Jean Le Rond d'Alembert. *Encyclopédie ou dictionnaire raisonné des sciences, des arts et des métiers, par une société de gens de lettres*. http://quod.lib.umich.edu/d/did/

George Washington Foundation. "Ferry Farm." http://www.kenmore.org/ff_home.html

Wood, Grant. *Parson Weems' Fable*, 1939. Oil on canvas, 38-3/8 × 50-1/8 inches. Amon Carter Museum, Fort Worth, TX. http://www.cartermuseum.org/works-of-art/1970–43

The Random House Dictionary of the English Language, second edition, unabridged, gives the following definitions:

Fact: something that actually exists; reality; truth. Something known to exist or to have happened. A truth known by actual experience or observation.

Fact finder: a person who searches impartially for the facts or actualities of a subject or situation.

Factoid: something fictitious or unsubstantiated that is presented as fact, devised especially to gain publicity and accepted because of constant repetition.

The Oxford English Dictionary, 1989, provides these definitions:

Fact: something that has really occurred or is actually the case; something certainly known to be of this character; hence, a particular truth known by actual observation or authentic testimony, as opposed to what is merely inferred, or to a conjecture or fiction; a datum of experience, as distinguished from the conclusions that may be based upon it. [In class. Lat. *factum* had occasionally the extended sense of "event, occurrence"; hence in scholastic Lat. was developed the sense above explained, which belongs to all the Romanic equivalents: Fr. *fait*, It. *fatto*, Sp. *hecho*.]

Factoid: (n) something that becomes accepted as a fact, although it is not (or may not be) true; spec. an assumption or speculation reported and repeated so often that it is popularly considered true; a simulated or imagined fact. (adj) Of or having the character of a factoid, quasi-factual; spec. designating writing (esp. journalism) which contains a mixture of fact and supposition or invention presented as accepted fact.

Part One: On Memory and History

7 *"Memory, from which comes"* Jean Le Rond d'Alembert, *Preliminary Discourse to the Encyclopedia of Diderot*, trans. Richard N. Schwab (Chicago: Univ. of Chicago Press, 1995), 143.

1. BATTLES AND BIGWIGS

The Start of History

10 *"Alphabetic writing is the last"* David Diringer, *The Book before Printing: Ancient, Medieval and Oriental* (New York: Dover, 1982), 76.

Daniels, Peter. "Writing Systems." *World Book Encyclopedia*, 2009.

Fischer, Steven. *A History of Writing*. London: Reaktion Books, 2001.

Ancient Crossroads

10 *"If you draw lines"* Marguerite Del Giudice, "Persia, Ancient Soul of Iran," *National Geographic*, August 2008. http://ngm.nationalgeographic.com/2008/08/iran-archaeology/del-giudice-text

Balcer, Jack Martin. "Persia, Ancient." *World Book Encyclopedia*, 2009.

Halsall, Paul, ed. "Persia." *Internet Ancient History Sourcebook*. Fordham University. http://www.fordham.edu/halsall/ancient/asbook05.html

The Rome of China

British Museum. "The First Emperor: China's Terracotta Army." http://www.britishmuseum.org/the_museum/news_and_press_releases/press_releases/2007/the_first_emperor.aspx

China Culture. "Lantian Man in Shaanxi." http://www.chinaculture.org/gb/en_artqa/2003-09/24/content_39044.htm

China Internet Information Center. "The Mausoleum of the First Emperor of the Qin Dynasty and Terracotta Warriors and Horses." September 12, 2003. http://www.china.org.cn/english/kuaixun/74862.htm

Lubow, Arthur. "Terra Cotta Warriors on the March." *Smithsonian*, July 2009. http://www.smithsonianmag.com/history-archaeology/On-the-March-Terra-Cotta-Soldiers.html

The Face of Amateur Archaeology

Fischman, Josh. "The Real Trojan War." *U.S. News & World Report*, May 24, 2004.

Harrington, Spencer. "Behind the Mask of Agamemnon." *Archaeology* 52, no. 4 (July /August 1999). http://www.archaeology.org/9907/etc/mask.html

"Heinrich Schliemann." *Science and Its Times*. Vol. 5, *1800–1899*. Farmington Hills, MI: Gale, 2000. Reproduced in *Biography Resource Center*. Farmington Hills, MI: Gale, 2009.

Pristine Civilization

13 *"interactions through the region"* John Noble Wilford, "Mother Culture, or Only a Sister?" *New York Times*, March 15, 2005.

Asociacion de Gestores del Patrimonio Historico y Cultural de Mazatlan. "The Mesoamerican Ballgame—Ulama." http://www.ulama.freehomepage.com/index.html

Diehl, Richard A. *The Olmecs: America's First Civilization*. London: Thames and Hudson, 2004.

Latin American Studies. "Olmecs." http://www.latinamericanstudies.org/olmecs.htm

Lawler, Andres. "Beyond the Family Feud." *Archaeology*, March/April 2007: 21–25.

Wilford, John Noble. "Writing May Be Oldest in Western Hemisphere." *New York Times*, September 15, 2006. http://www.nytimes.com/2006/09/15/science/15writing.html

Go Goth

13 *"dresses exclusively in black"* My NPR colleague Dorothy Hickson reports seeing this T-shirt at music clubs: "I'm only wearing black until they come up with a darker color." E-mail message, July 2009.

Halsall, Paul, ed. "Early Germanic States." *Internet Medieval Sourcebook*. Fordham University. http://www.fordham.edu/halsall/sbook1f.html

Todd, Malcolm. "Goths." *World Book Encyclopedia*, 2009.

Barbarians at the Gate

Bull, George. "The Sack of Rome." In *Michelangelo: A Biography*, 203–211. London: Viking Press, 1995.

Lees-Milne, James. "The Sacks of Rome." In *St. Peter's: The Story of St. Peter's Basilica in Rome*. Boston: Little, Brown, 1967.

Lost Knowledge

Bibliotheca Alexandrina. http://www.bibalex.org/English/index.aspx

Hannam, James. "The Mysterious Fate of the Great Library of Alexandria." Bede's Library, 2003. http://www.bede.org.uk/library.htm

Polastron, Lucien. *Books on Fire: The Destruction of Libraries Throughout History*. Rochester, VT: Inner Traditions, 2004.

Dating Epochs

15 *"The Christian calendar no longer"* Kofi Annan, "Common Values for a Common Era," *Civilization*, June 28, 1999.

Duncan, David Ewing. *Calendar: Humanity's Epic Struggle to Determine a True and Accurate Year*. New York: Bard, 1998.

Safire, William. "B.C./A.D. or B.C.E./C.E.?" *New York Times*, August 17, 1997.

Lovers Asunder

15 *"Dear Héloïse"* Abelard to Philintus. Israel Gollancz and Honnor Morten, eds. *The Love Letters of Abelard and Héloïse*, 1901. http://www.sacred-texts.com/chr/aah/index.htm

16 *"I will still love you"* Héloïse to Abelard. Ibid.

Abelard, Peter. *Historia Calamitatum: The Story of My Misfortunes*. Translated by Henry Adams Bellows. St. Paul, MN: T. A. Boyd, 1922. http://www.fordham.edu/halsall/basis /abelard-histcal.html

Clanchy, M. T. *Abelard: A Medieval Life*. Oxford, UK: Blackwell, 1997.

"Peter Abelard." *Stanford Encyclopedia of Philosophy*, August 3, 2004. http://plato.stanford.edu/entries/abelard/

Cradle Books

16 *"they belong to the childhood"* Svend Dahl, *History of the Book* (Metuchen, NJ: Scarecrow Press, 1968), 113.

Barber, Phil. "An Introduction to Incunabula." Historic Pages. http://www.historicpages.com/texts/incun1.htm

Ellenbogen, Rudolph. "Book." *World Book Encyclopedia*, 2009.

Romano, Frank. "Johannes Gutenberg." *World Book Encyclopedia*, 2009.

My friend and NPR colleague Scott Simon has a great affection for the semicolon. He has graciously allowed me to include his thoughts on the matter:

> The semicolon is the broadcaster's best friend; and I'm not forgetting coffee. The semicolon is a pause inserted between two statements where the finality of a period would create a script that might sound like a series of choppy observations, and the insertion of a comma, which I have done here, would create a sentence that is exhausting to both speak and hear, although grammatically correct.
>
> (Some broadcasters use a series of dots [an ellipsis] as pauses. I prefer semicolons.)
>
> Broadcasters like semicolons because they permit us to speak sentences that continue a narrative line without the interruption of conjunctions, like but or and. They enable us to breathe. No doubt the semicolon has crept into my written prose, too; at this point, it's how I think.
>
> It's interesting that at least a couple of modern writers who notably use semicolons—Edwin O'Connor; George Orwell—had backgrounds in broadcasting. It's possible that the semicolon seeped into their literary technique the way that Hemingway transported telegraph language into his prose. Not to compare myself to O'Connor or Orwell; or especially Hemingway.

Out of Africa

Franklin, John Hope, and Alfred Moss Jr., *From Slavery to Freedom*. New York: McGraw-Hill, 2000.

Hornsby, Alton. *Chronology of African American History*. 2nd ed. Farmington Hills, MI: Gale, 1997.

No Prenups?

Fraser, Antonia. *The Wives of Henry VIII*. New York: Alfred A. Knopf, 1992.

Weir, Alison. *The Six Wives of Henry VIII*. New York: Grove Weidenfeld, 1991.

Naming the Big Apple

"Anglo-Dutch Wars." *Encyclopedia Britannica*. Vol. 1, 15th ed., 2003.

Laise, Steve. "Nieuw Amsterdam to New York." New York Harbor Parks. http://nyharborparks.org/podcasts/rs-newamsterdam.html

The New-York Historical Society. https://www.nyhistory.org/web/

The Cost of Wars

Belasco, Amy. "The Cost of Iraq, Afghanistan, and Other Global War on Terror Operations Since 9/11." Congressional Research Service, May 15, 2009. http://www.fas.org/sgp/crs/natsec/RL33110.pdf

Clodfelter, Michael. *Warfare and Armed Conflict: A Statistical Encyclopedia of Casualty and Other Figures, 1494–2007*. 3rd ed. Jefferson, NC: McFarland, 2008.

Daggett, Stephen. "Costs of Major U.S. Wars." Congressional Research Service, July 24, 2008. http://www.fas.org/sgp/crs/natsec/RS22926.pdf

National Priorities Project. "Total Cost of Wars since 2001." http://costofwar.com/

U.S. Department of Defense. "U.S. Casualty Status: Operation Iraqi Freedom and Operation Enduring Freedom." http://www.defenselink.mil/news/casualty.pdf

The Gateway Gap

19 *"Boone with about thirty axmen"* William W. Luckett, "Cumberland Gap National Historical Park," *Tennessee Historical Quarterly* 23, no. 4 (December 1964). http://www.nps.gov/history/history/online_books/cuga/luckett/index.htm

19 *"These mountains are in the wilderness"* Ibid.

Cumberland Gap National Historical Park. http://www.nps.gov/cuga/index.htm

Filson, John. *The Discovery, Settlement and Present State of Kentucke.* Wilmington, DE: John Adams, 1784. http://digitalcommons.unl.edu/cgi/viewcontent.cgi?article=1002&context=etas

Longfellow, Rickie. "The Cumberland Gap." U.S. Department of Transportation, Federal Highway Administration, Highway History. http://www.fhwa.dot.gov/infrastructure/back0204.cfm

Shattuck, Tom N. *The Cumberland Gap Area Guidebook.* 5th ed. Middlesboro, KY: Bell County Historical Society, 2005.

Eighteenth-Century Networking

Fischer, David Hackett. *Paul Revere's Ride.* New York: Oxford Univ. Press, 1994.

Built by Bondage

21 *"No narrative on the construction"* H. Con. Res.135, S. Con. Res.24: "Placement of Marker in Capitol Visitor Center to Acknowledge Role of Slave Labor in Construction of Capitol." 2009.

Allen, William C. "History of Slave Laborers in the Construction of the United States Capitol." Office of the Architect of the Capitol, June 1, 2005. http://clerk.house.gov/art_hitory/art_artifacts/slave_labor_reportl.pdf

Bordewich, Fergus. *Washington: The Making of the American Capital.* New York: Amistad, 2008.

Office of the Architect of the Capitol. "A Brief Construction History." http://www.aoc.gov/cc/capitol/capitol_construction.cfm

Battling for Booze

21 *"an informal currency"* "Whiskey Rebellion," *Encyclopedia Britannica Online*, 2010. http://www.britannica.com/EBchecked/topic/641925/Whiskey-Rebellion

Asimov, Eric. "The Pour: Whiskey vs. Whisky." *New York Times*, December 4, 2008.

Blue, Anthony. *The Complete Book of Spirits: A Guide to Their History, Production, and Enjoyment.* New York: HarperCollins, 2004.

Global Security. "Whiskey Rebellion." http://www.globalsecurity.org/military/ops/whiskey_rebellion.htm

Hogeland, William. *The Whiskey Rebellion.* New York: Scribner's, 2006.

Presidential Secrets Revealed

Ketcham, Ralph. *James Madison: A Biography.* Charlottesville, VA: Univ. of Virginia Press, 1990.

Shenkman, Richard, and Kurt Reiger. *One Night Stands with American History.* New York: William Morrow, 1980.

U.S. National Park Service. "Presidential Trivia." http://www.nps.gov/pub_aff/pres/trivia.htm

Young, Jeff. *The Fathers of American Presidents.* Jefferson, NC: McFarland, 1997.

To the Pacific

22 *"The object of your mission"* Gary Moulton, "The Journals of the Lewis and Clark Expedition," University of Nebraska. http://lewisandclarkjournals.unl.edu/

23 *"We are in view"* Ibid.

Ambrose, Stephen. *Undaunted Courage: Meriwether Lewis, Thomas Jefferson, and the Opening of the American West*. New York: Simon and Schuster, 1997.

Lewis and Clark Fort Mandan Foundation. "Discovering Lewis and Clark." http://lewis-clark.org/

Library of Congress. "Jefferson's Instructions for Meriwether Lewis." http://www.loc.gov/exhibits/lewisandclark/transcript57.html

Moulton, Gary. "Lewis and Clark Expedition." *World Book Encyclopedia*, 2009.

National Geographic. "The Lewis and Clark Journey Log." http://www.nationalgeographic.com/lewisandclark/

Melancholy Meriwether

24 *"I fear, O I fear"* Stephen Ambrose, *Undaunted Courage: Meriwether Lewis, Thomas Jefferson, and the Opening of the American West* (New York: Simon and Schuster, 1997), 466.

24 *"Of courage undaunted"* Ibid., 474.

Books a Million

24 *"with nearly 145 million"* Library of Congress, "Fascinating Facts." http://www.loc.gov/about/facts.html

Numismatically Speaking

Bureau of Engraving and Printing. "FAQ_Library: U.S. Currency." http://www.moneyfactory.gov/faqlibrary.html

Federal Reserve Bank of San Francisco. "Fun Facts about Money." http://www.frbsf.org/federalreserve/money/funfacts.html

Federal Reserve Board. "Currency and Coins Services." http://www.federalreserve.gov/paymentsystems/coin_data.htm

Library of Congress. "Business Reference Services: Money." http://www.loc.gov/rr/business/money/paper.html

U.S. Department of the Treasury. "Currency FAQs." http://www.ustreas.gov/education/faq/currency/denominations.shtml

Presidents in the Line of Fire

Hunt, Gaillard, ed. *The Writings of James Madison, 1808–1819*. Vol. 8. New York: Putnam, 1908.

Lord, Walter. *The Dawn's Early Light*. New York: W. W. Norton, 1972.

Artist, Inventor, Bigot

26 *"proverbial through the world"* S. F. B. Morse, *Foreign Conspiracy against the Liberties of the United States* (New York: Leavitt, Lord, 1835), 47.

26 *The "great body of emigrants"* Ibid., 57.

26 *"We have in the country"* Ibid., 166.

27 *"Are there not in this relation"* S. F. B. Morse, "Ethical Position of Slavery," 1863, quoted in Yale, Slavery, and Abolition, "Morse College." http://www.yaleslavery.org/WhoYaleHonors/morse.html

Dillon, George L. "S. F. B. Morse: *Gallery of the Louvre*." University of Washington. http://faculty.washington.edu/dillon/Morse_Gallery/

Genzmer, George H. "Samuel Finley Breese Morse (1791–1872)." In *Dictionary of American Biography*. Edited by the American Council of Learned Societies. New York: Scribner's, 1990. Reproduced in *Biography Resource Center*. Farmington Hills, MI: Gale, 2009.

Golway, Terry. "Return of the Know-Nothings." *America*, March 29, 2004. http://www.americamagazine.org/content/article.cfm?article_id=3508&comments=1

Potter, George. *To the Golden Door: The Story of the Irish in Ireland and America*. Boston: Little, Brown, 1960.

Smithsonian Institution. "The Morse Telegraph." History Wired. http://historywired.si.edu/object.cfm?ID=306

The First and the Last Man Killed

Brock, R. A., ed. "Last Man Killed in Civil War." *Southern Historical Society Papers* 34 (1906).

Swanberg, William. *First Blood.* New York: Scribner's, 1957.

Trudeau, Noah Andre. *Out of the Storm: The End of the Civil War, April–June 1865.* Boston: Little, Brown, 1994.

The Kidnapped President

28 *"steal the bones"* "Horrible, Dastardly Attempt to Despoil the Lincoln Monument: Thieves Trying to Steal the Bones of the Martyr President," *Chicago Daily Tribune*, November 8, 1876.

Craughwell, Thomas. *Stealing Lincoln's Body.* Cambridge, MA: Harvard Univ. Press, 2007.

Illinois Historic Preservation Agency. "Lincoln's Tomb." http://www.illinoishistory.gov/hs/lincoln_tomb.htm

Robertson, Deane, and Peggy Robertson. "The Plot to Steal Lincoln's Body." *American Heritage*, April/May 1982.

The Great Hunger

28 *"wretched, rebellious and utterly dependent"* Cecil Woodham-Smith, *The Great Hunger: Ireland, 1845–1849* (London: Hamilton, 1962), 39.

28 *"would not kill more than one million"* Ibid., 376.

Famine Museum, Strokestown, Roscommon, Ireland. http://www.strokestownpark.ie/museum.html

Fegan, Melissa. *Literature and the Irish Famine, 1845–1919.* Oxford, UK: Oxford Univ. Press, 2002.

Holocaust Education Curriculum. "The Great Irish Famine." http://www.nde.state.ne.us/SS/Irish/Irish_pf.html

The Prince of Cranks

29 *"literature as in politics"* John D. Hicks, "Ignatius Donnelly," in *Dictionary of American Biography*, ed. American Council of Learned Societies (New York: Scribner's, 1990). Reproduced in *Biography Resource Center.* Farmington Hills, MI: Gale, 2009.

Biographical Directory of the U.S. Congress. "Ignatius Donnelly." http://bioguide.congress.gov/scripts/biodisplay.pl?index=D000417

Contemporary Authors Online. "Ignatius Donnelly." Reproduced in *Biography Resource Center.* Farmington Hills, MI: Gale, 2009.

Donnelly, Ignatius. *Atlantis: The Antediluvian World.* New York: Harper and Brothers, 1882. http://www.sacred-texts.com/atl/ataw/index.htm

Pederson, Jay P., ed. "Ignatius Donnelly." *St. James Guide to Science Fiction Writers.* 4th ed. Farmington Hills, MI: St. James Press, 1996. Reproduced in *Biography Resource Center.* Farmington Hills, MI: Gale, 2009.

The King of Censors

29 *"possessed of a curious"* Mark Van Dorn, "Anthony Comstock," in *Dictionary of American Biography*, ed. American Council of Learned Societies (New York: Scribner's, 1990). Reproduced in *Biography Resource Center.* Farmington Hills, MI: Gale, 2009.

30 *"Comstockery is the world's standing joke"* "Bernard Shaw Resents Action of Librarian," *New York Times*, September 26, 1905.

Gazit, Chana. "The Pill." *American Experience.* PBS, February 24, 2003. http://www.pbs.org/wgbh/amex/pill/peopleevents/e_comstock.html

A Visit from the Merry Monarch

30 *"It would not be courtesy"* "Kalakaua: A Few Chicagoans Go Out to Meet Him." *Chicago Daily*, December 11, 1874.

Staton, Ron. "Iolani Palace: America's Only Royal Residence." Associated Press, February 14, 2004.

U.S. Department of State. Visits to the U.S. by Foreign Heads of State and Government. http://2001-2009.state.gov/r/pa/ho/34912.htm

The Golden Door

31 *"rosy-cheeked"* "Landed on Ellis Island," *New York Times*, January 2, 1892.

Ellis Island. "Annie Moore." http://www.ellisisland.org/genealogy/Annie_Moore.asp

———. "Annual Report 2009." http://www.ellisisland.org/EIinfo/Annual_Report_2009.pdf

———. "History." http://www.ellisisland.org/genealogy/ellis_island_history.asp

The Bonus Expeditionary Force

Dickson, Paul, and Thomas Allen. *The Bonus Army: An American Epic.* New York: Walker, 2004.

Kast, Sheila. "Soldier against Soldier: The Story of the Bonus Army." *Weekend Edition Sunday.* NPR, February 13, 2005. http://www.npr.org/templates/story/story.php?storyId=4494446

Library of Congress. "Bonus Army March." http://www.loc.gov/exhibits/treasures/trm203.html

Temp Jobs

32 *"The largest number"* Ken Rudin, "Four Senate Appointees, Two More to Come: Is That a Record?" *Political Junkie Blog.* NPR, August 13, 2009. http://www.npr.org/blogs/politicaljunkie/2009/08/those_appointed_senate_seats.html

Biographical Directory of the United States Congress. http://bioguide.congress.gov/biosearch/biosearch.asp

Throwing Off the Shackles

33 *"The General Assembly"* UN General Assembly, Fifteenth Session, "Declaration on the Granting of Independence to Colonial Countries and Peoples," Resolution 1514, December 14, 1960. http://www.un.org/documents/ga/res/15/ares15.htm

U.S. Department of State. "Background Notes." http://www.state.gov/r/pa/ei/bgn/index.htm

Presidential Nanas

"President Kennedy's Grandmother Dies at 98." Associated Press, August 9, 1964.

Rudin, Ken. "JFK Did Have a Living Grandparent While in WH." *Political Junkie Blog.* NPR, April 13, 2009. http://www.npr.org/blogs/politicaljunkie/2009/04/jfk_did_have_a_living_grandpar.html

Smith, Ben. "Madelyn Dunham's Vote Will Count." Politico.com, November 3, 2008. http://www.politico.com/blogs/bensmith/1108/Madelyn_Dunhams_vote_will_count.html

A Rare Honor

H.J. Res. 37, "Conferring Honorary Citizenship of the United States on Anne Frank." http://thomas.loc.gov/cgi-bin/bdquery/z?d110:h.j.res.00037:

Public Law 111–94, "Proclaiming Casimir Pulaski to Be an Honorary Citizen of the United States." http://thomas.loc.gov/cgi-bin/bdquery/z?d111:HJ00026:%7C/bss/111search.html%7C

U.S. Senate. "Honorary Citizens of the United States." http://www.senate.gov/pagelayout/reference/three_column_table/HonoraryCitizens_US.htm

He Should Have Said It

Brokaw, Tom. "The Secret Man: History and Identity of Deep Throat" (interview with William Goldman). *Dateline.* NBC, July 6, 2005.

Schorr, Daniel. "Follow the Money." *Weekend Edition Sunday.* NPR, June 15, 1997.

Plenty of Presidents

White House. "The Presidents." http://www.whitehouse.gov/about/presidents/

Killed in the Line

Committee to Protect Journalists. "Journalists Killed since 1992." http://cpj.org/killed/

———. "2009 Prison Census." http://cpj.org/imprisoned/2009.php

Party Changers

Biographical Directory of the United States Congress. http://bioguide.congress.gov

Rudin, Ken. "Senate Party-Switchers of the Last Half-Century." *Political Junkie Blog*. NPR, April 28, 2009. http://www.npr.org/blogs/politicaljunkie/2009/04/notable_senate_party_switches.html

SCOTUS: Confirmed or Rejected

37 *"Since the Supreme Court"* U.S. Senate, "Supreme Court Nominations, 1789–present." http://www.senate.gov/pagelayout/reference/nominations/reverseNominations.htm

Rudin, Ken. "Most No Votes against Supreme Court Nominees." *Political Junkie Blog*. NPR, July 31, 2009. http://www.npr.org/blogs/politicaljunkie/2009/07/most_no_votes_against_supreme.html

2. DEVIATIONS AND WONDERS

Planet Earth 101

National Aeronautics and Space Administration (NASA). "Earth's Facts and Figures." http://solarsystem.nasa.gov/planets/profile.cfm?Object=Earth&Display=Facts&System=Metric

Forest Primeval

Białowieża Forest. http://www.bialowiezaforest.eu/

United Nations Educational, Scientific, and Cultural Organization (UNESCO). "Białowieża Forest." UNESCO World Heritage Sites. http://whc.unesco.org/en/list/33/

Lunar Labels

Geiger, Peter, ed. *The Farmers' Almanac*. Lewiston, ME: Almanac, 2010. http://www.farmersalmanac.com/full-moon-names

Kallman, Tim. *Ask an Astrophysicist*. Goddard Space Flight Center. http://imagine.gsfc.nasa.gov/docs/ask_astro/answers/970314a.html

The Greatest Lakes

Great Lakes Historical Society. http://www.inlandseas.org/

U.S. Environmental Protection Agency. "Great Lakes." http://epa.gov/greatlakes/

A Deep Blue Lake

Oregon State University. "Crater Lake Data Clearinghouse." Oregon Explorer. http://oregonexplorer.info/craterlake

U.S. National Park Service. "Crater Lake." http://www.nps.gov/crla

Deep in the Ocean

Mariana Trench. http://www.marianatrench.com/

National Science Foundation. "The Abyss: Deepest Part of the Oceans No Longer Hidden." June 2, 2009. http://www.nsf.gov/news/news_summ.jsp?cntn_id=114913

U.S. Fish and Wildlife Service. "Marianas Trench Marine National Monument." http://www.fws.gov/marianastrenchmarinemonument/MTMNM%20brief.pdf

Jaws

42 *a "gradual reduction"* Florida Museum of Natural History, *International Shark Attack File*. http://www.flmnh.ufl.edu/fish/Sharks/ISAF/ISAF.htm

42 *"which would strengthen"* Dan Klotz, "Pew Brings Survivors to Congress to Seek Protections for Sharks That Attacked Them." Pew Charitable Trusts, July 15, 2009. http://www.pewtrusts.org/news_room_detail.aspx?id=54142

Shark Attack Survivors. http://sharkattacksurvivors.com/
Stop Shark Finning. http://www.stopsharkfinning.net/

Jaws and Julia

Central Intelligence Agency. "A Look Back: Julia Child, Life Before French Cuisine." December 13, 2007. https://www.cia.gov/news-information/featured-story-archive/2007-featured-story-archive/julia-child.html
Kilian, Michael. "Child's Kitchen Belongs on Smithsonian Menu." *Chicago Tribune*, August 29, 2002.
Stamberg, Susan. "The Lady Was a Spy." *Morning Edition*. NPR, April 4, 2002. http://www.npr.org/programs/morning/features/2002/apr/spies/

Arid Areas

Geology. "World's Largest Desert." http://geology.com/records/largest-desert.shtml
Hutchinson, Charles. "Introduction: The 'Greening' of the Sahel." *Journal of Arid Environments* 63 (2005): 535–537.
———. "The Sahelian Desertification Debate: A View from the American South-West." *Journal of Arid Environments* 33 (1996): 519–524.

Flatland

44 *"What do we hope to achieve?"* Olivia Lang, "Maldives Leader in Climate Change Stunt." *BBC News*, October 17, 2009. http://news.bbc.co.uk/2/hi/south_asia/8312320.stm

Bradnock, Robert W. "Maldives." *World Book Encyclopedia*, 2009.
Candappa, Dayan. "Map of Island Paradise Needs to Be Redrawn." Reuters, January 11, 2005.
Central Intelligence Agency. "Maldives." *CIA World Fact Book*, 2010. https://www.cia.gov/library/publications/the-world-factbook/geos/mv.html
Nash, J. Madeleine. "Where the Waters Are Rising: A Close-Up Look at the Low-Lying Maldives, Where Global Warming Hits the Seawall." *Time*, April 25, 2005.
World Atlas. Maldives Maps. http://www.worldatlas.com/webimage/countrys/asia/mv.htm

Chew on This

Hansen, Liane. "Chicle: A Chewy Story of the Americas." *Weekend Edition Sunday*. NPR, July 12, 2009. http://www.npr.org/templates/story/story.php?storyId=106439600
Mathews, Jennifer. *Chicle: The Chewing Gum of the Americas—from the Ancient Maya to William Wrigley*. Tucson, AZ: Univ. of Arizona Press, 2009.
Wrigley Company. "About Gum." http://www.wrigley.com/global/about-us/about-gum.aspx

Put That in Your Pipe

44 *"Siva brought the marijuana plant"* Ernest Abel, *Marihuana, the First Twelve Thousand Years* (New York: Plenum Press, 1980), 17.

Booth, Martin. *Cannabis: A History*. New York: St. Martin's Press, 2005.
Cooper, Charles, and Declan McCullagh. "America's Love-Hate History with Pot." *CBS News*, July 13, 2009. http://www.cbsnews.com/stories/2009/07/13/national/main5154550.shtml
Duncan, David F. "A Human Need to Alter One's State of Consciousness." Addiction Info, April 19, 2005. http://www.addictioninfo.org/articles/183/1/Humans-Need-To-Alter-Consciousness/Page1.html
Gettman, Jon. "Marijuana Production in the United States, 2006." *Bulletin of Cannabis Reform*, December 2006. http://www.drugscience.org/Archive/bcr2/MJCropReport_2006.pdf

Lunar Lagomorph

45 *"The Buddha was wandering"* Jules Cashford, *The Moon: Myth and Image* (New York: Basic Books, 2003), 190.

Ezpeleta, Alicia. *Rabbits Everywhere*. New York: Abrams, 1996.

Harley, Timothy. *Moon Lore*. London: Sonnenschein, 1885. http://www.gutenberg.org/files/27228/27228-h/27228-h.htm

Volcanic Explosivity

46 *"A cloud . . . was ascending"* Pliny the Younger to Tacitus, letter 65 in *Harvard Classics*, vol. 9, part 4, *Letters*, ed. Charles W. Eliot (New York: Bartleby.com, 2001). http://www.bartleby.com/9/4/1065.html

Jones, Rick. "Visiting Pompeii." *Current Archaeology*. http://www.archaeology.co.uk/world-features/visiting-pompeii/all-pages.htm

Osservatorio Vesuviano. "The Eruptive History of Vesuvius." http://www.ov.ingv.it/inglese/vesuvio/storia/storia.htm

U.S. Geological Service. "Mount St. Helens Eruptive History." http://vulcan.wr.usgs.gov/Volcanoes/MSH/EruptiveHistory/framework.html

———. "Volcanic Explosivity Index." Volcano Hazards Program. http://volcanoes.usgs.gov/images/pglossary/vei.php

Freak Waves

46 *"more than 2 times"* National Weather Service Ocean Prediction Center, "Rogue Waves." http://www.opc.ncep.noaa.gov/perfectstorm/mpc_ps_rogue.shtml

46 *it "looked as if"* Colin Nickerson, "A Bit of White-Knuckle Time: Ocean Liner Rides Out Giant Wave off Canada," *Boston Globe*, September 16, 1995.

Broad, William. "Rogue Giants at Sea." *New York Times*, July 11, 2006.

Hall, Chris. "Freak Waves." *Beacon* 185 (2005). http://www.skuld.com/upload/News%20and%20Publications/Publications/Beacon/Beacon%202005%20185/Freak%20waves.pdf

Muller, Peter, Chris Garrett, and Al Osborne. "Rogue Waves, the 14th 'Aha Huliko'a Hawaiian Winter Workshop." *Oceanography* 18, no. 3 (September 2005): 66–75.

National Weather Service. "The Story of the Edmund Fitzgerald." http://www.crh.noaa.gov/mqt/fitzgerald/fitzb.php

Underwater Caves

47 *"Named for their vibrant"* Kelsey Ramos, "Dean's Blue Hole," *Los Angeles Times*. http://www.latimes.com/travel/la-tr-offbeattraveler17-pg,0,6375576.photogallery

Bahama Caves Research Foundation. http://www.bahamascaves.com/blueholes.html

Iliffe, Thomas. "Anchialine Caves and Cave Fauna of the World: Bahamas." Texas A&M University. http://www.tamug.edu/cavebiology/Bahamas/BahamaIntro.html

McGaw, Tamara. "Blue Holes of the Bahamas: Tidal Underwater Caves in the Caribbean." Suite 101. http://marinebiologyoceanography.suite101.com/article.cfm/blue_holes_of_the_bahamas

Sometimes Speed Is of the Essence

48 *"blitzes from 0 to 60"* Arthur St. Antoine, "First Test: 2009 Chevrolet Corvette ZR1," *Motor Trend*, October 18, 2008. http://www.motortrend.com/roadtests/coupes/112_0810_2009_chevrolet_corvette_zr1_first_test/index.html

Cheetah Conservation Fund. "Cheetah Fact Sheet." http://www.cheetah.org/?nd=cheetah_facts

Cupp, E. W. "Dragonfly." *World Book Encyclopedia*, 2009.

Merritt, Thomas. "Fastest Runner." In *Book of Insect Records*. Gainesville: Univ. of Florida, 2001. http://entnemdept.ifas.ufl.edu/walker/ufbir/chapters/chapter_39.shtml

National Geographic Society. "Sailfish (*Istiophorus platypterus*)." http://animals.nationalgeographic.com/animals/fish/sailfish.html

"Sailfish Profile." *Sailfish*, 2007. http://www.sailfishmagazine.com/about/main.htm

Shour, Mark. "Tiger Beetle Tales." *Extension News* (Iowa State University), September 25, 2006. http://www.extension.iastate.edu/news/2006/sep/071501.htm

Smithsonian Institution. "Bug Info: The Most Incredible Insects." http://www.si.edu/Encyclopedia_si/snmnh/buginfo/incredbugs.htm

U.S. Fish and Wildlife Service. "All about the Peregrine Falcon." Endangered Species Program. http://www.fws.gov/endangered/recovery/peregrine/QandA.html

Van Riper, Charles, and Sandra Van Riper. "Peregrine Falcon." *World Book Encyclopedia*, 2009.

Wielebnowski, Nadja. "Cheetah." *World Book Encyclopedia*, 2009.

The Roots of Red Hair

Garreau, Joel. "Red Alert! An Often Misunderstood Minority Finds It's Become a Mane Attraction." *Washington Post*, March 19, 2002.

Ha, Tom, and Jonathan Rees. "The Melanocortin 1 Receptor: What's Red Got to Do with It?" *Journal of the American Academy of Dermatology* 45 (2001): 961–964. http://www.derm.med.ed.ac.uk/PDF/Whats%20red%20got%20to%20do%20with%20it.pdf

Rees, Jonathan. "The Roots of Red Hair." The Human Genome. Wellcome Trust, April 2, 2003. http://genome.wellcome.ac.uk/doc_WTD020874.html

Sacharov, Allen. *The Redhead Book.* Takoma Park, MD: Word of Mouth Press, 1982.

3. FISH OR WEAPON?

The Highest Honor

49 *"highest expression of"* Congressional Gold Medal Recipients. http://clerk.house.gov/art_history/house_history/goldMedal.html

Stathis, Stephen W. *Congressional Gold Medals, 1776–2002*. Hauppauge, NY: Novinka Books, 2003.

A Special Span

50 *"The preparations are thus"* "Two Great Cities United: The Bridge Formally Opened." *New York Times*, May 25, 1883.

McCullough, David. *The Great Bridge: The Epic Story of the Building of the Brooklyn Bridge*. New York: Simon and Schuster, 1983.

New York City Department of Transportation. "Bridge Information." http://www.nyc.gov/html/dot/html/faqs/faqs_bridge.shtml

Fish or Weapon?

Fish Base. "Family Torpedinidae: Electric Rays." http://www.fishbase.org/Summary/Family Summary.cfm?Family=Torpedinidae

Kirby, Geoff. "A History of the Torpedo: The Early Days." *Journal of the Royal Navy Scientific Service* 27, no. 1 (1999).

Payne, Craig. "Torpedo." *World Book Encyclopedia*, 2009.

Rockets' Red Glare

Congreve, William. *A Treatise on the General Principles, Powers and Facility of Application of the Congreve Rocket System as Compared with Artillery*. London: Longman, Rees, Orme, Brown, and Green, 1827. Reprint, Chestnut Hill, MA: Adamant Media, 2005.

"Congreve Rocket." *Encyclopedia Britannica*. Vol. 3, 15th ed., 2003.

"What Is a Congreve Rocket?" *Harper's*, July 1854.

Bombs Bursting in Air

51 *a "shell . . . filled with bullets"* A. Marshall, "The Invention and Development of the Shrapnel Shell," *Journal of the Royal Artillery* 10, no. 1 (January 1920): 12.

52 *"hence on this simple circumstance"* Ian Frazier, "The Unsettling Legacy of General Shrapnel," *Mother Jones*, September–October 2003, 38.

52 *"any metal fragment"* Ibid.
52 *"a disappointed man"* Ibid.

Lissack, Ormond. *Ordnance and Gunnery: A Textbook Prepared for the Cadets of the United States Military Academy*. West Point, NY: John Wiley & Sons, 1915. http://www.archive.org/stream/ordnancegunneryt00lissrich/ordnancegunneryt00lissrich_djvu.txt

From Featherie to Polymer

Golf Europe. "A History of the Golf Ball." http://www.golfeurope.com/almanac/history/golf_ball.htm
Titleist. "Tech Art or Cave Art?" http://www.titleist.com/technology/details.asp?id=17
Veilleux, Tom. "How Do Dimples in Golf Balls Affect Their Flight?" *Scientific American*, September 19, 2005. http://www.scientificamerican.com/article.cfm?id=how-do-dimples-in-golf-ba

Hard as Rock

Dettman, Matthew. "Concrete." *World Book Encyclopedia*, 2009.
DuTemple, Lesley. *The Pantheon*. Minneapolis, MN: Lerner, 2003.
Portland Cement Association. "Cement and Concrete Basics." http://www.cement.org/basics/

The White City

Applebaum, Stanley. *The Chicago World's Fair of 1893: A Photographic Record*. New York: Dover Books, 1980.
Museum of Science and Industry. "Museum History." http://www.msichicago.org/about-the-museum/museum-history/

The White House

54. *"many Americans were opposed"* Hugh Sidey, "A Republic's Palace," *Time*, November 3, 1986, 24.

U.S. National Park Service. "The White House." http://www.nps.gov/nr/travel/wash/dc31.htm
White House. "History." http://www.whitehouse.gov/about/history/
White House Historical Association. "White House Facts." http://www.whitehousehistory.org/whha_history/history_facts-trivia.html

Rising from the Ashes

55 *"the most conspicuous structure"* "Laws Will Add to Magnificence of Fairmont Hotel," *San Francisco Chronicle*, March 4, 1906.

"Julia Morgan." In *Dictionary of American Biography*. Edited by the American Council of Learned Societies. New York: Scribner's, 1990. Reproduced in *Biography Resource Center*. Farmington Hills, MI: Gale, 2009.
"Julia Morgan." In *International Dictionary of Architects and Architecture*. Doreen Yarwood, Randall J. Van Vynckt, and Suhail Butt, eds. Farmington Hills, MI: St. James Press, 1993. Reproduced in *Biography Resource Center*. Farmington Hills, MI: Gale, 2009.
Sullivan, Mary Ann. "The Fairmont Hotel." Bluffton University. http://www.bluffton.edu/~sullivanm/jmfairmont/jmfairmont.html

Pleasant Transit

Devoss, David. "End of the Road." *Smithsonian*, May 2008. http://www.smithsonianmag.com/travel/da-natchez-trace.html
Longfellow, Rickie. "California's Pacific Coast Highway." U.S. Department of Transportation, Highway History. http://www.fhwa.dot.gov/infrastructure/back0403.cfm
Merritt Parkway Conservancy. "Origins of the Merritt Parkway." http://merrittparkway.org/pages/history.asp
Radde, Bruce. *The Merritt Parkway*. New Haven, CT : Yale Univ. Press, 1993.

U.S. Department of Transportation, Federal Highway Administration. "Scenic Byways Program." http://www.byways.org/explore/

A City for "Useful Manufactures"

Paterson History. "Paterson, New Jersey: A History." http://www.patersonhistory.com/index.html

"Silk City—Paterson, New Jersey." Rt23.com, North Jersey's Internet Magazine.http://www.rt23.com/history/Paterson_NJ-silk_city.shtml

Zax, Leonard. "The Great Falls and a City's Future: Park Plan Had Broad, Bipartisan Support." *Passaic Herald News*, April 5, 2009.

The Salad Dressing of the St. Lawrence

56 *"To become an official"* 1000 Islands International Tourism Council. http://www.visit1000islands.com/visitorinfo/?page_id=4

Lunman, Kim. "The Mystery of the Thousand Islands Dressing." *Thousand Islands Life*, November 14, 2008. http://www.thousandislandslife.com/BackIssues/Archive/tabid/393/articleType/ArticleView/articleId/25/The-Mystery-of-the-Thousand-Islands-Dressing.aspx

All Things Peanut

Iowa State University Library. "The Legacy of George Washington Carver," 1998. http://www.lib.iastate.edu/spcl/gwc/home.html

Mackintosh, Barry. "George Washington Carver and the Peanut: New Light on a Much-Loved Myth." *American Heritage*, August 1977. http://www.americanheritage.com/articles/magazine/ah/1977/5/1977_5_66.shtml

National Park Service. "American Visionaries: George Washington Carver." http://www.nps.gov/history/museum/exhibits/Tuskegee/gwcarts.htm

Pinkett, Harold. "George Washington Carver." In *Dictionary of American Biography*. Edited by the American Council of Learned Societies. New York: Scribner's, 1990. Reproduced in *Biography Resource Center*. Farmington Hills, MI: Gale, 2009.

Spoiled Milk

Capasso, Luigi. "Bacteria in Two-Millennia-Old Cheese, and Related Epizoonoses in Roman Populations." *Journal of Infection* 45, no. 2 (August 2002): 122–127.

Homer. *The Odyssey*. New York: Harper & Row, 1967.

Lucey, John. "Cheese." *World Book Encyclopedia*, 2009.

Ultimate Ungulates. "Ungulates of the World: Species Fact Sheet." http://www.ultimateungulate.com/ungulates.html

Italian Food Translated

Black, Jane. "The Trail of Tiramisu." *Washington Post*, July 11, 2007.

Piedigrotta Italian Bakery and Pastry Shop. "The Past." http://www.piedigrottabakery.com/subpages/history.html

Rebora, Piero. *Cassell's Italian Dictionary*. New York: Macmillan, 1984.

Something to Write On

Dahl, Svend. *History of the Book*. Metuchen, NJ: Scarecrow Press, 1968.

Francko, David. "Papyrus." *World Book Encyclopedia*, 2009.

Hillas, Roger. "The History of the Book: Long before Gutenberg, Somebody Had to Invent Chapters, Page Numbers, Even Word Spacing." *Washington Post*, April 10, 1996.

Keller, D. Stephen. "Paper." *World Book Encyclopedia*, 2009.

Norman, Jeremy. "From Cave Paintings to the Internet: A Chronological and Thematic Database on the History of Information and Media—Paper/Papyrus/Parchment/Vellum Timeline." History of Science. http://www.historyofscience.com/G2I/timeline/index.php?category=Paper+%2F+Papyrus+%2F+Parchment+%2F+Vellum

"Parchment." *World Book Encyclopedia*, 2009.

Steinway Grand

Chapin, Miles. *88 Keys: The Making of a Steinway Piano.* New York: Clarkson Potter, 1997.

Roney, Maya. "The Making of a Steinway Piano." *Businessweek*, March 6, 2007. http://www.businessweek.com/bwdaily/dnflash/content/mar2007/db20070305_637888.htm

Part Two: On Reason and Science

61 *"Reason, from which comes"* Jean Le Rond d'Alembert, *Preliminary Discourse to the Encyclopedia of Diderot*, trans. Richard N. Schwab (Chicago: Univ. of Chicago Press, 1995), 148.

4. LINKS IN THE CHAIN OF BEING

The Great Chain of Being

64 *the "contingent chain of becoming"* William Bynum, "The Great Chain of Being after Forty Years," *History of Science* 13 (1975): 2.

Aristotle. *History of Animals*. London: George Bell & Sons, 1897.

Weiner, Philip, ed. "Chain of Being." In *Dictionary of the History of Ideas*. Vol. 1. New York: Scribner's, 1973.

One God

64 *"Theists believe that"* "Monotheism," *Stanford Encyclopedia of Philosophy*, October 26, 2009. http://plato.stanford.edu/entries/monotheism/

Falk, Nancy E. "Theism." *World Book Encyclopedia*, 2009.

Two Natures

64 *"the ultimate recovery"* Kile Jones, "A Comparison between Manichean and Christian Views of Evil," *Circle of Ancient Iranian Studies*, December 27, 2006. http://www.cais-soas.com/CAIS/Religions/iranian/Manichaeism/comp_manich_christ_evil.htm

"Dualism." *Stanford Encyclopedia of Philosophy*, October 10, 2007. http://plato.stanford.edu/entries/dualism/

Three Fates

64 *"divinities of the duration"* William Smith, ed., *A Dictionary of Greek and Roman Biography and Mythology* (Boston: Little, Brown, 1867), 2: 1109, 1110. http://quod.lib.umich.edu/cgi/t/text/pageviewer-idx?c=moa;cc=moa;rgn=full%20text;idno=ACL3129.0002.001;didno=ACL3129.0002.001;view=image;seq=00001119

65 *"those women who shape"* John Lindow, *Norse Mythology: A Guide to the Gods, Heroes, Rituals, and Beliefs* (New York: Oxford Univ. Press, 2001), 243.

65 *"aged and hideous women"* Smith, *Dictionary*, 1111.

McLean, Adam. *The Triple Goddess: An Exploration of the Archetypal Feminine.* Grand Rapids, MI: Phanes Press, 1989.

Four Truths

65 *"suffering is part of life"* Juliane Schober, "Buddhism," *World Book Encyclopedia*, 2009.

Bodhi, Bhikkhu (Block, Jeffrey). "The Noble Eightfold Path: The Way to the End of Suffering." Access to Insight. http://www.accesstoinsight.org/lib/authors/bodhi/waytoend.html

D'Epiro, Peter, and Mary Desmond Pinkowish. "Four Noble Truths." In *What Are the Seven Wonders of the World? And 100 Other Great Cultural Lists—Fully Explicated.* New York: Doubleday, 1998.

Thanissaro, Bhikkhu (DeGraff, Geoffrey). "The Four Noble Truths: A Study Guide." Access to Insight. http://www.accesstoinsight.org/lib/study/truths.html

Five Pillars

66 *the Five Pillars of Islam* Islam FAQ. http://www.islamfaq.org/html/read_the_faq.html

Cornell, Vincent. "Islam." *World Book Encyclopedia*, 2009.

Ibrahim, I. A. *A Brief Illustrated Guide to Understanding Islam*. Houston, TX: Darussalam Publications, 1997. http://www.islamic-council.com/okdown1/islam-guide.pdf

Islamic Center. "The Five Pillars of Islam." http://www.theislamiccenter.com/node/30

A Six-Pointed Star

Frankel, Ellen, and Betsey Platkin Teutsch. *The Encyclopedia of Jewish Symbols*. Northvale, NJ: Jason Aronson, 1992.

Jewish Virtual Library. "Star of David." http://jewishvirtuallibrary.org/jsource/Judaism/star.html

Wigoder, Geoffrey, ed. "Magen David." In *New Encyclopedia of Judaism*. New York: New York Univ. Press, 2002.

Seven Happiness Beings

67 *"journey harmoniously together"* Travel to Japan, "The Seven Lucky Gods of Japan." http://www.travel-to-japan.com/the-seven-lucky-gods-of-japan/

Sakata, Shane. "Seven Gods of Good Fortune." *Nihon Sun*, January 22, 2009. http://www.nihonsun.com/2009/01/22/seven-gods-of-good-fortune/

Wohl, Samantha. "Seven Lucky Gods of Japan." UCLA Center for East Asian Studies. http://www.international.ucla.edu/eas/lessons/wohl/gods.pdf

Eight Immortals

67 *"male, female, the old"* People's Republic of China, Ministry of Culture, "The Eight Immortals," China Culture. http://211.147.20.24/library/2008-02/04/content_25144.htm

68 *"the fish-shaped drum"* "Traditions: Myths and Legends—Eight Immortals," Shanghai News and Press Bureau. http://traditions.cultural-china.com/en/13Traditions43.html

Travel China Guide. "Temple of the Eight Immortals." http://www.travelchinaguide.com/attraction/shaanxi/xian/ba-xian-an-monastery.htm

Nine for Hindus

68 *"closely associated with the process"* Pankaj Dixit, "Navratras: Story of Cosmic Evolution," *Times of India*. http://www.hinduwisdom.info/articles_hinduism/112.htm

68 *"the emanating power"* "Navaratri: In the Festival of 'Nine Nights' Hindus across the Globe Worship the Feminine Form of the Supreme," *Hinduism Today*, December 2008. http://www.hinduismtoday.com/modules/smartsection/item.php?itemid=3073

Hindu Temple of Central Illinois. "Temple Festivals: Navaratri." http://www.hinduheritage.org/Default.aspx?pageId=51338

"Nine Beliefs of Hinduism." *Hinduism Today*. http://www.hinduismtoday.com/modules/wfchannel/index.php?wfc_cid=19

Sivananda, Sri Swami. "All about Hinduism." Divine Life Society, 1999. http://www.dlshq.org/download/hinduismbk.pdf

Ten Commandments

69 *Ten Commandments chart* Cliff Walker and Jyoti Shankar. "Which Ten Commandments?" *Positive Atheism Breau*, July 1999. http://www.positiveatheism.org/crt/whichcom.htm

Lattin, Don. "Just Which Commandments Are the 10 Commandments?" *San Francisco Chronicle*, August 26, 2003.

Myers, Jim. "Which Ten Commandments?" Biblical Heritage Center. http://www.biblicalheritage.org/Bible%20Studies/10%20Commandments.htm

Soul Guides

71 *"emblematic of the passage"* George Dennis, *The Cities and Cemeteries of Etruria*, 3rd ed. (London: John Murray, 1883), 168.

Ashoka. "Kishitigarbha (Jizo)." *Faces of Compassion.* http://www.ashokaedu.net/samples/Bodhisattvasample1.htm

Biedermann, Hans. *Dictionary of Symbolism: Cultural Icons and the Meanings behind Them.* Translated by James Hulbert. New York: Penguin Books, 1992.

National Gallery of Australia. "The Aboriginal Memorial." http://nga.gov.au/AboriginalMemorial/malarra.cfm

"Psychopomps." http://www.psychopomps.org/

Strong, Laura. "Psychopomp Stories: Contemplating Death in a Spiritually Diverse Society." http://www.psychopomps.org/psychopomp-stories/abstract.html

Jesus and Mary

72 *"The most Blessed Virgin Mary"* Pius IX, *Ineffabilis Deus*, December 8, 1854. http://www.papalencyclicals.net/Pius09/p9ineff.htm

Catechism of the Catholic Church, 1993. http://www.vatican.va/archive/ENG0015/__P1K.HTM

Cow Protection

73 *"The cause of cow-protection"* Mohandas K. Gandhi, *Hindu Dharma* (Ahmedabad, India: Navajivan, 1978), 110.

"Hinduism." *Encyclopedia Britannica.* 15th ed., 2003, vol. 20.

The Piasa

73 *"While skirting some rocks"* Jacques Marquette, "The Mississippi Voyage of Jolliet and Marquette," in *Early Narratives of the Northwest, 1634–1699*, ed. Louise P. Kellogg (New York: Charles Scribner's Sons, 1917), 248–249. http://www.wisconsinhistory.org/turningpoints/search.asp?id=370

73 *"bird who devours man"* Southwestern (Piasa) High School, "The Legend of the Piasa Bird." http://www.piasabirds.com/piasalegend.html

Bayliss, Clara. "The Significance of the Piasa." *Transactions of the Illinois State Historical Society for the Year 1908.* Springfield: Illinois State Historical Library, 1909.

Great River Road. "Visitors Guide to the Piasa Bird." http://www.greatriverroad.com/Cities/Alton/PiasaBird.htm

The Numbers of the Faithful

Adherents. "Major Religions of the World Ranked by Number of Adherents." http://www.adherents.com/Religions_By_Adherents.html

American Jewish Committee. *American Jewish Year Book, 2008.* http://www.ajcarchives.org/main.php?GroupingId=40

Don't Annoy the Gods

74 *They were "relentless"* Philip Wiener, ed., "Sin and Salvation," in *Dictionary of the History of Ideas* (New York: Scribner's, 1973), 4:228.

Jinxed

75 *"idea that a malign glance"* Alan Dundes, ed., *The Evil Eye: A Casebook* (Madison: University of Wisconsin Press, 1992), vii.

75 *"all made the sign"* Bram Stoker, *Dracula: A Mystery Story* (New York: W. R. Caldwell, 1897), 6.

Elworthy, Frederick. *The Evil Eye: An Account of This Ancient and Widespread Superstition.* London: John Murray, 1895. Reprint, *The Evil Eye: The Classic Account of an Ancient Superstition.* New York: Dover, 2004. http://www.sacred-texts.com/evil/tee/index.htm

Gurel, Perin. "Nazar, the Evil Eye." *Dergi: Yale Friends of Turkey*, Spring 2008. http://www.yale.edu/yuft/dergiYFTmagazine08.pdf

Koyen, Jeff. "The Evil Eye." *Fortean Times*, July 2002. http://www.forteantimes.com/features/articles/241/the_evil_eye.html

Lucky Seven

75 *"Seven is an odd"* Robert C. Solomon, ed. *Wicked Pleasures: Meditations on the Seven 'Deadly' Sins* (Lanham, MD: Rowman and Littlefield, 1999), 1, 4.

Dell, Kristina. "The Most Popular Wedding Day Ever." *Time*, June 7, 2007.

Haupt, Jennifer. "Lucky Number Seven: Why Are We Fascinated with the Number Seven?" *Psychology Today*, November 19, 2009.

Usborne, Simon. "Is This Your Lucky Number? Seventy-Seven Things You Need to Know about 07." *Independent*, December 31, 2006. http://www.independent.co.uk/news/uk/this-britain/is-this-your-lucky-number-seventyseven-things-you-need-to-know-about-07–430258.html

5. LETTERS IN PLAIN SIGHT

A Man of Puzzles

Indiana University. "Alumni Profile: Will Shortz." http://alumni.indiana.edu/profiles/alumni/wshortz.shtml

National Public Radio. "About Will Shortz." http://www.npr.org/programs/wesun/puzzle/will.html

The Infinity of Lists

78 *"The list is the origin"* Susanne Beyer and Lothar Gorris, "We Like Lists Because We Don't Want to Die," *Spiegel International*, November 11, 2009. http://www.spiegel.de/international/zeitgeist/0,1518,659577,00.html

Louvre Museum. "The Louvre Invites Umberto Eco." http://www.louvre.fr/llv/exposition/detail_exposition.jsp?CONTENT%3C%3Ecnt_id=10134198674146631&CURRENT_LLV_EXPO%3C%3Ecnt_id=10134198674146631&bmLocale=en

Louvre Museum. "Vertige de la liste." (in French) http://www.louvre.fr/media/repository/ressources/sources/pdf/src_document_55774_v2_m56577569831249072.pdf

Hometown Names

Dickson, Paul. *Labels for Locals: What to Call People from Abilene to Zimbabwe*. Springfield, MA: Merriam-Webster, 1997.

They Carried the Mail

79 *"Neither snow, nor rain"* U.S. Postal Service, "Postal Facts, 2010." http://www.usps.com/communications/newsroom/postalfacts.htm

Bowyer, Mathew. *They Carried the Mail: A Survey of Postal History and Hobbies*. Washington, DC: Robert B. Luce, 1972.

U.S. Post Office Department. *History of U.S. Postage Stamps, Postal Cards and Stamped Envelopes*. Washington, DC: U.S. Government Printing Office, 1970.

U.S. Postal Service. *2009 Annual Report*. http://www.usps.com/financials/_pdf/annual_report_2009.pdf

Main Street, U.S.A.

U.S. Postal Service. "Postal Facts, 2010." http://www.usps.com/communications/newsroom/postalfacts.htm

Project Gutenberg

80 *"To encourage the creation"* "Project Gutenberg." http://www.gutenberg.org/wiki/Gutenberg:About

80 *"The Gutenberg Press"* Nicholas Tomaiuolo, "U-Content: Project Gutenberg, Me, and You," *Searcher*, January 2009. http://www.infotoday.com/searcher/jan09/Tomaiuolo.shtml

Project Gutenberg. "The Declaration of Independence." http://www.gutenberg.org/etext/1

Vara, Vauhini. "Project Gutenberg Fears No Google." *Wall Street Journal*, December 10, 2005. http://online.wsj.com/public/article/SB113415403113218620-U_OqLOmApoaSvNpy5SjNwvhpW5w_20061209.html

The Implements of Communication

81 *"a pen in which the point"* "Ballpoint," *Random House Dictionary of the English Language*, 2nd ed., 1987.

Diringer, David. "Inks, Pens, and Other Writing Tools." In *The Book before Printing*, 544–563. New York: Dover, 1982.

Writing Instrument Manufacturers Association. http://www.wima.org/

Alternate Writing

81 *"as the ox turns"* M. C. Hawatson, ed., *The Oxford Companion to Classical Literature* (New York: Oxford Univ. Press, 1989), 94.

82 *"Parker uses the back and forth"* "CD Reviews," *Birmingham Post* (UK), April 14, 2008.

Unsyentifik, Unskolarli, Ilojikal Speling

82 *"that wud clas"* Melvil Dewey, *Dewey Decimal Classification and Relative Index*, 19th ed. (Albany, NY: Forest Press, 1979), 67. http://www.spellingsociety.org/news/media/dewey.php

Online Computer Library Center. "OCLC and the Library Hotel Settle Trademark Complaint." News release, November 24, 2003. http://www.oclc.org/news/releases/20031124.htm

Wiegand, Wayne. *Irrepressible Reformer: A Biography of Melvil Dewey*. Chicago: American Library Association, 1996.

Alpha Bravo Charlie

British Broadcasting Corporation. "The NATO Phonetic Alphabet." *BBC News*. http://www.bbc.co.uk/dna/h2g2/A8245910

Communications Specialists, Ltd. http://www.comm-spec.com/phonetic-alphabet.php

Demarest, Chris L. *Alpha, Bravo, Charlie: The Military Alphabet*. New York: Simon and Schuster, 2005.

"Emma." *Oxford English Dictionary*. Oxford, UK: Oxford Univ. Press, 1989.

National Aeronautics and Space Administration. "Hurricanes." *NASA World Book*. http://www.nasa.gov/worldbook/hurricane_worldbook.html

Funny Papers on the Radio

83 *"Now, talking about newspapers"* Ben Manilla, "NYC Mayor LaGuardia's Legendary Radio Readings," *All Things Considered*, NPR, November 30, 2008. http://www.npr.org/templates/story/story.php?storyId=97621982

"'Uncle Fiorello' Reads the Comics." *New York Times*, July 2, 1945.

A Deadline for Real

84 *"A railing round the inside"* Albert Riddle, *The Life, Character and Public Service of James A. Garfield* (Cleveland, OH: W. W. Williams, 1880), 305.

Metcalf, Allan, and David Barnhart. *America in So Many Words: Words That Have Shaped America*. New York: Houghton Mifflin Harcourt, 1999.

A Few Billion from the People

Center for Responsive Politics. "2008 Overview of Campaign Fundraising and Spending." http://www.opensecrets.org/bigpicture/stats.php

Global Security. "USS *Carter*." http://www.globalsecurity.org/org/news/2005/050218-uss-carter.htm

Insurance Information Institute. "Hurricane Katrina." http://www.iii.org/media/research/katrina1year/

United Nations. "General Assembly Adopts $3.2 Billion 2005–2006 Peacekeeping Budget." Fifty-ninth General Assembly. Press release, June 23, 2005. http://www.un.org/News/Press/docs/2005/ga10356.doc.htm

The Cost per Vote

Barbaro, Michael, and David W. Chen. "Mayor's Political Quest Is Costliest Ever in U.S." *New York Times*, October 24, 2009.

Kugler, Sara. "NYC Mayor Bruised by Surprisingly Close Victory." Associated Press, November 4, 2009.

Lombardi, Frank. "Mike's Election Cost Him $108M—That's $185 a Vote." *New York Daily News*, January 16, 2010.

Thrush, Glenn. "Bloomberg: $180–$252 per Vote." Politico, November 4, 2009. http://www.politico.com/blogs/glennthrush/1109/Blommberg_180252_per_vote.html

SOTU Loquaciousness

85 *"shall from time to time"* U.S. Constitution, Article II, Section 3, Clause 1. http://www.law.cornell.edu/constitution/constitution.articleii.html#section3

Clerk of the House of Representatives. "House History: State of the Union Address." http://clerk.house.gov/art_history/house_history/stateunion.html

Initial Letters

86 *"Distinctions are not always made"* "Preface," *Acronyms, Initialisms and Abbreviations Dictionary*, 42nd ed. Farmington Hills, MI: Gale, 2009.

Acronym Finder. http://www.acronymfinder.com/

Little Old Ladies Laugh Out Loud

Acronym Finder. http://www.acronymfinder.com

Dictionnaire des Acronymes. http://acronymes.info/

Please Don't BTQ

87 *"is a form of logical"* Beg the Question. http://begthequestion.info/

Kirwan, Christopher. "Begging the Question." In *The Oxford Companion to Philosophy*. Edited by Ted Honderich. 2nd ed. Oxford, UK: Oxford Univ. Press, 2005.

Quinion, Michael. "Beg the Question." World Wide Words. http://www.worldwidewords.org/qa/qa-beg1.htm

Safire, William. "On Language: Take My Question Please!" *New York Times*, July 26, 1998.

My Favorite Punctuation

Strumpf, Michael, and Auriel Douglas. *The Grammar Bible: Everything You Always Wanted to Know about Grammar but Didn't Know Whom to Ask*. 3rd ed. New York: Henry Holt, 2004.

U.S. Government Printing Office Style Board. "Punctuation." In *U.S. Government Style Manual*. 30th ed. Washington, DC: U.S. Government Printing Office, 2008. http://www.gpoaccess.gov/stylemanual/browse.html

The Department of Redundancies Department

Burton, Gideon. "The Forest of Rhetoric." Brigham Young University. http://rhetoric.byu.edu/

Firesign Theater. "The Department of Redundancies Department." *Don't Crush That Dwarf, Hand Me the Pliers!* (C-30102). Columbia Records, 1970.

A Lot of Letters

"Floccinaucinihilipilification." *Oxford English Dictionary*. Oxford, UK: Oxford Univ. Press, 1989.

Quinion, Michael. "Floccinaucinihilipilification." World Wide Words. http://www.worldwidewords.org/weirdwords/ww-flo2.htm

The word also has its own Web site: http://www.floccinaucinihilipilification.com/

All the Others

Guinagh, Kevin. *Dictionary of Foreign Phrases and Abbreviations*. New York: Wilson, 1972.

Endangered Languages

89 *"a unique part of human"* "Ancient Island Language Dies," *Hindustan Times*, February 5, 2010.

Lewis, M. Paul, ed. "Endangered Languages." In *Ethnologue: Languages of the World*. 16th ed. Dallas: SIL International, 2009. http://www.ethnologue.com/nearly_extinct.asp

United Nations Educational, Scientific, and Cultural Organization (UNESCO). "Safeguarding Endangered Languages." http://www.unesco.org/culture/ich/index.php?pg=00136

Euskera Spoken

Koerner, Brendan. "How Do Basque and Spanish Differ?" *Slate*, May 30, 2003.

Strafford, Peter. "Great Survivors Trace History Back to the Stone Age." *Times* (London), October 26, 1990.

Urla, Jackie. "Voice of the People Recast as Language of Terrorism." *Times* (London), August 29, 2003.

Walters, Colin. "Story of the First Europeans?" *Washington Times*, November 7, 1999.

The Forest of Rhetoric

90 *"antanaclasis: the repetition of a word"* Gideon Burton, "*Silva Rhetoricae* (The Forest of Rhetoric)," Brigham Young University. http://rhetoric.byu.edu/

Mixed Metaphors

92 *"Mr. Speaker, I smell a rat"* Brian Maye, "An Irishman's Diary," *Irish Times*, February 14, 2000.

Burton, Gideon. "*Silva Rhetoricae* (The Forest of Rhetoric)." Brigham Young University. http://rhetoric.byu.edu/

Grammar Girl. "Mixed Metaphors." December 6, 2008. http://grammar.quickanddirtytips.com/mixed-metaphors.aspx

6. SIN VERSUS VIRTUE

Sin against Virtue

"Lesson Sixth: Of Sin and Its Kinds." *Baltimore Catechism No. 3*. New York: Benziger Brothers, 1895. http://www.gutenberg.org/files/14553/14553.txt

Green with What?

Here are the official definitions of jealousy and envy according to *The Oxford English Dictionary* (Oxford: Oxford Univ. Press, 1989):

> Envy: (n) The feeling of mortification and ill-will occasioned by the contemplation of superior advantages possessed by another. . . . A longing for the advantages enjoyed by another person. (v) To feel displeasure and ill-will at the superiority of (another person) in happiness, success, reputation, or the possession of anything desirable; to regard with discontent another's possession of (some superior advantage that one would like to have for oneself).
>
> Jealousy: Solicitude or anxiety for the preservation or well-being of something; vigilance in guarding a possession from loss or damage. . . . The state of mind arising from the suspicion, apprehension, or knowledge of rivalry in love, etc. Fear of being supplanted in the affection, or distrust of the fidelity, of a beloved person, esp. a wife, husband, or lover.

The First Charter of Human Rights

94 *"This cylinder has sometimes"* British Museum, "Cyrus Cylinder." http://www.britishmuseum.org/explore/highlights/highlight_objects/me/c/cyrus_cylinder.aspx

94 *"As for the population of Babylon"* Irving Finkel, "Cyrus Cylinder translation," British Museum http://www.britishmuseum.org/explore/highlights/article_index/c/cyrus_cylinder_-_translation.aspx

94 *"This proclamation reflects Cyrus' desire"* United Nations, "Statement of Secretary General U Thant at Presentation of Gift from Iran to United Nations," October 14, 1971. http://www.livius.org/a/1/inscriptions/cyrus.pdf

Ghasemi, Shapour. "The Cyrus the Great Cylinder." Iran Chamber Society. http://www.iranchamber.com/history/cyrus/cyrus_charter.php

Curse You, Book Stealer

95 *"Quisquis quem tetigerit"* Marc Drogin, *Anathema! Medieval Scribes and the History of Book Curses* (Totowa, NJ: Allanheld and Schram, 1983), 17.

95 *"O reader, turn the leaves gently"* Ibid., 21.

95 *"If anyone take away"* Ibid., 88.

Virginia Commonwealth University. "Book Curses." VCU Libraries, Preservation Department. http://www.library.vcu.edu/preservation/curse.html

Let My People Go

96 *"Approximately 800,000 people"* Central Intelligence Agency, "Population," *CIA World Factbook, 2010.* https://www.cia.gov/library/publications/the-world-factbook/geos/xx.html

Anti-Slavery International. http://www.antislavery.org/english/default.aspx

Free the Slaves. "Slavery Today." http://www.freetheslaves.net/Page.aspx?pid=301

International Labor Conference. "A Global Alliance against Forced Labor." Report of the director-general, 93rd session, 2005. http://www.ilo.org/public/english/standards/relm/ilc/ilc93/pdf/rep-i-b.pdf

General Tubman of the Railroad

96 *"I had reasoned this out in my mind"* Sarah H. Bradford, *Harriet: The Moses of Her People* (New York: George R. Lockwood and Son, 1886). http://www.gutenberg.org/dirs/etext06/8htub10h.htm

96 *"one of the bravest persons"* Ibid.

96 *"Expecting John Brown"* Ibid.

97 *"She braved every danger"* Harriet Tubman. http://www.harriettubman.com/tab.html

Bradford, Sarah H. *Scenes in the Life of Harriet Tubman*. Auburn, NY: W. J. Moses, 1869. http://docsouth.unc.edu/neh/bradford/bradford.html

"Harriet Tubman." *Notable Black American Women*. Vol. 1. Farmington Hills, MI: Gale, 1992. Reproduced in *Biography Resource Center*. Farmington Hills, MI: Gale, 2009.

Institute for New York State History. "The Life of Harriet Tubman." http://www.nyhistory.com/harriettubman/life.htm

Lakewood Public Library. "Women in History: Harriet Tubman." http://www.lkwdpl.org/wihohio/tubm-har.htm

Larson, Kate Clifford. *Bound for the Promised Land: Harriet Tubman, Portrait of an American Hero*. New York: Ballantine Books, 2004. http://www.harriettubmanbiography.com/

Library of Congress. "Harriet Tubman." http://www.loc.gov/rr/program/bib/tubman/

National Park Service. "Aboard the Underground Railroad." http://www.nps.gov/history/nr/travel/underground/

From the Handbook of Robotics

97 *The word* robot Karel Čapek, "Who Did Actually Invent the Word 'Robot' and What Does It Mean?" http://capek.misto.cz/english/robot.html

97 *"A robot may not injure"* Isaac Asimov, *The Three Laws of Robotics* in *I, Robot* (New York: Gnome Press, 1950).

97 *"One of the stock plots"* Isaac Asimov, "Introduction," in *The Rest of the Robots* (New York: Doubleday, 1964), 10–11.

Who Can Be a Justice?

98 *"The judicial Power of the United States"* The Constitution of the United States, Article III, Section 1. http://www.law.cornell.edu/constitution/constitution.articleiii.html

The Secret Ballot

99 *"By 1896, Americans"* Jill Lepore, "Annals of Democracy: Rock, Paper, Scissors—How We Used to Vote," *New Yorker*, October 13, 2008, 95.

Ackerman, S. J. "The Vote That Failed." *Smithsonian*, November 1998.

Phillips, Adam. "History of the Secret Ballot Revealed." Voice of America, November 3, 2008. http://www1.voanews.com/english/news/american-life/a-13–2008–11–03-voa35.html?textmode=0

And Throw Away the Key

King's College. "World Prison Brief." London, 2010. http://www.kcl.ac.uk/depsta/law/research/icps/worldbrief/

Sabol, William J., Heather C. West, and Matthew Cooper. "Prisoners in 2008." *Bureau of Justice Statistics Bulletin*. U.S. Department of Justice, December 2009. http://bjs.ojp.usdoj.gov/content/pub/pdf/p08.pdf

Walmsley, Roy. *World Prison Population List*. 8th ed. London: King's College International Centre for Prison Studies, 2009. http://www.kcl.ac.uk/depsta/law/research/icps/downloads/wppl-8th_41.pdf

How Much Should I Pay Myself?

Brudnick, Ida A. "Salaries of Members of Congress: A List of Payable Rates and Effective Dates, 1789–2008." Congressional Research Service, February 21, 2008. http://www.senate.gov/reference/resources/pdf/97–1011.pdf

National Taxpayers Union. "Salaries for Members of Congress, Supreme Court Justices, and the President." http://www.ntu.org/main/page.php?PageID=23

U.S. House of Representatives. "Historical Table of Congressional Salaries." January 2009. http://www.house.gov/daily/salaries.htm

U.S. Senate. "Senate Salaries since 1789." http://www.senate.gov/artandhistory/history/common/briefing/senate_salaries.htm

7. MODUS MUNDI

I Seem to Be a Verb

101 *"technology had a redeeming"* E. J. Applewhite, "Who Was Buckminster Fuller?" Buckminster Fuller Institute. http://www.bfi.org/about-bucky/biography/who-was-buckminster-fuller-ej-applewhite

101 *"I live on Earth at present"* R. Buckminster Fuller, *I Seem to Be a Verb* (New York: Bantam Books, 1970), 1.

102 *"And because the meaning"* R. Buckminster Fuller, *And It Came to Pass—Not to Stay* (New York: Macmillan, 1976), 102.

Buckminster Fuller Institute. "Design Science." http://www.bfi.org/design-science/definitions-and-resources/design-science-amy-edmondson

The State of Plasma

102 *"Plasma temperatures"* Timothy E. Eastman, "Perspectives on Plasmas, the Fourth State of Matter," Plasmas International. http://www.plasmas.org/what-are-plasmas.htm

103 *"the ionized gas contains"* Irving Langmuir, "Oscillations in Ionized Gases," *Proceedings of the National Academy of Sciences* 14, no. 8 (August 1, 1928): 628. http://www.pnas.org/content/14/8/627

103 *"how to make"* "Microwave Grape Plasma." http://c3po.barnesos.net/homepage/lpl/grapeplasma/

Coalition for Plasma Science. "What Is Plasma?" http://www.plasmacoalition.org/what.htm

Elementary, My Dear Gell-Mann

103 *"In 1963, when I assigned"* Murray Gell-Mann, *The Quark and the Jaguar: Adventures in the Simple and the Complex* (New York: Henry Holt, 1994), 180.

103 *"for his contributions"* Nobel Foundation, "Murray Gell-Mann: The Nobel Prize in Physics, 1969." http://nobelprize.org/nobel_prizes/physics/laureates/1969/gell-mann-bio.html

March, Robert. "Quark." *World Book Encyclopedia*, 2009.

Singh, Simon. "The Big Bang Machine: Large Hadron Collider at CERN." *Guardian*, June 30, 2008.

Fullerenes and Buckyballs

104 *"A fullerene"* Nobel Foundation, "The Nobel Prize in Chemistry, 1996." http://nobelprize.org/nobel_prizes/chemistry/laureates/1996/presentation-speech.html

104 *"the almost unlimited potential"* Texas State Legislature, House Concurrent Resolution No. 83, 1997. http://www.legis.state.tx.us/tlodocs/75R/billtext/html/HC00083H.htm

Allen, Kim. "Fullerenes." http://kimallen.sheepdogdesign.net/Fuller/index.html

Fischer, John E. "Carbon." *World Book Encyclopedia*, 2009.

Hare, Jonathan. "Bucky Balls—Carbon 60." Vega Science Trust. http://www.vega.org.uk/video/programme/163

Stoddart, Alison. "Interview: Technology in a Bottle." *Highlights in Chemical Technology.* Royal Society of Chemistry, August 28, 2007. http://www.rsc.org/Publishing/ChemTech/Volume/2007/09/jim_heath_interview.asp

A Gas Can Be Noble

105 *"In chemistry and alchemy"* "Noble Gases," *Encyclopedia Britannica*, vol. 8, 15th ed., 2003. http://www.britannica.com/EBchecked/topic/416955/noble-gas

Los Alamos National Laboratory, Chemical Division. Periodic Table of the Elements. http://periodic.lanl.gov/default.htm

Marsden, Steve. "The Noble Gases." Chemistry Resources for Students and Teachers. http://www.chemtopics.com/elements/noble/noble.htm

Royal Society of Chemistry. "Chemical Data: The Noble Gases." http://www.rsc.org/chemsoc/visualelements/Pages/data/intro_groupviii_data.html

Shakhashiri, Bassam Z. "Gases of the Air." Science Is Fun. http://scifun.chem.wisc.edu/chemweek/PDF/airgas.pdf

The Seven Billion

Population Reference Bureau. "2009 World Population Data Sheet." http://www.prb.org/pdf09/09wpds_eng.pdf

U.S. Census Bureau. "U.S. and World Population Clocks." http://www.census.gov/main/www/popclock.html

Who They Are and What They Do

106 *"over two-thirds"* Central Intelligence Agency, "The World," *CIA World Factbook, 2010.* https://www.cia.gov/library/publications/the-world-factbook/geos/xx.html

Bulls and Bears on Wall Street

Beattie, Andrew. "A Trip through Index History." Investopedia. http://www.investopedia.com/articles/07/history-indexes.asp

Dow Jones Averages. "The Dow through History and Interactive Timeline." http://www.djaverages.com/?view=ilc

New York Stock Exchange. "Dow Jones Industrial Average History." http://www.nyse.tv/dow-jones-industrial-average-history-djia.htm

A New York Minute

Word Net. "New York Minute." http://wordnetweb.princeton.edu/perl/webwn?s=new%20york%20minute

How Many Cubic Dekameters in a Gill?

107 *"it has been slow"* Central Intelligence Agency, "Weights and Measures," *CIA World Factbook, 2010.* https://www.cia.gov/library/publications/the-world-factbook/appendix/appendix-g.html

108 *"Conversions between unit systems"* U.S. Metric Association. http://lamar.colostate.edu/~hillger/

108 *"ensure the propagation"* General Conference on Weights and Measures. http://www.bipm.org/en/convention/cgpm/

108 *"NASA lost a $125 million"* "NASA's Metric Confusion Caused Mars Orbiter Loss," CNN, September 30, 1999. http://www.cnn.com/TECH/space/9909/30/mars.metric/

Barrow, Bruce B. "Metric System." *World Book Encyclopedia*, 2009.

China Was First

108 *"The four inventions"* Deng Yinke, *Ancient Chinese Inventions*, trans. Wang Pingxing (Beijing: China Intercontinental Press, 2005), 14.

109 *"the most moving program"* "Four Great Inventions at Olympic Opening Warmly Welcomed," *People's Daily*, August 15, 2008. http://english.peopledaily.com.cn/90001/90776/6476950.html

People's Republic of China, Ministry of Culture. "Four Great Inventions of Ancient China." http://www.chinaculture.org/gb/en_aboutchina/node_137.htm

You Must See These Wonders

109 *"that had been recently revealed"* "Seven New Wonders of the World," *USA Today*, October 27, 2006.

109 *the "greatest civil engineering achievements"* American Society of Civil Engineers, "Seven Wonders of the Modern World." http://www.asce.org/history/seven_wonders.cfm

D'Epiro, Peter, and Mary Desmond Pinkowish. *What Are the Seven Wonders of the World? And 100 Other Great Cultural Lists—Fully Explicated.* New York: Doubleday, 1998.

Dreyfus and the Tour de France

McGann, Bill, and Carol McGann. *The Story of the Tour de France.* Vol. 1, *1903–1964.* Indianapolis, IN: Dog Ear, 2006.

Thompson, Christopher. *The Tour de France: A Cultural History.* Berkeley: University of California Press, 2006.

Tour de France. http://www.letour.fr/us/homepage_horscourseTDF.html

Just a Friendly Game

111 *"When they lined up"* "Gee! What a Game Is This! Ty Cobbs of the House Play Baseball," *Boston Daily Globe*, July 17, 1909.

111 *"partly as the result"* "Solons Play Ball: Minority Shows That It Can Swat the Leather," *Washington Post*, July 17, 1909.

Baseball Reference. "John Kinley Tener." http://www.baseball-reference.com/players/t/tenerjo01.shtml?redir

Clerk of the U.S. House of Representatives, Office of History and Preservation. "House History: Congressional Baseball Game." http://clerk.house.gov/art_history/house_history/baseball/index.html

Roll Call. "Congressional Baseball Game." http://www.rollcall.com/sports/baseball.html

A Freak Pitch

"Chapman Suffers Skull Fracture." *New York Times*, August 17, 1920. http://www.nytimes.com/packages/html/sports/year_in_sports/08.17.html

Sowell, Mike. *The Pitch That Killed.* New York: Macmillan, 2004.

Ward, Geoffrey, and Ken Burns. *Baseball: An Illustrated History*. New York: Alfred A. Knopf, 1996.

Uniquely True-Going in Australia

Arndt, Dinah. "Trugo, Trugo-Ing, Trugone; Death Knell for Sport." *Age*, April 1, 2009.

Murphy, Justin. "The Game of Trugo." Australian Broadcasting Corporation, August 1, 2004.

Victorian Trugo Association. Yarraville, Australia. http://home.vicnet.net.au/~vtrugo/index.html

Dying from the Heat

113 *"If the air were highly compressed"* George Chapel, "Gorrie's Fridge," Apalachicola Area Historical Society, University of Florida Department of Physics. http://www.phys.ufl.edu/~ihas/gorrie/fridge.htm

Architect of the Capitol. "National Statuary Hall Collection: John Gorrie." http://www.aoc.gov/cc/art/nsh/gorrie.cfm

Morse, Minna Scherlinder. "Chilly Reception." *Smithsonian*, July 2002. http://www.smithsonianmag.com/history-archaeology/Chilly_Reception.html?c=y&page=1

From Senusret to Suez

Suez Canal Authority. "Canal Characteristics." http://www.canal.gov.eg/sc.aspx?show=12

———. "Canal History." http://www.canal.gov.eg/sc.aspx?show=8

Can Queen Victoria Eat Cold Apple Pie?

Heiken, Grant, Renato Funicello, and Donatella de Rita. *The Seven Hills of Rome: A Geological Tour of the Eternal City* (Princeton, NJ: Princeton Univ. Press, 2005).

Squeezed into South Dakota

Janssen, Sarah, ed. *World Almanac and Book of Facts, 2010*. New York: World Almanac Books, 2010.

What Ice Can Tell Us

115 *"We're checking out"* Chaz Firestone, "Ice Hunt for Old Air," *Nature* 463 (January 27, 2010): 408. http://www.nature.com/news/2010/100127/full/463408a.html

Amos, Jonathan. "Deep Ice Tells Long Climate Story." *BBC News*, September 4, 2006. http://news.bbc.co.uk/2/hi/science/nature/5314592.stm

Byrd Polar Research Center. Ohio State University's Ice Core Paleoclimatology Research Group. http://bprc.osu.edu/Icecore/

National Oceanic and Atmospheric Administration (NOAA). Ice Core Gateway. http://www.ncdc.noaa.gov/paleo/icgate.html

"National Science Foundation's West Antarctic Ice Sheet Divide (WAIS Divide) Ice Core Project." http://www.waisdivide.unh.edu/Reference/Download.pm/621/Document

Riebeek, Holli. "Paleoclimatology: The Ice Core Record." NASA Earth Observatory, December 19, 2005. http://earthobservatory.nasa.gov/Features/Paleoclimatology_IceCores/

White, Jim. "International Greenland Ice Coring Effort Sets New Drilling Record in 2009." University of Colorado Office of News Services, August 26, 2009. http://www.colorado.edu/news/r/d293a239083e3826bcc014e5df4671f7.html

Salt and Ice

Kramer, Jim. "How Does Ice Melt?" Icenator. http://www.icenator.com/ice-melt.htm

Michigan State University. "Why Does Salt Melt Ice?" *Ask Science Theatre*. http://www.pa.msu.edu/sciencet/ask_st/030492.html

Peeples, Bob. "Using Salt to Melt Ice." MadSci Network, November 9, 1998. http://www.madsci.org/posts/archives/nov98/910675052.Ch.r.html

Ides, Kalends, and Nones

116 *"in a confusing system"* David Ewing Duncan, *Calendar: Humanity's Epic Struggle to Determine a True and Accurate Year* (New York: Avon Books, 1998), 38.

Dupont, Florence. *Daily Life in Ancient Rome*. Translated by Christopher Woodall. Malden, MA: Blackwell, 1993.

Grout, James. "The Julian Calendar." In *Encyclopaedia Romana*. University of Chicago. http://penelope.uchicago.edu/~grout/encyclopaedia_romana/calendar/juliancalendar.html

As Time Goes By

117 *"Unfortunately, no U.S. Web page"* U.S. Naval Observatory, Time Service Department. http://tycho.usno.navy.mil/tzones.html

Map of World Time Zones. http://www.timezoneguide.com/tzmap.php

Military and Civilian Time Designations. "Greenwich Mean Time." https://www.greenwichmeantime.com/info/timezone.htm

National Institute of Standards and Technology, Time and Frequency Division. http://tf.nist.gov/

TZ Database. "Sources for Time Zone and Daylight Saving Time Data." http://www.twinsun.com/tz/tz-link.htm

"Standard Time." *United States Code*. Title 15, *Commerce and Trade*, chapter 6, subchapter 9. http://tycho.usno.navy.mil/260.html

I Can't See for Miles

117 *"letters, however small and dim"* American Association for the Advancement of Science, "Physical Science in the Time of Nero," in *Science* (New York: Science Press, 1910), 32:515. http://books.google.com/books?id=GpICAAAAYAAJ&pg=PA515&dq=seneca+globe+books&cd=7#v=onepage&q=seneca%20globe%20books&f=false

117 *"glass lenses for spectacles"* Jose M. Vaquero and M. Vazquez, *The Sun Recorded through History* (New York: Springer, 2009), 104.

Chilvers, Ian, ed. "Tomaso da Modena." In *The Oxford Dictionary of Art*. New York: Oxford Univ. Press, 2004. http://www.enotes.com/oxford-art-encyclopedia/tomaso-da-modena

Drewry, Richard D. "What Man Devised That He Might See." Teagle Optometry. http://www.teagleoptometry.com/history.htm

A Sticky Syndrome

118 *"a condition resulting"* Society of American Archivists, "Sticky Shed Syndrome." http://www.archivists.org/glossary/term_details.asp?DefinitionKey=3071

118 *"sticky tape damage"* Library of Congress, "Sticky Shed Syndrome in Magnetic Tapes: Characterization, Diagnosis, and Treatment." Preservation Research Projects. http://www.loc.gov/preserv/rt/projects/sticky_shed.html

Ciletti, Eddie. "If I Knew You Were Coming I'd Have Baked a Tape," 1998. http://www.tangible-technology.com/tape/baking1.html

———. "Sleep Like an Egyptian." *Mix*, July 1, 2002. http://mixonline.com/mag/audio_sleep_egyptian/index.html

Rarey, Rich. "Baking Old Tapes Is a Recipe for Success." *Radio World*, October 1995. Part 1: http://euonline.org/members/reprints/baketap1.htm. Part 2: http://euonline.org/members/reprints/baketap2.htm

Rivers, Mike. "Baking Magnetic Tape to Overcome the Sticky-Shed Syndrome." Audio Restoration. http://www.audio-restoration.com/baking.php

8. UGLY BAGS OF MOSTLY WATER

All Pongidae

Brown, David. "Among Many Peoples, Little Genomic Variety," *Washington Post*, June 22, 2009.

Pritchard, Jonathan, et al. "The Role of Geography in Human Adaptation." *PLoS* [Public Library of Science] *Genetics*, June 2009. http://www.plosgenetics.org/article/info%3Adoi%2F10.1371%2Fjournal.pgen.1000500

Wilson, Don, and DeeAnn Reeder, eds. "Hominoidea." In *Mammal Species of the World*. 3rd ed. Baltimore: Johns Hopkins Univ. Press, 2005. http://www.bucknell.edu/msw3/browse.asp?id=12100786

Take Me to Your Insect

Entomological Society of America. "Insect Trivia." http://www.entsoc.org/resources/faq.htm

Smithsonian Institution. "Number of Insects (Species and Individuals)." Bug Info Index. *Encyclopedia Smithsonian*. http://www.si.edu/Encyclopedia_SI/nmnh/buginfo/bugnos.htm

Enlightened Beetles

Museum of Science (Boston). "Firefly Watch." https://www.mos.org/fireflywatch/

Ohio State University. "The Firefly Files." C. A. Triplehorn Insect Collection. http://iris.biosci.ohio-state.edu/projects/FFiles/

Thanks for the Topsoil

121 *"intestines of the earth"* Thomas Taylor, *The Treatises of Aristotle* (London: Robert Wilks, 1808), 371.

121 *"dramatically alter soil structure"* Clive Edwards, "Soil Biology: Earthworms," U.S. Department of Agriculture, Natural Resources Conservation Service. http://soils.usda.gov/SQI/concepts/soil_biology/earthworms.html

Earthworm Digest. http://www.wormdigest.org

Parrack, Keely. "The Mighty Worm." *Christian Science Monitor*, June 21, 2005.

Big Ugly Birds

121 *"iconic . . . worshipped and despised"* John Nielsen, *Condor: To the Brink and Back—the Life and Times of One Giant Bird* (New York: HarperCollins, 2006), 1.

Zoological Society of San Diego. "California Condor Conservation." http://cacondorconservation.org/index.cfm

Beautiful Little Butterflies

De Pencier, Nick. "The Incredible Journey of the Butterflies." *Nova*. PBS, January 27, 2009. http://www.pbs.org/wgbh/nova/butterflies/

Kansas Biological Survey. *Monarch Watch*. University of Kansas. http://www.monarchwatch.org/

Young, Allen. "Monarch Butterfly Is Ideal National Symbol." Letter to the editor. *New York Times*, August 22, 1987.

A Monotreme Mammal

Australian Platypus Conservancy. "The Platypus." http://www.platypus.asn.au/

Pettigrew, John. "Electroreception in Monotremes." *Journal of Experimental Biology* 202 (1999): 1447–1454. http://jeb.biologists.org/cgi/reprint/202/10/1447.pdf

Tasmania Department of Primary Industries, Parks, Water, and Environment. "Platypus: Introduction to an Iconic Mammal." http://www.dpiw.tas.gov.au/inter.nsf/WebPages/BHAN-53573T?open (includes video and audio of platypus)

University of Tasmania. "The Platypus." http://www.medicine.utas.edu.au/research/mono/Platpage.html

A Horse of a Different Color

Carey, Stefanie. "The Seahorse." Microscopy-UK. http://www.microscopy-uk.org.uk/mag/artnov06macro/sc-macro.html

International Institute for Species Exploration. "Top 10 New Species, 2009." Arizona State University. http://species.asu.edu/2009_species03

Jones, Adam G. "Pipefish and Seahorse Research." Texas A&M University. http://www.bio.tamu.edu/USERS/ajones/seahorse.html

"Kingdom of the Seahorse." *Nova*. PBS, April 15, 1997. http://www.pbs.org/wgbh/nova/seahorse/

University of British Columbia. "Project Seahorse." http://seahorse.fisheries.ubc.ca/

American Dromedaries

Lesley, Lewis. *Uncle Sam's Camels*. Cambridge, MA: Harvard Univ. Press, 1929.

U.S. Army Transportation Museum. "The U.S. Army Camel Corps, 1855–1866." http://www.transchool.eustis.army.mil/museum/transportation%20museum/camel.htm

Grunting Cows

International Union for Conservation of Nature and Natural Resources. "*Bos Mutus*." IUCN Red List of Threatened Species, version 2009.1. http://www.iucnredlist.org/details/2892/0

International Yak Society. http://www.iyak.us/

Taylor, C. Richard. "Yaks." *World Book Encyclopedia*, 2009.

Ultimate Ungulates. "*Bos Grunniens*: Fact Sheet." http://www.ultimateungulate.com/Artiodactyla/Bos_grunniens.html

"Yak Racing Held in Quinghai Tibetan-Inhabited Area." *China Tibet Online*, July 7, 2009. http://chinatibet.people.com.cn/6694772.html

Crossbred Dogs

Dog Breed Info Center. "Coydog." http://www.dogbreedinfo.com/coydog.htm

Flaim, Denise. "Hybrids Cross Popular Notions." *Newsday*, May 8, 2006.

Birds of War

125 *"The Pharaohs of Egypt"* Jeffrey Ulbrich, "H-Tech French Army Still Has Faithful Pigeons," Associated Press, December 13, 1985.

125 *"is a large, bronze medallion"* People's Dispensary for Sick Animals, "Pigeons Role of Honour." http://www.pdsa.org.uk/page309_3.html

Blume, Mary. "The Hallowed History of the Carrier Pigeon." *New York Times*, January 30, 2004.

"Switzerland's Army Disbands Carrier Pigeon Service." Associated Press, July 3, 1996.

Ugly Bags of Mostly Water

125 *"Because of nature's water cycle"* Thomas Keinath, "Water," *World Book Encyclopedia*, 2009.

Southwestern Water Conservation District. "Water Facts." http://www.waterinfo.org/resources/water-facts

Water. "Water Facts." http://water.org/facts

The Chemistry of Humans

Schirber, Michael. "The Chemistry of Life: The Human Body." *Live Science*, April 16, 2009. http://www.livescience.com/health/090416-cl-human-body.html

How the Nose Knows

Flatow, Ira. "Smell." *Talk of the Nation, Science Friday*. NPR, March 10, 2000. http://www.sciencefriday.com/pages/2000/Mar/hour2_031000.html

Gawker Media. New York City Subway Smells Map. http://gawker.com/maps/smell/

Olfactory Biosciences. Olfactory Perception Altering Technologies. Noxo. http://www.noxoinfo.com/

Sense of Smell Institute. "Smell 101: How Does the Sense of Smell Work?" http://www.senseofsmell.org/feature/smell101/lesson1/01.php

Cleanliness Was Next to Impossible

127 *"cleannesse of bodie"* Francis Bacon, *The Advancement of Learning* (Sioux Falls, SD: NuVision, 2005), 112.

128 *"During the mid-1960s"* Suellen Hoy, "Hygiene, Personal," in *The Oxford Companion to United States History*, ed. Paul S. Boyer (New York: Oxford Univ. Press, 2001), 356.

Bushman, Richard, and Claudia Bushman, "The Early History of Cleanliness in America," *Journal of American History* 74, no. 4 (March 1988): 1213–1238.

Hoy, Suellen. *Chasing Dirt: The American Pursuit of Cleanliness*. New York: Oxford Univ. Press, 1995.

Scrubbing Bubbles

Bower, Lynn Marie. "Basic Housekeeping: Soaps vs. Detergents." Housekeeping Channel. http://www.housekeepingchannel.com/a_767-Soaps_Vs._Detergents

Karr, Paul. "Detergent and Soap." *World Book Encyclopedia*, 2009.

Soap and Detergent Association. "Soap History." http://www.sdahq.org/cleaning/history/

Wine as Ancient Health Food

129 *"ancient Egyptians settled on"* Jennifer Viegas, "Herbal Wines Healed Ancient Egyptians," *Discovery News*, April 14, 2009. http://dsc.discovery.com/news/2009/04/14/egyptian-wine.html

129 *"Wine is fit for man"* University of Pennsylvania Museum of Archaeology and Anthropology, "5100-Year-Old Chemical Evidence for Ancient Medicinal Remedies Discovered in Ancient Egyptian Wine Jars," May 26, 2009. http://penn.museum/press-releases/164–5100-year-old-chemical-evidence-for-ancient-medicinal-remedies-discovered-in-ancient-egyptian-wine-jars.html

McGovern, Patrick E., Armen Mirzoian, and Gretchen R. Hall. "Ancient Egyptian Herbal Wines." *Proceedings of the National Academy of Sciences* 106, no. 18 (May 5, 2009): 7361–7366. http://www.pnas.org/content/106/18/7361.full

Todt, Ron. "Study: Herbs Added to 5,100-Year-Old Egyptian Wine," Associated Press, April 13, 2009.

Ah-Choo!

129 *"Everyone knows the first signs"* National Institutes of Health, Institute of Allergy and Infectious Diseases. "Common Cold." http://www3.niaid.nih.gov/topics/commonCold

129 *"people often catch cold"* Library of Congress. "Benjamin Franklin: In His Own Words." http://www.loc.gov/exhibits/treasures/franklin-scientist.html

McCoy, Lori. "Rhinovirus: An Unstoppable Cause of the Common Cold." *Science Creative Quarterly*, August 2004. http://www.scq.ubc.ca/rhinovirus-an-unstoppable-cause-of-the-common-cold/

Ellis, Harold. "Review of *Cold Wars: The Fight against the Common Cold* by David Tyrrell and Michael Fielder." *British Medical Journal*, January 4, 2003.

The Deadliest Virus

Page 130 image: transmission micrograph of the Ebola virus. Hemorrhagic fever, RNA virus. Photo credit: Dr. Frederick A. Murphy. Content providers: CDC/Dr. Frederick A. Murphy, 1976.

130 *"Although Yambuku would seem"* Joseph McCormick, Susan Fisher-Hoch, and Leslie Alan Horvitz, *Level 4: Virus Hunters of the CDC* (New York: Barnes and Noble, 1996), 55.

130 *"Death comes from a combination"* Jason S. Bardi, "Death Called a River," *News and Views Weekly*, Scripps Research Institute, January 14, 2002. http://www.scripps.edu/newsandviews/e_20020114/ebola1.html

King, John W. "Ebola Virus." Web MD, April 2, 2008. http://emedicine.medscape.com/article/216288-overview

Lather, Rinse, Repeat

130 *"Several hair specialists"* "How to Shampoo the Hair," *New York Times*, May 10, 1908. http://query.nytimes.com/mem/archive-free/pdf?_r=2&res=9904E5DA143EE233A25753C1A9639C946997D6CF

131 *"If you wash your hair"* Allison Aubrey, "When It Comes to Shampoo, Less Is More," *Morning Edition*, NPR, March 19, 2009. http://www.npr.org/templates/story/story.php?storyId=102062969&ps=rs

Masterson, Kathleen. "Engineering a Good Hair Day." NPR, March 18, 2009. http://www.npr.org/templates/story/story.php?storyId=102067582

Plasticized Hair

131 *Hairspray is "a solution"* Fred Senese, "What Is Hairspray Made Of?" General Chemistry Online, Frostburg (Maryland) State University. http://antoine.frostburg.edu/chem/senese/101/consumer/faq/hairspray-ingredients.shtml

Arizona State University. International Institute for Species Exploration. http://species.asu.edu/2009_species10

Environmental Working Group. "Cancer in a Can: What the Chemical Industry Kept Secret about Vinyl Chloride in Hair Spray." *Chemical Industry Archives*, March 27, 2009. http://www.chemicalindustryarchives.org/dirtysecrets/hairspray/1.asp

"Hairspray Is Linked to Common Genital Birth Defect, Says Study." *Health and Medicine Week*, December 8, 2008.

"New Angiosarcoma Research from George Washington University Outlined." *Cancer Weekly*, March 24, 2009.

"New Bacteria Contaminate Hairspray." *Health and Medicine Week*, March 17, 2008.

Zzzzzzz

132 *"eight sweet hours"* Patrick L. Barry and Tony Phillips, "NASA-Supported Sleep Researchers Are Learning New and Surprising Things about Naps," Science at NASA, June 3, 2005. http://science.nasa.gov/headlines/y2005/03jun_naps.htm

132 *"Don't think you will be"* Jennifer Fisher Wilson, "Night Terrors: What Happens When We Sleep, What Happens When We Don't, and Why Naps Are Good," *TheSmart Set* (Drexel University), January 31, 2008. http://www.thesmartset.com/article/article01310801.aspx

Harvard Medical School, Division of Sleep Medicine. "Healthy Sleep." http://healthysleep.med.harvard.edu/

National Sleep Foundation. "Napping." http://www.sleepfoundation.org/article/sleep-topics/napping

Rosekind, M. R., et al. "Alertness Management: Strategic Naps in Operational Settings." *Journal of the Sleep Research Society*, 1995. http://human-factors.arc.nasa.gov/zteam/PDF_pubs/strat_naps.pdf

Calculus: Mouth, Not Math

American Dental Association. "Oral Health Topics: Plaque." http://www.ada.org/public/topics/plaque.asp

University of Leeds Dental Institute. "Introduction to Dental Plaque." http://www.dentistry.leeds.ac.uk/OROFACE/PAGES/micro/micro2.html

Web MD. "Oral Health Guide: Plaque and Your Teeth." http://www.webmd.com/oral-health/guide/plaque-and-your-teeth

Face Bugs

Conniff, Richard. "Body Beasts: No Man Is an Island, He Is an Ecosystem." *National Geographic*, December 1998. http://ngm.nationalgeographic.com/ngm/9812/fngm/index.html

Roque, Manolette R., and Barbara L. Roque. "Demodicosis." Web MD, April 7, 2008. http://emedicine.medscape.com/article/1203895-overview

Umar, M. Halit. "Demodex: An Inhabitant of Human Hair Follicles, and a Mite Which We Live with in Harmony." *Micscape*, May 2000. http://www.microscopy-uk.org.uk/mag/indexmag.html?http://www.microscopy-uk.org.uk/mag/artmay00/demodex.html

Worsley School. "Eyelash Creatures." http://www.worsleyschool.net/science/files/eyelash/creatures.html

9. THE WILD BLUE YONDER AND WHAT'S BELOW

Solar Circle

134 *"consisted of four concentric circles"* Madhusree Mukerjee, "Circles for Space, German 'Stonehenge' Marks Oldest Observatory," *Scientific American*, December 8, 2003. http://www.scientificamerican.com/article.cfm?id=circles-for-space

135 *"When the site was finally opened"* Ulrich Boser, "Solar Circle," *Archaeology* 59, no. 4 (July–August 2006): 31.

Boser, Ulrich. "Solar Circle." *Archaeology* 59, no. 4 (July–August 2006): 30–35.

The First Sky Map

135 *"These symbols are part of"* "Secrets of the Star Disk," BBC, January 29, 2004. http://www.bbc.co.uk/science/horizon/2004/stardisctrans.shtml

Cramer, Anna. "The World Is a Disk: The Sky Disk of Nebra, Germany's 3600-Year-Old Astronomical Clock." *German Life* 14, no. 5 (February–March 2008).

Mukerjee, Madhusree. "Circles for Space: German 'Stonehenge' Marks Oldest Observatory." *Scientific American*, December 8, 2003. http://www.scientificamerican.com/article.cfm?id=circles-for-space

The Wild Blue Yonder

136 *"I do not know"* John Tyndall, *New Fragments* (New York: Appleton, 1896), 232.

136 *"All religious theories"* John Tyndall, "Address Delivered before the British Association Assembled at Belfast, with Additions 1874." Victorian Web. http://www.victorianweb.org/science/science_texts/belfast.html

Athenaeum. "John Tyndall." http://www.lexicorps.com/Tyndall.htm

"John Tyndall." *World of Scientific Discovery*. Farmington Hills, MI: Gale, 2006. Reproduced in *Biography Resource Center*. Farmington Hills, MI: Gale, 2009.

NASA Earth Observatory. "John Tyndall (1820–1893)." http://earthobservatory.nasa.gov/Features/Tyndall/

We Are Not Alone

137 *"the idea of the universe"* Michael D. Lemonick, "The Time 100: Edwin Hubble," *Time*, March 29, 1999. http://www.time.com/time/magazine/article/0,9171,990615,00.html

137 *"the velocity at which"* Peter Coles, ed., *The Routledge Companion to the New Cosmology* (London: Routledge, 2001), 10.

137 *"has revolutionized astronomy"* NASA, "The Hubble Space Telescope." http://hubble.nasa.gov/

137 *"Equipped with his five senses"* Edwin P. Hubble, *The Nature of Science and Other Lectures* (San Marino, CA: Huntington Library, 1954).

Englebert, Phillis, ed. "Edwin Hubble." *Astronomy and Space: From the Big Bang to the Big Crunch*. Detroit, MI: U*X*L, 2008. Reproduced in *Biography Resource Center*. Farmington Hills, MI: Gale, 2009.

Hubble, Edwin. "A Relation between Distance and Radial Velocity among Extra-Galactic Nebulae." *Proceedings of the National Academy of Sciences* 15, no. 3 (January 17, 1929).

National Aeronautics and Space Administration. Hubble Site. http://hubblesite.org/

Space Fireflies

137 *"I am in a big mass"* NASA Manned Spacecraft Center, "Results of the First U.S. Manned Orbital Space Flight, February 20, 1962," 161, 195–196. http://www.jsc.nasa.gov/history/mission_trans/MA06_TEC.PDF

138 *"The 'fireflies' reported"* Gene Kranz, *Failure Is Not an Option* (New York: Simon and Schuster, 2000), 91.

Space Junk

138 *"for miles and miles"* Eric M. Jones, "EVA-2 Closeout and the Golf Shots," *Apollo 14 Lunar Surface Journal*, 1995. http://history.nasa.gov/alsj/a14/a14.clsout2.html

139 *"collision with even a small piece"* NASA Orbital Debris Program Office. http://www.orbitaldebris.jsc.nasa.gov/faqs.html

Broad, William. "Orbiting Junk, Once a Nuisance, Is Now a Threat." *New York Times*, February 6, 2007.

Madrigal, Alexis. "How to Track Space Junk Online." *Wired*, March 12, 2009. http://www.wired.com/wiredscience/2009/03/howtojunk/

Terrill, Delbert, Jr. "Project West Ford [Project Needles]." In *The Air Force Role in Developing International Outer Space Law*. Maxwell Air Force Base, AL: Air University Press, 1999.

Balanced in Space

139 *"five special points"* National Aeronautics and Space Administration, "The Lagrange Points." http://map.gsfc.nasa.gov/mission/observatory_l2.html

139 *"producing our new Standard Model"* Wilkinson Microwave Anisotropy Probe. http://map.gsfc.nasa.gov/

139 *"freeway in space"* National Aeronautics and Space Administration, "Interplanetary Superhighway Makes Space Travel Simpler," July 17, 2002. http://www.nasa.gov/mission_pages/genesis/media/jpl-release-071702.html

European Space Agency. "What Are Lagrange Points?" February 12, 2009. http://www.esa.int/esaSC/SEMM17XJD1E_index_0.html

Grossman, Lisa. "Why Future Astronauts May Be Sent to 'Gravity Holes.'" *New Scientist*, August 29, 2009. http://www.newscientist.com/article/dn17713-why-future-astronauts-may-be-sent-to-gravity-holes.html

National Aeronautics and Space Administration. "The James Webb Space Telescope." http://www.jwst.nasa.gov/

A Thing High Up

140 *"heated to incandescence"* National Aeronautics and Space Administration, "Solar System: Meteors and Meteorites." http://solarsystem.nasa.gov/planets/profile.cfm?Object=Meteors&Display=OverviewLong

140 *"a thing high up"* "Meteor," *Online Etymology Dictionary*. http://www.etymonline.com/index.php?term=meteor

International Meteor Organization. "Glossary." http://www.imo.net/glossary

Jenniskens, Peter. "Meteor." *World Book Encyclopedia*, 2009.

The Costliest, Deadliest, and Most Intense

Blake, Eric, and Edward Rappaport. *The Deadliest, Costliest, and Most Intense United States Tropical Cyclones from 1851 to 2006*. Miami: National Weather Service, 2007. http://www.nhc.noaa.gov/pdf/NWS-TPC-5.pdf

National Weather Service. National Hurricane Center. http://www.nhc.noaa.gov/

The Same, Only Different

141 *a "non-frontal synoptic scale"* NOAA Hurricane Research Division. "What Is a Hurricane, Typhoon, or Tropical Cyclone?" http://www.aoml.noaa.gov/hrd/tcfaq/A1.html

Emanuel, Kerry A. "Hurricane." *World Book Encyclopedia*, 2009.

NASA Goddard Space Flight Center. "Hurricane, Typhoon and Tropical Cyclone Tracking." http://gcmd.nasa.gov/records/Storm_Tracking.html

The Great London Fog

142 *"It had a yellow tinge"* "Days of Toxic Darkness," *BBC News*, December 5, 2002. http://news.bbc.co.uk/2/hi/uk_news/2542315.stm

142 *"The association between health"* Michelle L. Bell, Devra L. Davis, and Tony Fletcher, "A Retrospective Assessment of Mortality from the London Smog Episode of 1952: The Role of Influenza and Pollution," *Environmental Health Perspectives* 11, no. 1 (January 2004): 6. http://www.ehponline.org/members/2003/6539/6539.pdf

Environmental Institute of Houston. "The History of Air Quality." http://prtl.uhcl.edu/portal/page/portal/EIH/archives/projects/TFORS/history

Nielsen, John. "The Killer Fog of '52." *All Things Considered.* NPR, December 11, 2002. http://www.npr.org/templates/story/story.php?storyId=873954

"1952: London Fog Clears after Days of Chaos." *On This Day* (9 December). BBC. http://news.bbc.co.uk/onthisday/hi/dates/stories/december/9/newsid_4506000/4506390.stm

U.K. National Weather Service. "Case Study: The Great Smog of 1952." http://www.metoffice.gov.uk/education/teens/casestudy_great_smog.html

Plastic Soup

142 *"Marine debris is"* National Oceanic and Atmospheric Administration, "Marine Debris." http://marinedebris.noaa.gov/info/welcome.html

142 *"In the week"* Robin McKie, "Eco-Warrior Sets Sail to Save Oceans from 'Plastic Death,'" *Observer*, April 12, 2009.

143 *"It's a swirling"* Marco R. Della Cava, "Birds, Boats Threatened by Great Garbage Patch," *USA Today*, November 19, 2009.

143 *"If it's calm"* Alison Stewart, "Garbage Mass Is Growing in the Pacific," *The Bryant Park Project*, NPR, March 26, 2008.

Algalita Marine Research Foundation. http://www.algalita.org/

Arthur, Courtney, Joel Baker, and Holly Bamford, eds. *Proceedings of the International Research Workshop on the Occurrence, Effects, and Fate of Microplastic Marine Debris, September 9–11, 2008* (University of Washington, Tacoma). Silver Spring, MD: NOAA, 2009. http://marinedebris.noaa.gov/projects/pdfs/Microplastics.pdf

Chick, Kristen. "The Pacific Isn't the Only Ocean Collecting Plastic Trash." *Christian Science Monitor*, June 19, 2009.

Greenpeace. "The Trash Vortex." http://www.greenpeace.org/international/campaigns/oceans/pollution/trash-vortex%20

Hoshaw, Lindsey. "Afloat in the Ocean: Expanding Islands of Trash." *New York Times*, November 10, 2009.

The Measure of Great Rivers

143 *"constantly changing"* National Park Service, "Mississippi River Facts." http://www.nps.gov/miss/riverfacts.htm

144 *"compared to other"* National Park Service, "Missouri National Recreational River." http://www.nps.gov/mnrr/index.htm

144 *"cannot be tamed"* Mark Twain, *Life on the Mississippi*, 1883, quoted in Sandi Zellmer and Christine Klein, "Mississippi River Stories: Lessons from a Century of Unnatural Disasters," *SMU* [Southern Methodist University] *Law Review* 60: 1492. http://digitalcommons.unl.edu/cgi/viewcontent.cgi?article=1012&context=lawfacpub

U.S. Army Corps of Engineers. "Missouri River Basin Water Management Information." http://www.nwdmr.usace.army.mil/rcc/index.html

U.S. Geological Survey. "Lengths of the Major Rivers." http://ga.water.usgs.gov/edu/riversofworld.html

———. "Missouri River Water Information Portal." http://ne.water.usgs.gov/missouririverwq/index.html

Minuscule Blooms

Caughey, Andrea. "Munch a Bunch of Wolffia: Thimble Full after Thimble Full, the Wildflower Packs a Punch." *San Diego Union-Tribune*, November 15, 1984.

Library of Congress Science Reference Services. "Everyday Mysteries." http://www.loc.gov/rr/scitech/mysteries/smallestflower.html

Missouri Botanical Garden. "Practical Duckweed." http://www.mobot.org/jwcross/duckweed/practical_duckweed.htm

Washington State Department of Ecology. "Free-Floating Plants." http://www.ecy.wa.gov/programs/wq/plants/plantid2/descriptions/wol.html

Water Gardeners International. "The Genus Wolffia." http://www.victoria-adventure.org/aquatic_plants/wolffia/page1.html

Giant Meat Flowers

144 *"More bizarre than beautiful"* Edward Ross, "*Rafflesia*: The Super Flower," *California Wild*, Summer 2003. http://researcharchive.calacademy.org/calwild/2003summer/stories/rafflesia.html

Library of Congress Science Reference Services. "Everyday Mysteries." http://www.loc.gov/rr/scitech/mysteries/flower.html

Southern Illinois University Department of Plant Biology. "*Rafflesia Arnoldii*." Parasitic Plant Connection. http://www.parasiticplants.siu.edu/Rafflesiaceae/Raff.arn.page.html

Ancient Evergreens

145 *"can live for more"* World Wildlife Fund, "Ancient Alerces: 3,000 Year Old Trees and Other Marvels." http://www.worldwildlife.org/what/wherewework/southernchile/index.html

145 *"The reddish brown wood"* Gymnosperm Database, "*Fitzroya Cupressoides*." http://www.conifers.org/cu/fi/

ARKive. "Alerce (*Fitzroya Cupressoides*)." http://www.arkive.org/alerce/fitzroya-cupressoides/info.html

Conservation Land Trust. http://www.theconservationlandtrust.org/eng/proyectos_pumalin.htm

Enciclopedia de la Flora Chilena. "*Fitzroya Cupressoides* (Alerce)." http://www.florachilena.cl/Niv_tax/Gimnospermas/Cupressaceae/Fitzroya/Fitzroya.htm

Park Pumalín. http://www.parquepumalin.cl/content/eng/index.htm

Herbal Remedies Used Up

146 *"among the most precious gifts"* Pliny the Elder, "Laser: Thirty-nine Remedies," in *The Natural History*, ed. John Bostock, vol. 22, *The Properties of Plants and Fruits* (Medford, MA: Tufts University Perseus Digital Library, n.d.), n.p. http://www.perseus.tufts.edu/hopper/text?doc=Perseus%3Atext%3A1999.02.0137%3Abook%3D22%3Achapter%3D49

146 *"We have so many sure-fire drugs"* John M. Riddle, *Contraception and Abortion from the Ancient World to the Renaissance* (Cambridge, MA: Harvard University Press, 1992), 25.

Tatman, John. "Silphium: Ancient Wonder Drug?" John Jencek Ancient Coins and Antiquities. http://ancient-coins.com/resourcedetail.asp?rsc=8

Killer Weed

146 *"snuffed, chewed, drunk"* Walter, Mariko Namba, and Eva Jane Neumann Fridman, *Shamanism: An Encyclopedia of World Beliefs, Practices, and Culture* (Santa Barbara, CA: ABC-CLIO, 2004), 2:388.

146 *"Their bodies are notably preserved"* Sander L. Gilman and Xun Zhou, eds., *Smoke: A Global History of Smoking* (London: Reaktion Books, 2004), 11.

146 *"tobacco was either grown"* Jordan Goodman, *Tobacco in History: The Cultures of Dependence* (London: Routledge, 1994), 36.

147 *"Only the mode of delivery"* Judith Mackay and Michael Eriksen, *The Tobacco Atlas* (Geneva, Switzerland: World Health Organization, 2002), 18. http://whqlibdoc.who.int/publications/2002/9241562099.pdf

Billings, E. R. *Tobacco: Its History, Varieties, Culture, Manufacture and Commerce.* Hartford, CT: American, 1875. http://www.gutenberg.org/files/24471/24471-h/24471-h.htm

Borio, Gene. "The Tobacco Timeline." http://www.tobacco.org/History/Tobacco_History.html

Lawrence, Ghislaine. "Tobacco Smoke Enemas." *Lancet* 359, no. 9315 (April 20, 2002): 1442.

Random Facts. "Forty Random Facts about Smoking." http://facts.randomhistory.com/2009/02/17_smoking.html

Wilbert, Johannes. *Tobacco and Shamanism in South America.* New Haven, CT: Yale Univ. Press, 1987.

The Wine of the Bean

Buzby, Jean, and Stephen Haley. "Coffee Consumption over the Last Century." *Amber Waves*, June 2007. http://www.ers.usda.gov/AmberWaves/June07/PDF/Coffee2.pdf

Coffee Research Institute. "Coffee History." http://www.coffeeresearch.org/coffee/history.htm

National Geographic. "Coffee: Beyond the Buzz." http://www.nationalgeographic.com/coffee/ax/frame.html

U.S. Department of Agriculture. "Food Availability (per Capita) Data System." http://www.ers.usda.gov/Data/FoodConsumption/

The Drink of the Gods

148 *"a combination of"* William I. Lengeman, "Confessions of a Reluctant Yerba Mate Drinker," *Epicurean.* http://www.epicurean.com/articles/yerba-mate.html

Aviva Yerba Mate. http://www.yerba-mate.com/yerbamate.htm

Conis, Elena. "Yerba Mate: Sip, Don't Gulp; Consuming a Lot of the Tea May Bring a Higher Risk of Certain Cancers." *Los Angeles Times*, March 16, 2009.

My Mate World. http://www.mymateworld.com/

Yerba Mate Association of the Americas. http://www.yerbamateassociation.org/index.php

Fruit or Vegetable?

Giant Watermelons. http://www.giantwatermelons.com/

"It's Official: Watermelon Is the State Veggie." *Oklahoman*, April 25, 2007.

National Watermelon Association. http://www.nationalwatermelonassociation.com/

National Watermelon Promotion Board. http://www.watermelon.org/watermelon_funfacts.asp

Produce Oasis. "Watermelons." http://www.produceoasis.com/Items_folder/Fruits/Watermelon.html

Roach, John. "Watermelon Juice May Be the Next 'Green' Fuel." *National Geographic News*, August 28, 2009.

"Square Fruit Stuns Japanese Shoppers." *BBC News*, June 15, 2001. http://news.bbc.co.uk/2/hi/asia-pacific/1390088.stm

USDA Agricultural Research Service. "Biofuel Research: Watermelon, Using Everything for Food and Fuel." http://www.ars.usda.gov/Research/docs.htm?docid=17470

USDA Natural Resources Conservation Service. http://plants.usda.gov/java/profile?symbol=CILAL

Watermelon Thump in Luling, Texas. http://www.watermelonthump.com/

Pink and White Petals

National Cherry Blossom Festival. "History of the Trees and the Festival." http://nationalcherryblossomfestival.org/cms/index.php?id=574

National Park Service. "History of the Cherry Trees." http://www.nps.gov/cherry/cherry-blossom-history.htm

Glistening Ice Plants

149 *"glistening, hairlike parts"* George Yatskievych, "Ice Plant," *World Book Encyclopedia*, 2009.

149 *"main impacts are"* Global Invasive Species Database, "*Carpobrotus Edulis.*" http://www.issg.org/database/species/ecology.asp?si=1010&fr=1&sts=

Do It Yourself. "Ice Plants Can Dominate Your Landscape." http://www.doityourself.com/stry/ice-plants-can-dominate-your-landscape

Duncombe, Pete. "Ice Plants." Cactus and Succulent Society of America. http://www.cssainc.org/index.php?option=com_content&task=view&id=234&Itemid=212

Garden Web. "Planting Ice Plants, If and When." *Southwestern Gardening Forum.* http://forums.gardenweb.com/forums/load/swest/msg0817422226773.html

Lithops. http://www.lithops.info

USDA Natural Resources Conservation Service. "Carpobrotus Chilensis (Sea Fig)" *Plants Profile.* http://plants.usda.gov/java/profile?symbol=CACH38

———. "Mesembryanthemum Crystallinum L. (Common Iceplant)." *Plants Profile.* http://plants.usda.gov/java/profile?symbol=MECR3

The Tiniest Park

150 *"the only leprechaun colony"* Portland Parks and Recreation, "Mill Ends Park." http://www.portlandonline.com/parks/finder/index.cfm?PropertyID=265&action=ViewPark

Anderson, Jennifer. "Stumptown Stumper." *Portland Tribune*, August 25, 2006.

An Uncommon Park

City of Boston. "Freedom Trail: Boston Common." http://www.cityofboston.gov/FreedomTrail/bostoncommon.asp

"History of Boston Common." *Boston Globe*, September 30, 2007. http://www.boston.com/news/local/massachusetts/articles/2007/09/30/history_of_boston_common/

Consuming Minerals

151 *a "naturally occurring"* U.S. Geological Survey. "Mineral Facts and FAQs." Western Mineral Resources Science Center. http://minerals.usgs.gov/west/factfaq.htm

Minerals Information Institute. "Every American Born Will Need . . .," May 2009. http://mii.org/pdfs/2009miiMineralsBaby.pdf

A Barrel of Energy

151 *"measures the disappearance"* "U.S. Weekly Product Supplied." *Topics for Petroleum Consumption/Sales.* http://tonto.eia.doe.gov/dnav/pet/pet_cons_top.asp

U.S. Energy Information Administration. "Gasoline Facts." http://tonto.eia.doe.gov/ask/gasoline_faqs.asp

———. "Oil (Petroleum) Basics." http://tonto.eia.doe.gov/kids/energy.cfm?page=oil_home-basics

Oil Futures

152 *"those quantities of petroleum"* Central Intelligence Agency, "Country Comparison: Oil—Proved Reserves," *CIA World Factbook, 2010.* https://www.cia.gov/library/publications/the-world-factbook/rankorder/2178rank.html

Swann, Richard. "BP Report Sees New 'Center of Gravity' for World Energy." *Platt's Oilgram News*, June 11, 2009.

Sweet Medicines

152 *"the heating of coal"* "Coal Tar," *Encyclopedia Britannica*, vol. 3, 15th ed., 2003.

152 *"by causing the skin"* Web MD, "Coal Tar Topical Uses." http://www.webmd.com/drugs/mono-1056-COAL+TAR+-+TOPICAL.aspx?drugid=4183&drugname=coal+tar+top

"Coal Tar." *The Columbia Encyclopedia*. 6th ed., 2008.

What's in Your Food?

152 *"People have been using"* USDA Food Safety and Inspection Service, "Additives in Meat and Poultry Products." http://www.fsis.usda.gov/fact_sheets/Additives_in_Meat_&_Poultry_Products/index.asp

Center for Science in the Public Interest. "Food Additives." http://www.cspinet.org/reports/chemcuisine.htm

Nutrition Data. "Food Additives." http://www.nutritiondata.com/topics/food-additives

Part Three: On Imagination, Poetry, and Art

155 *"Imagination, from which comes"* Jean Le Rond d'Alembert, *Preliminary Discourse to the Encyclopedia of Diderot*, trans. Richard N. Schwab (Chicago: Univ. of Chicago Press, 1995), 156.

10. PERFECT CIRCLES

The Start of Art

157 *"reached a level"* John Ives Sewell, *A History of Western Art* (New York: Holt, Rinehart & Winston, 1963), 13–14.

158 *"the earliest unequivocal evidence"* Laura Anne Tedesco, "Lascaux (ca. 15,000 B.C.)," *Heilbrunn Timeline of Art History*, Metropolitan Museum of Art, August 2007. http://www.metmuseum.org/TOAH/hd/lasc/hd_lasc.htm

Bradshaw Foundation. "Cave Art of France." *French Cave Paintings Archive*. http://www.bradshawfoundation.com/france/index.php

EuroPreArt Database. "European Prehistoric Art: Past Signs and Present Memories." http://www.europreart.net/

Ministère de la Culture et de la Communication. "Lascaux: A Visit to the Cave." http://www.lascaux.culture.fr/#/en/00.xml/index3.html

Sacred Destinations. "Lascaux Caves." http://www.sacred-destinations.com/france/lascaux-caves

What Is Art?

158 *"Art enables men"* Paul Weiss, *The World of Art* (Carbondale: Southern Illinois Univ. Press, 1961), 4–5.

Carroll, Noel. *Philosophy of Art: A Contemporary Introduction*. London: Routledge, 1999.

The Goddesses of Inspiration

158 *The Nine Muses* William Smith, ed., *A Dictionary of Greek and Roman Biography and Mythology* (Boston: Little, Brown, 1867), 1124–1126. http://quod.lib.umich.edu/cgi/t/text/pageviewer-idx?c=moa;cc=moa;idno=acl3129.0002.001;size=l;frm=frameset;seq=1134

Atsma, Aaron, ed. "Mousai." Theoi Project. http://www.theoi.com/Ouranios/Mousai.html

Littleton, C. Scott. "Muses." *World Book Encyclopedia*, 2009.

Too Much Excitement

159 *"I was in a sort"* Stendhal, *Naples and Florence: A Journey from Milan to Reggio* (London: H. Colburn, 1818), quoted in Maria Chatzichristodoulou, Janis Jefferies, and Rachel Zerihan, *Interfaces of Performance*. (Burlington, VT: Ashgate, 2009), 196–197.

Amancio, Edson Jose. "Dostoevsky and Stendhal's Syndrome." *Arquivos de Neuro-Psiquiatria* 63, no. 4 (2005): 1099–1103. http://www.scielo.br/pdf/anp/v63n4/a34v63n4.pdf

Guy, Melinda. "The Shock of the Old." *Frieze*, January–February 2003. http://www.frieze.com/issue/article/the_shock_of_the_old/

A Perfect Circle

160 *"Giotto . . . took a paper"* Giorgio Vasari, "Giotto," in *Lives of the Most Eminent Painters, Sculptors and Architects*, vol. 1, *Cimabue to Agnolo Gaddi* (London: Macmillan, 1912), 78. http://www.gutenberg.org/files/25326/25326-h/25326-h.htm#Page_69

Ladis, Andrew. *Victims and Villains in Vasari's Lives*. Chapel Hill: Univ. of North Carolina Press, 2008).

In a Man's World

Bohlen, Celestine. "Elusive Heroine of the Baroque: Artist Colored by Distortion, Legend and a Notorious Trial." *New York Times*, February 18, 2002. http://www.nytimes.com/2002/02/18/theater/elusive-heroine-baroque-artist-colored-distortion-legend-notorious-trial.html?pagewanted=all

Lilith Gallery of Toronto. "Artemisia Gentileschi." Art History Archive. http://www.arthistoryarchive.com/arthistory/baroque/Artemisia-Gentileschi.html

Parker, Christine. *The Life and Art of Artemisia Gentileschi*. http://www.artemisia-gentileschi.com/index.shtml

Done with Mirrors

162 *"For centuries the technique"* Web Gallery of Art, "Glossary." http://www.wga.hu/database/glossary/glossary.html#c

Hockney, David. *Secret Knowledge: Rediscovering the Lost Techniques of the Old Masters*. London: Thames and Hudson, 2001.

Kohn, David. "Was It Done with Mirrors?" *60 Minutes*. CBS, August 3, 2003. http://www.cbsnews.com/stories/2003/01/16/60minutes/main536814.shtml

Mo Tzu. "Cultural China." Shanghai News and Press Bureau. http://www.cultural-china.com/chinaWH/html/en/33History575.html

Powers, Richard. "Best Idea: Eyes Wide Open." *New York Times*, April 18, 1999. http://www.nytimes.com/1999/04/18/magazine/best-idea-eyes-wide-open.html

Steadman, Philip. "Vermeer and the Camera Obscura." *British History in Depth*. BBC, November 5, 2009. http://www.bbc.co.uk/history/british/empire_seapower/vermeer_camera_01.shtml

Sweet, David L. "Secret Knowledge: Rediscovering the Lost Techniques of the Old Masters." *Art in America*, April 2002. http://findarticles.com/p/articles/mi_m1248/is_4_90/ai_84669338/

The Madman of Arles

Browning, Frank. "Who Really Cut Off Van Gogh's Ear?" *All Things Considered*. NPR, May 10, 2009. http://www.npr.org/templates/story/story.php?storyId=103990820

Kaufmann, Hans, and Rita Wildegans. *Van Gogh's Ohr: Paul Gauguin und der Pakt des Schweigens* [Van Gogh's Ear: Paul Gauguin and the Pact of Silence]. Berlin, Germany: Osburg Verlag, 2008.

"Vincent van Gogh." *Authors and Artists for Young Adults*. Vol. 29. Farmington Hills, MI: Gale, 1999. Reproduced in *Biography Resource Center*. Farmington Hills, MI: Gale, 2009.

Maori *Moko*

163 *"You may be robbed"* Lisa Altieri and Emiko Omori, *Skin Stories: The Art and Culture of Polynesian Tattoo*. PBS. May 4, 2003. http://www.pbs.org/skinstories/index.html

Cowan, James. "Netana Whakaari." In *The New Zealand Wars: A History of the Maori Campaigns and the Pioneering Period*. Vol. 2, *The Hauhau Wars (1864–72)*, 445. Wellington,

New Zealand: Rowen, 1923. http://www.nzetc.org/tm/scholarly/Cow02NewZ-fig-Cow02NewZ445a.html

Museum of New Zealand. "Origins of *Tā Moko*." http://www.tepapa.govt.nz/Education/OnlineResources/Moko/Pages/Origins.aspx

New Zealand in History. "The Maori: The Tattoo (*Tā Moko*)." http://history-nz.org/maori3.html

Robley, Horatio Gordon. *Moko, or Maori Tattooing*. London: Chapman and Hall, 1896. http://books.google.com/books?id=hV8uAAAAYAAJ&pg=PR5&dq=Major+General+Robley+moko#v=onepage&q=&f=false

Seduction of the Innocent

"Fredric Wertham." *St. James Encyclopedia of Popular Culture*. Vol. 5. Farmington Hills, MI: St. James Press, 2000. Reproduced in *Biography Resource Center*. Farmington Hills, MI: Gale, 2009.

Menand, Louis. "The Horror." *New Yorker*, March 31, 2008.

Wertham, Fredric. *Seduction of the Innocent*. New York: Rinehart, 1954.

Everyone a Rembrandt

165 *"I don't know what America"* Smithsonian Institution, "Paint by Number: Accounting for Taste in the 1950s," National Museum of American History. http://americanhistory.si.edu/paint/rembrandt.html

Paint by Number Museum. http://www.paintbynumbermuseum.com/

No Straight Lines

165 *"The straight line is godless"* Friedensreich Hundertwasser, *Mouldiness Manifesto: Against Rationalism in Architecture*, trans. Andrew Feenberg (Burnaby, British Columbia, Canada: Simon Fraser University, 1958). http://www.sfu.ca/~andrewf/MOULDINESS_MANIFESTO.htm

166 *"Even now, I am still struck"* Susanna Loof, "Despite the Tourists, Residents Love Living in Unique Building," Associated Press, September 7, 2005.

166 *"Art must be precious"* Walter Koschatzky, with Janine Kertesz, *Friedensreich Hundertwasser: The Complete Graphic Work, 1951–1986*, trans. Charles Kessler (New York: Rizzoli, 1986), 12.

166 *"Everything is so infinitely"* Friedensreich Hundertwasser, "Hundertwasser on Hundertwasser." http://www.hundertwasser.at/english/hundertwasser/hwueberhw.php

Hundertwasserhaus. http://www.hundertwasserhaus.com/

Pawley, Martin. "Friedensreich Hundertwasser: Maverick Architect Building against the Grain." *Guardian*, April 14, 2000. http://www.guardian.co.uk/news/2000/apr/14/guardianobituaries2

Nourished by Marble Dust

166 *"he breathed the dust"* Will Durant, *The Renaissance: A History of Civilization in Italy from 1304–1576* (New York: Simon and Schuster, 1953), 5:469.

166 *"if I have anything of the good"* Giorgio Vasari "Michelagnolo Buonarroti" in *Lives of the Most Eminent Painters, Sculptors and Architects*. Vol. 9, *Michelangelo to the Flemings* (London: Macmillan, 1915), 4.

166 *"oil-painting was a woman's"* George Bull, *Michelangelo: A Biography* (New York: St. Martin's Press, 1995), 271.

Stone, Irving. *I, Michelangelo, Sculptor*. New York: Doubleday, 1962.

The Greatest Rivalry

166 *"very great disdain"* "Giorgio Vasari: Life of Leonardo da Vinci, 1550," *Medieval Sourcebook*, Fordham University. http://www.fordham.edu/halsall/source/vasari1.html

166 *"Leonardo was elegant"* Ed Wright, *A Left-Handed History of the World* (New York: Barnes and Noble, 2007), 66.

167 *"The sculptor in creating"* Leonardo da Vinci, Notebooks (2 vols.), ed. Edward MacCurdy (London: Cape, 1938), quoted in Gill, Anton, *Il Gigante: Michelangelo, Florence, and the David, 1492–1504* (New York: St. Martin's Press, 2003), 209.

Hibbard Howard, *Michelangelo* (Boulder, CO: Westview Press, 1974), 74–75.

Museo d'Arte e Scienza. "Leonardo the Ingenious Painter." http://www.leonardodavincimilano.com/linkTrattato-en.htm

Cultural Vandalism

168 *"roughly half of what now survives"* British Museum, "What Are the Elgin Marbles?" http://www.britishmuseum.org/explore/highlights/article_index/w/what_are_the_elgin_marbles.aspx

Casey, Christopher. "Grecian Grandeurs and the Rude Wasting of Old Time: Britain, the Elgin Marbles, and Post-Revolutionary Hellenism." *Foundations*, October 30, 2008. http://ww2.jhu.edu/foundations/?p=8

"Elginism." http://www.elginism.com/

Emerling, Susan. "Is Greece Losing Its Elgin Marbles?" *Foreign Policy*, August 21, 2009.

Hellenic Electronic Center. "The Parthenon Marbles." http://www.greece.org/parthenon/marbles/

Jenkins, Ian. "Cleaning and Controversy: The Parthenon Sculptures, 1811–1939." British Museum. http://www.britishmuseum.org/research/research_publications/online_research_publications/cleaning_and_controversy.aspx

Carving a Mountain

168 *"To protect and preserve"* Crazy Horse Memorial. http://www.crazyhorsememorial.org/

Higbee, Paul. "Carving Crazy Horse." *American Profile*, May 27, 2001. http://www.americanprofile.com/article/1033.html

"Korczak Ziolkowski." *Authors and Artists for Young Adults*. Vol. 57. Farmington Hills, MI: Gale, 2004. Reproduced in *Biography Resource Center*. Farmington Hills, MI: Gale, 2009.

The Art of Packaging

169 *"In a materialistic age"* "Christo and Jeanne-Claude." http://christojeanneclaude.net/

169 *"a golden river"* Ibid.

169 *"the quality of love"* Pagliasotti, James. "An interview with Christo and Jeanne-Claude." *Eye-Level*, January 4, 2002, available at http://www.christojeanneclaude.net/eyeLevel.shtml

Bourdon, David. *Christo*. Edited by Susan Astwood. Rev. ed. New York: Harry N. Abrams, 2000.

"Christo and Jeanne-Claude." *Contemporary Artists*. 5th ed. Farmington Hills, MI: St. James Press, 2001. Reproduced in *Biography Resource Center*. Farmington Hills, MI: Gale, 2009.

Grimes, William. "Jeanne-Claude, Christo's Collaborator on Environmental Canvas, Is Dead at 74," *New York Times*, November 19, 2009. http://www.nytimes.com/2009/11/20/arts/design/20jeanne-claude.html?_r=1&scp=1&sq=%22jeanne%20claude%22&st=cse

Brunelleschi's Dome

170 *"an inner hemispherical dome"* "Filippo Brunelleschi," *Medici: Godfathers of the Renaissance*. PBS, February 11, 2004. http://www.pbs.org/empires/medici/renaissance/brunelleschi.html

Atkins, Jim. "*Il Duomo*: Brunelleschi and the Dome of Santa Maria del Fiore." 12 episodes. *Adventures in Architecture*, January 25–December 19, 2008.

"The Cathedral of Santa Maria del Fiore." http://www.duomofirenze.it/index-eng.htm

Farfan, Maria Patricia. "Dome Structures: Santa Maria del Fiore (Florence)." McGill University. http://www.arch.mcgill.ca/prof/sijpkes/arch374/winter2001/sfarfa/ensayo1.htm

King, Ross. *Brunelleschi's Dome: How a Renaissance Genius Reinvented Architecture.* New York: Walker, 2000.

Opera di S. Maria del Fiore di Firenze. http://www.operaduomo.firenze.it/english/

Mimetic Architecture

170 *"oldest functioning example"* Joan Marie Arbogast, *Buildings in Disguise: Architecture That Looks Like Animals, Food, and Other Things* (Honesdale, PA: Boyd Mills Press, 2004), 6.

Lucy the Elephant. http://www.lucytheelephant.org/

Dinny the Apatosaurus. http://www.weirdca.com/location.php?location=109

Longaberger Company. http://www.longaberger.com/homeOffice.aspx

National Fresh Water Fishing Hall. http://www.freshwater-fishing.org/museuminfo.html

Peachoid. http://www.ohiobarns.com/othersites/watertowers/sc/WT%2040–11peach.html

Scary Waterspouts

172 *"that savage monster"* Homer, *The Iliad*, trans. Samuel Butler (Roslyn, NY: Walter J. Black, 1942), 92.

Arnold, Walter S. "Gargoyles." Stone Carver. http://www.stonecarver.com/gargoyle.html

Chiffriller, Joe. "Gargoyles." New York Carver. http://www.newyorkcarver.com/gargoyles.htm

"Chrysler Building." http://www.nyc-architecture.com/MID/MID021.htm

Gargoyle Gothica. http://www.gargoylegothica.com/

Princeton University. "Gargoyles." http://etcweb.princeton.edu/CampusWWW/Communications/Gargoyles.pdf

Washington National Cathedral. "Gargoyles: Self-Guided Tours." http://www.nationalcathedral.org/visit/selfguidedTours.shtml

———. "Grotesques: Darth Vader." http://www.nationalcathedral.org/about/darthVader.shtml

Washington University. "Gargoyle Gallery." http://library.wustl.edu/units/spec/archives/gargoyle/

A Secret Spire

"Chrysler Building." *New York Times*, n.d. http://topics.nytimes.com/topics/reference/timestopics/subjects/c/chrysler_building/index.html

Eliot, Marc. "Chrysler Building." In *Down 42nd Street: Sex, Money, Culture, and Politics at the Crossroads of the World*, 28–31. New York: Warner Books, 2001.

Great Buildings. "Chrysler Building." http://www.greatbuildings.com/buildings/Chrysler_Building.html

Megerian, Christopher, and Cam Mosgrove. "The Chrysler Building: An Engineering Reform and an Architectural Revolution." Needham High School. http://nhs.needham.k12.ma.us//cur/Baker_00/2002_p5/Baker-p5-cm_cm/The%20Chrysler%20Building

New York History. "Chrysler Building." http://www.newyorkhistory.info/42nd-Street/chryslerbuilding.html

Zacharek, Stephanie. "The Chrysler Building: New York's Most Glorious Skyscraper, Its Art Deco Eagles Poised for Flight, Is a Timeless Work of Jazz Age Poetry in Steel." *Salon*, February 25, 2002. http://www.salon.com/ent/masterpiece/2002/02/25/chrysler/

11. RHAPSODIES IN BLOOM

An Audible Sign of Life

173 *"In the beginning was the voice"* Otto Jespersen, *Language: Its Nature, Development and Origin* (New York: Macmillan, 1949), 435.

173 *"The technique of singing"* "Singing," *Encylopedia Britannica*, vol. 10, 15th ed., 2003.

173 *"The human voice is really"* John Koopman, "A Brief History of Singing," Lawrence University Conservatory of Music, 1999. http://www.lawrence.edu/fast/koopmajo/brief.html

The Sound of Music

Campbell, Michael. *Popular Music in America*. Boston: Schirmer Cengage Learning, 2009.

Constantinidis, Sylvia. "Elements of Music." History of Music. http://historyofmusic.tripod.com/id6.html

Van Dijke, Gilbert Hoek. "Essays on Pitch, Tuning and the Physics of Musical Tone." House of Musical Traditions, November 19, 2008. http://www.hmtrad.com/catalog/articles/theory.html

Music of the Winds

Harmonic Wind Harps. Audio File of a Wind Harp. http://www.harmonicwindharps.com/sound/aeolus%20125.mp3

Harpmaker. http://www.harpmaker.net/windharp.htm

Joly, Greg. "About Wind Harps." http://www.harmonicwindharps.com/about.htm

Kennedy, Michael, ed. "Aeolian harp." In *The Oxford Dictionary of Music*. New York: Oxford Univ., 1994.

Lienhard, John H. "Aeolian Vibration." *Engines of Our Ingenuity*. University of Houston. http://www.uh.edu/engines/epi1653.htm

Eeee-Oooo-Eeee

Big Briar. "Moog Music." http://www.bigbriar.com/

Conway, Chris. "Theremin Concert at Filk Consonance 2006." http://www.geekhackfilk.com/gallery/albums/consonance2006/theremin_small.mov

Moog Music. "History of the Theremin." http://www.moogmusic.com/history.php?cat_id=2

Oddmusic. "Lev Sergeivitch Termen: Electronic Music Pioneer." http://www.oddmusic.com/theremin/

Theremin World. "Theremin FAQ." http://www.thereminworld.com/faq.asp

The Sibyl of the Rhine

176 *"I heard the voice"* Hildegard, *Scivias*, trans. Jane Bishop (Mahwah, NJ: Paulist Press, 1996), 59.

176 *"that divine melody of praise"* Hildegard to the Prelates of Mainz in *The Letters of Hildegard of Bingen*, trans. Joseph L. Baird and Radd K. Ehrman (Oxford, UK: Oxford Univ. Press, 1994), 1:78.

Benedictine Abbey of St. Hildegard. http://www.abtei-st-hildegard.de/english/hildegard/index.php

Halsall, Paul, ed. "The Life and Works of Hildegard von Bingen (1098–1179)." Fordham University. http://www.fordham.edu/halsall/med/hildegarde.html

Hildegard. *Hildegard of Bingen*. http://www.hildegard.org/

International Society of Hildegard von Bingen Studies. http://www.hildegard-society.org/

Maddocks, Fiona. *Hildegard of Bingen: The Woman of Her Age*. New York: Doubleday, 2001.

Mather, Olivia Carter. "The Music of Hildegard von Bingen." *The ORB: Online Reference Book for Medieval Studies*, June 15, 2003. http://the-orb.net/encyclop/culture/music/mather.htm

Mershman, F. "St. Hildegard." In *The Catholic Encyclopedia*. Vol. 7. New York: Robert Appleton, 1910. Available online at New Advent. http://www.newadvent.org/cathen/07351a.htm

Papa Bach

176 *"he vitalized the polyphonic music"* Phil Goulding, *Classical Music* (New York: Ballantine, 1992), 97.

J. S. Bach Home Page. http://www.jsbach.org/biography.html

Library of Congress. "Felix Mendelssohn: Reviving the Works of J. S. Bach." In *Performing Arts Encyclopedia*. http://memory.loc.gov/diglib/ihas/loc.natlib.ihas.200156436/default.html

Teaching Little Fingers to Play

178 *"Czerny was warmer"* Harold C. Schonberg, *The Great Pianists from Mozart to the Present* (New York: Simon and Schuster, 1963), 95.

Czerny, Charles. *Letters to a Young Lady, on the Art of Playing the Pianoforte*. trans. J. A. Hamilton. New York: Firth, Pond, 1851. http://books.google.com/books?id=oTQuAAAAYAAJ&printsec=frontcover&dq=inauthor:%22Carl+Czerny%22&lr=&as_drrb_is=b&as_minm_is=0&as_miny_is=1800&as_maxm_is=0&as_maxy_is=1950&as_brr=3#v=onepage&q=&f=false

A Self-Playing Instrument

Baines, Anthony. "Player-Piano (Pianola)." In *The Oxford Companion to Musical Instruments*. New York: Oxford Univ. Press, 2002.

McLaughlin, Ian. "The Player Piano Page." http://www.pianola.com/index.htm

Pianola Institute. "History of the Pianola." http://www.pianola.org/history/history.cfm

Rhapsody in Blue

179 *"It was on the train"* Ron Cowen, "George Gershwin: He Got Rhythm," *Washington Post*, November 11, 1998. http://www.washingtonpost.com/wp-srv/national/horizon/nov98/gershwin.htm

180 *"By the end"* Rodney Greenberg, *George Gershwin* (London: Phaidon, 1998), 73.

Crawford, Richard. "George Gershwin." In *The New Grove Twentieth-Century American Masters*, 137–141. New York: W. W. Norton, 1988.

Goldberg, Isaac. *George Gershwin: A Study in American Music*. New York: Simon and Schuster, 1931.

Musical Embellishments

Hoffman, Miles. "Cadenzas: Ladling the Gravy on Classical Music." *Morning Edition*. NPR, November 26, 2009. http://www.npr.org/templates/story/story.php?storyId=120792490

Nicholas Temperley. "Cadenza." In *The Oxford Companion to Music*, ed. Alison Latham. (New York: Oxford Univ. Press, 2002).

Ross, Alex. "Taking Liberties: Reviving the Art of Classical Improvisation." *New Yorker*, August 31, 2009. http://www.newyorker.com/arts/critics/musical/2009/08/31/090831crmu_music_ross

Yankee Doodle Boy

182 *"My God, what an act"* Fred Anderson, "My God, What an Act to Follow!" *American Heritage*, July–August 1997.

Collins, David. "George M. Cohan in America's Theater." http://www.members.tripod.com/davecol8/

Internet Broadway Data Base. "George M. Cohan." http://www.ibdb.com/person.php?id=5829

Kenrick, John. "George M. Cohan." Musicals 101, 2004. http://www.musicals101.com/cohan.htm

Lubbock, Mark. "American Musical Theatre: An Introduction." In *The Complete Book of Light Opera*, 753–756. New York: Appleton-Century-Crofts, 1962. http://www.theatrehistory.com/american/musical030.html

The Subtle Beauty of the Guitar

183 *"I pride myself"* Andrés Segovia, *Segovia: An Autobiography of the Years 1893–1920*, trans. W. F. O'Brien (New York: Macmillan, 1976), ix.

Avraam, Vasilios. "In Memory of Andrés Segovia." *Guitarra*. http://www.guitarramagazine.com/andres_segovia_memory

Classical Guitar Net. "Andrés Segovia." http://www.classicalguitar.net/artists/segovia/

Henahan, Donal. "Andrés Segovia Is Dead at 94; His Crusade Elevated Guitar." *New York Times*, June 4, 1987. http://www.nytimes.com/learning/general/onthisday/bday/0221.html

Slonimsky, Nicolas, ed. "Andrés Segovia." *Baker's Biographical Dictionary of Musicians*. Centennial ed. New York: Schirmer, 2001. Reproduced in *Biography Resource Center*. Farmington Hills, MI: Gale, 2009.

A Music Hall on Goat Hill

183 *"The audience which assembled"* "It Stood the Test Well; First Concert in New Music Hall." *New York Times*, May 6, 1891.

Carnegie Hall Corporation. "Carnegie Hall Then and Now: One Hundred Years of Excellence, 1891–1991." http://www.carnegiehall.org/pdf/CHnowthen.pdf

The Wordless Chorus

184 *"have shown that this vocal art"* Lalage Cochrane, "Vocalise," in *The Oxford Companion to Music*, ed. Alison Latham (New York: Oxford Univ. Press, 2002), 1348.

Edwards, Brent Hayes. "Louis Armstrong and the Syntax of Scat." *Critical Inquiry* 28, no. 3 (Spring 2002). http://criticalinquiry.uchicago.edu/issues/v28/v28n3.edwards.html

Robinson, J. Bradford. "Scat Singing." In *The New Grove Dictionary of Jazz*, ed. Barry Kernfeld (New York: Oxford Univ. Press, 2001), 515–516.

The Mother of Gospel

185 *"I'll never give up"* Alden Whitman, "Mahalia Jackson, Gospel Singer and a Civil Rights Symbol, Dies," *New York Times*, January 28, 1972.

185 *"All her years"* Ibid.

"Mahalia Jackson." *Notable Black American Women*. Vol. 1. Farmington Hills, MI: Gale, 1992. Reproduced in *Biography Resource Center*. Farmington Hills, MI: Gale, 2009.

Rock and Roll Hall of Fame and Museum. "Mahalia Jackson." http://www.rockhall.com/inductee/mahalia-jackson

Slonimsky, Nicolas, ed. "Mahalia Jackson." *Baker's Biographical Dictionary of Musicians*. Centennial ed. New York: Schirmer, 2001. Reproduced in *Biography Resource Center*. Farmington Hills, MI: Gale, 2009.

Radio Perennials

Grand Ole Opry. "History of the Opry." http://www.opry.com/about/History.html

"Longest-Running Weekly Radio Programme." *Guinness World Records*, 2005. http://www.guinnessworldrecords.com/records/arts_and_media/tv_shows/longest_running_weekly_radio_programme_-_same_host.aspx

WNYC-AM. *Folksong Festival*. http://www.wnyc.org/shows/folksong/

In the Jungle, the Mighty Jungle

Malan, Rian. "In the Jungle." *Rolling Stone*, May 25, 2000.

Verster, Francois. "The Lion's Trail." *Independent Lens*. PBS, 2005. http://www.pbs.org/independentlens/lionstrail/index.html

Rock Launched

Dawson, Jim. *Rock around the Clock: The Record That Started the Rock Revolution*. San Francisco: Back Beat Books, 2005.

Rock and Roll Hall of Fame and Museum. "Bill Haley." http://www.rockhall.com/inductee/bill-haley

Egyptian Surfer Girl

Dinosaur Gardens. "The Mysteries of Miserlou." October 3, 2006. http://www.dinosaurgardens.com/archives/297

Hansen, Liane. "Misirlou: From Klezmer to Surf Guitar." *Weekend Edition Sunday*. NPR, January 8, 2006. http://www.npr.org/templates/story/story.php?storyId=5134530

When Did He Leave the Building?

"Al Dvorin, Announcer Who Dashed Fans' Hope with the Phrase 'Elvis Has Left the Building.' *Independent*, August 25, 2004.

"Elvis Fans to Dedicate Marker at MSA Site." *Indianapolis Star*, June 26, 2002.

Lollar, Michael. "Who First Said, 'Elvis Has Left the Building'?" *Commercial Appeal*, April 14, 1998.

"Radio Legend Horace Logan Dies at 86." Associated Press, October 13, 2002.

He Chose Poorly

188 *"We don't like their sound"* NationMaster. "The Decca Audition." http://www.nationmaster.com/encyclopedia/The-Decca-audition#cite_ref-0

Brian Poole and the Tremeloes Fan Site. http://www.geocities.com/fabgear6366/poole.htm

Davies, Hunter. "The Beatles." *Life*, September 13, 1968.

Roylance, Brian. *The Beatles Anthology*. San Francisco: Chronicle Books, 2000.

Feel the Music

189 *"Sound is simply vibrating air"* Evelyn Glennie, "Hearing Essay." http://www.evelyn.co.uk/Evelyn_old/live/hearing_essay.htm

189 *"She is a master"* "Evelyn Glennie," *Contemporary Musicians,* vol. 33 (Farmington Hills, MI: Gale Group, 2002). Reproduced in *Biography Resource Center* (Farmington Hills, MI: Gale, 2009).

189 *"please, enjoy the music"* Glennie, "Hearing Essay."

"Biography: Evelyn Glennie." http://www.evelyn.co.uk/Evelyn_old/live/long_biog.htm

Brown, Jeffrey. "Beat of a Different Drummer." *The NewsHour with Jim Lehrer*. PBS, June 14, 1999. http://www.pbs.org/newshour/bb/entertainment/jan-june99/drummer_6–14.html

Your Brain on Jazz

190 *"Changes in prefrontal activity"* Charles J. Limb and Allen R. Braun, "Neural Substrates of Spontaneous Musical Performance: An fMRI Study of Jazz Improvisation." *PLoS* [Public Library of Science] *ONE* 3, no. 2 (February 28, 2008): 1679. http://www.plosone.org/article/fetchArticle.action?articleURI=info:doi/10.1371/journal.pone.0001679

Brownlee, Christen. "Brain on Jazz: MRI Used to Study Spontaneity, Creativity." *Johns Hopkins University Gazette*, March 3, 2008. http://www.jhu.edu/~gazette/2008/03mar08/03jazz.html

Wenger, Jennifer. "In Jazz Improv, Large Portion of Brain's Prefrontal Region 'Takes Five' to Let Creativity Flow." National Institute on Deafness and Other Communication Disorders, February 26, 2008. http://www.nidcd.nih.gov/news/releases/08/02_26_08.htm

12. LOVE SONGS AND LOST WORDS

Little Songs of Love

Academy of American Poets. "Poetic Form: Sonnet." http://www.poets.org/viewmedia.php/prmMID/5791

Browning, Elizabeth Barrett. *Sonnets from the Portuguese*. Project Gutenberg e-book, September 14, 2004. http://www.gutenberg.org/files/2002/2002-h/2002-h.htm

Miller, Nelson. "Basic Sonnet Forms." Sonnets. http://www.sonnets.org/basicforms.htm

Shakespeare's Sonnets. http://www.shakespeares-sonnets.com/

Sixty-Six: The Journal of Sonnet Studies. http://bostonpoetry.com/66/

Lost Words of the Bard

192 *"to promote reading"* United Nations Educational, Scientific, and Cultural Organization, "World Book and Copyright Day, April 23." http://portal.unesco.org/culture/en/ev.php-URL_ID=5125&URL_DO=DO_TOPIC&URL_SECTION=201.html

Dobson, Michael, and Stanley Wells, eds. "Cardenio." In *The Oxford Companion to Shakespeare*. New York: Oxford Univ. Press, 2001.

Marche, Stephen. "Longing for Great Lost Works." *Wall Street Journal*, April 18, 2009.

Fairy-Tale Finders

193 *"to demonstrate the virtues"* Jack Zipes, ed., "Introduction," in *The Oxford Companion to Fairy Tales* (New York: Oxford Univ. Press, 2000), xxvi.

Ashliman, D. L. Grimm Brothers' Home Page. University of Pittsburgh. http://www.pitt.edu/~dash/grimm.html

Bottigheimer, Ruth B. "Grimm, Brothers." In *The Oxford Companion to Fairy Tales*, ed. Jack Zipes. New York: Oxford Univ. Press, 2000.

Brüder Grimm-Museum Kassel (Museum of the Brothers Grimm), Berlin. http://www.grimms.de/contenido/cms/front_content.php

Grimm Stories. http://www.grimmstories.com/

National Geographic. "Grimms' Fairy Tales," 1999. http://www.nationalgeographic.com/grimm/index2.html

Some Light on the Subject

Chafin, Kerry. "Limelight and the Development of Stage Lighting." *Theatre History*. Suite 101, September 2, 2009. http://theatrehistory.suite101.com/article.cfm/in_the_limelight

Stage Lighting Museum. "History: Limelight." http://www.stage-lighting-museum.com/museum/html/history-4/limelight-spot.html

University of Leeds School of Chemistry. "Demonstrations: Limelight." http://www.chem.leeds.ac.uk/delights/texts/Demonstration_19.htm

A Real Detective

Jackman, Philip. "Myth Conceptions: Many Britons Think Winston Churchill Was a Fictional Character and Sherlock Holmes Was a Real Person, Study Says." *Toronto Globe and Mail*, February 5, 2008.

Klinger, Leslie S. *The New Annotated Sherlock Homes*. New York: W. W. Norton, 2005.

Sherlock Holmes Museum. http://www.sherlock-holmes.co.uk/

Unreal Books

195 *"recorded in bibliographies"* Joan M. Reitz, "Ghost," *Online Dictionary for Library and Information Science*. http://lu.com/odlis/odlis_g.cfm

195 *"Announced in 1942"* Ibid.

Invisible Library. http://invislib.blogspot.com/

Kennedy, George. *Fictitious Authors and Imaginary Novels in French, English and American Fiction from the 18th to the Start of the 21st Century*. Lewiston, NY: Mellen Press, 2004.

Koontz, Dean. *The Book of Counted Sorrows*. Podcast Episode 25. http://www.deankoontz.com/entertainment/podcasts/podcast-episode-25-book-of-counted-sorrows-1

Park, Ed. "Welcome to the Invisible Library." *Los Angeles Times*, December 28, 2008. http://www.latimes.com/features/books/la-caw-astral-weeks28–2008dec28,1,6730759.story

The Father of Film

196 *"the teacher of us all"* "D. W. Griffith," *American Masters*, PBS, March 24, 1993. http://www.pbs.org/wnet/americanmasters/episodes/d-w-griffith/about-d-w-griffith/621/

196 *"established the motion picture"* Robert Sklar, "David Wark Griffith," in *Dictionary of American Biography*, ed. American Council of Learned Societies (New York: Scribner's, 1990). Reproduced in *Biography Resource Center* (Farmington Hills, MI: Gale, 2009).

197 *"To watch his work"* "D. W. Griffith," *American Masters*. PBS.

American Mutoscope & Biograph Company. "History." http://www.biographcompany.com/history_home.html

Drew, William M. "D. W. Griffith (1875–1948)." Gilda's Attic, August 10, 2002. http://www.gildasattic.com/dwgriffith.html

A Noble Actor

Bogle, Donald. *Bright Boulevards, Bold Dreams: The Story of Black Hollywood*. New York: Ballantine Books, 2006.

Internet Movie Data Base. "Noble Johnson." http://www.imdb.com/name/nm0425903/

Sampson, Henry. *The Ghost Walks: A Chronological History of Blacks in Show Business, 1865–1910*. Metuchen, NJ: Scarecrow Press, 1988.

'Twas Not Beauty Killed the Beast

"We should kill" Orville Goldner and George Turner, *The Making of King Kong: The Story behind a Film Classic* (Cranbury, NJ: A. S. Barnes, 1975), 173.

Four Universal Frankensteins

198 *"the foremost producers"* Carlos Clarens, *An Illustrated History of the Horror Film* (New York: Capricorn Books, 1967), 79.

Gifford, Denis. *A Pictorial History of Horror Films*. London: Hamlyn, 1973.

Rohrmoser, Andreas. "Frankenstein Films." http://universal.frankensteinfilms.com/

Underwood, Peter. *Karloff*. New York: Drake, 1972.

Yak's Greatest Stunt

B-Westerns. "Yakima Canutt." http://www.bwesterns.com/canutt.htm

Film Reference. "Yakima Canutt." http://www.filmreference.com/Writers-and-Production-Artists-Bo-Ce/Canutt-Yakima.html

Zorro's Fighting Legion. http://www.imagesjournal.com/issue04/infocus/zorrosfighting legion.htm

A Chilly Reception for Boris

200 *"for his important achievement"* "Boris Pasternak," *Contemporary Authors Online*. Reproduced in *Biography Resource Center* (Farmington Hills, MI: Gale, 2009).

"Boris Pasternak Obituary." *New York Times*, May 31, 1960.

Frenz, Horst, ed. "Boris Pasternak." In *Nobel Lectures, Literature 1901–1967*. Amsterdam: Elsevier, 1969. Available on the Nobel Foundation Web site. http://nobelprize.org/nobel _prizes/literature/laureates/1958/pasternak-bio.html

Fear on Trial

Counterattack. *Red Channels: The Report of Communist Influence in Radio and Television*. New York: American Business Consultants, 1950.

Faulk, John Henry. *Fear on Trial*. New York: Simon and Schuster, 1964.

Foshee, Page. "Faulk, John Henry." Texas State Historical Association. http://www.tsha online.org/handbook/online/articles/FF/ffa36.html

A Naked Literary Hoax

201 *"As one of Newsday's"* Henry Raymont, "Does Sex Sell? Ask 'Penelope Ashe,'" *New York Times*, August 7, 1969.

Museum of Hoaxes. "Naked Came the Stranger." http://www.museumofhoaxes.com/hoax /archive/permalink/naked_came_the_stranger/

Moral Fiction

202 *"true art is moral"* John Gardner, *On Moral Fiction* (New York: Basic Books, 1978), 5–6.

Vitale, Tom. "John Gardner: 'Literary Outlaw.'" *Weekend Edition Sunday*. NPR, February 22, 2004. http://www.npr.org/templates/story/story.php?storyId=1691510

Banned in the U.S.A.

203 *"an attempt to remove"* American Library Association, "Attempts to Ban Books in U.S. Continue," September 21, 2009. http://www.ala.org/ala/newspresscenter/news/pressreleases2009/september2009/bbw2009_oif.cfm

American Library Association. "Banned and Challenged Classics." http://www.ala.org/ala/issuesadvocacy/banned/frequentlychallenged/challengedclassics/reasonsbanned/index.cfm

———. "Number of Challenges, by Year, Reason, Institution and Initiator." http://www.ala.org/ala/issuesadvocacy/banned/frequentlychallenged/challengesbytype/index.cfm

In Conclusion

203 *"So we beat on"* F. Scott Fitzgerald, *The Great Gatsby* (New York: Scribner's, 1925).

203 *"Rest assured"* Pearl Buck, *The Good Earth* (New York: John Day, 1931).

203 *"He still held on"* Richard Wright, *Native Son* (New York: Harper, 1940).

203 *"His soul swooned"* James Joyce, *"The Dead"* in *Dubliners* (London: Grant Richards, 1914).

203 *"But the effect"* George Eliot, *Middlemarch* (Edinburgh and London: Blackwood, 1871).

203 *"He went past"* MacKinlay Kantor, *Andersonville* (New York: World Publishing, 1955).

204 *"Then I added 'Blah'"* Jack Kerouac, *The Dharma Bums* (New York: Viking Press, 1958).

204 *"I stand on the deck"* Frank McCourt, *Angela's Ashes* (New York: Scribner's, 1996).

204 *"And the pearl lay"* John Steinbeck, *The Pearl* (New York: Viking Press, 1947).

204 *"O Agnes"* Charles Dickens, *The Personal History of David Copperfield* (London: Bradbury and Evans, 1850).

204 *"But I can and will"* Tom Robbins, *Still Life with Woodpecker* (New York: Bantam Books, 1980).

204 *"In the world according to her father"* John Irving, *The World According to Garp* (New York: Dutton, 1978).

Index

Colophon

Type faces: Adobe Caslon Pro, Caslon Antique, and Caslon 224 Black
Designer: Forty-five Degree Design
Pounds of paper used for first printing: 15,762
Number of facts: 277
Number of words: 73,535
Time spent researching and writing: 818.5 hours
Unique sources cited (books, articles, Web sites, people): 709